a certain age

women growing older

edited by

MARILYN POOLE & SUSAN FELDMAN

Taylor & Francis Group
LONDON AND NEW YORK

First published 1999 by Allen & Unwin

Published 2020 by Routledge
2 Park Square, Milton Park, Abingdon, Oxon OX14 4RN
605 Third Avenue, New York, NY 10017

First issued in hardback 2021

Routledge is an imprint of the Taylor & Francis Group, an informa business

Editorial arrangement copyright © Marilyn Poole
& Susan Feldman 1999
Copyright © in individual chapters remains with the authors

All rights reserved. No part of this book may be reprinted or reproduced or utilised in any form or by any electronic, mechanical, or other means, now known or hereafter invented, including photocopying and recording, or in any information storage or retrieval system, without permission in writing from the publishers.

Notice:
Product or corporate names may be trademarks or registered trademarks, and are used only for identification and explanation without intent to infringe.

National Library of Australia
Cataloguing-in-Publication entry:

 A certain age: women growing older.

 Bibliography.
 Includes index.
 ISBN 1 86448 996 0.

 1. Aged women. 2. Middle aged women. 3. Aging. I. Poole,
 Marilyn. II. Feldman, Susan, 1945- .

305.26

Set in 10/12 pt Garamond by DOCUPRO, Sydney

Publisher's Note

The publisher has gone to great lengths to ensure the quality of this reprint but points out that some imperfections in the original copies may be apparent.

ISBN 13: 978-0-367-71730-8 (hbk)
ISBN 13: 978-1-86448-996-5 (pbk)

contents

Contributors v
Preface ix

Part One   Positioning
1 Positioning older women 3
   Susan Feldman & Marilyn Poole
2 Policy's black box: mass media, women and ageing 17
   Anne Ellison
3 Meanings of home in the lives of older women
   (and men) 36
   Cherry Russell
4 Mauve is an old woman's colour: women's visual
   representations of menopause 56
   Marilys Guillemin

Part Two   Participating
5 Learning at the end of your life: a pedagogy of
   relocation 73
   Barbara Kamler
6 It's a lovely feeling: older women's fitness programs 87
   Marilyn Poole
7 Pebbles and hugs: older women in small business 101
   Heather Horrocks

8 The improvised careers of older women: gendered ageism at work? 117
   Rosslyn Reed
9 Social capital, volunteerism and older women 134
   Concetta Benn, Therese McCarthy & Wendy Weeks

Part Three   Relating

10 Making the most of my life: a conversation with Dot Peters 155
   Marilyn Poole & Susan Feldman
11 'No more dinners only lunches': older widowed women relating to the world 165
   Susan Feldman
12 The ache of frequent farewells 182
   Cora Vellekoop Baldock
13 The expectation of love in older age: towards a sociology of intimacy 193
   Anne Riggs & Bryan S. Turner

Index 209

contributors

Cora Vellekoop Baldock is Professor of Sociology (holder of a Personal Chair) at Murdoch University, Perth. She has written extensively on issues relating to women's paid and unpaid work. Her publications include *Volunteers in Welfare* (Allen & Unwin, 1990). She is a Dutch–Australian, and her chapter in this book is largely based on her own experiences.

Concetta Benn has had forty years experience as a caseworker, community development worker, social policy development worker, teacher, administrator and social change agent. Between 1957 and 1995 she has held many senior community, academic and public service positions, including Associate Director, Social Policy & Research (Brotherhood of St Laurence); Director, Social Development Division (Department of Premier & Cabinet); Deputy Director-General (Community Services Victoria) and Professor of Social Work (University of Melbourne). Concetta has received two Honoris Causa doctorates, from University of Melbourne in 1992 and Royal Melbourne Institute of Technology in 1993.

Anne Ellison lectures in Politics of the Media and Public Policy Making at University of Melbourne. She is currently completing her PhD dissertation on women and ageing. Anne also studies women in Australian politics, and is the author of several articles on Pauline Hanson.

Susan Feldman is the Director of the Alma Unit for Women and Ageing, a teaching and research unit located in the Centre for the Study of Health and Society, University of Melbourne. She has had twenty years experience in health and welfare research and policy development. Susan co-edited *Family Violence, Everybody's Business, Somebody's Life* (Federation Press, 1991) and more recently *Something that Happens to Other People* (Vintage Press, 1996). She is currently undertaking a PhD exploring the health and well-being of older Australian women who are widows.

Marilys Guillemin has had an eclectic background in microbiology, education and sociology of science and technology. Her doctoral work examined women's understanding of menopause and the use of menopause clinics in the management of menopause. Her current position is in the Alma Unit for Women and Ageing at the Centre for the Study of Health and Society, University of Melbourne. Her broad research interests are in the areas of sociology of health and technology, the social construction of medical technologies and practices and the use of qualitative research in health. She is currently working on research examining women and heart disease, menopause and the shaping of medical practices and technologies during the period 1930–1980.

Heather Horrocks has been active in politics and the women's movement for over thirty years. In 1992 she collaborated on a collection of women parliamentarians' speeches, *At Home in the House*, and in 1996 edited a volume of the speeches of the Hon. Barry Jones, *Work in Progress*. She is currently working on a women's adventure storybook.

Barbara Kamler is Associate Professor in Language and Literacy Education at Deakin University, where she teaches and researches writing pedagogy, language and gender, critical literacies and critical discourse analysis. A central focus of her work has been to develop critical frameworks for examining the social and cultural construction of language in school and community settings. Her most recent research examines cultural narratives of ageing produced by older women aged seventy to eighty-five, with a particular focus on women's self-representation and the documentation of ageing from the perspective of older women. She has published widely and her most recent books include *Constructing Gender and Difference: Critical Research Perspectives on Early Childhood*. (Hampton Press, 1998) and *Relocating the Personal: A Critical Writing Pedagogy* (SUNY Press, 1999).

contributors / vii

Therese McCarthy is a social worker who has worked for the past fifteen years in health and welfare services in Victoria. From 1988 to 1995 she was involved in the movement against sexual assault as part of a team of counsellor-advocates, and then as a professional educator on changes to Victoria's rape laws. From 1995 to 1997 she was Executive Director of Victorian Court Network.

Dot Peters is the granddaughter of Yarra Yarra people who lived on the Aboriginal reserve at Healesville, Victoria. She has lived in the area for most of her life. She is involved in a broad range of community activities and believes that older people should be role models for the younger generation.

Marilyn Poole is a Senior Lecturer in the School of Social Inquiry, Deakin University. Marilyn has published extensively on women's issues. She has written a chapter on older women and exercise (based on her research on older women involved in Vicfit programs) for M. Ang-Lygate *et al.* (eds), *Desperately Seeking Sisterhood* (Taylor & Francis, 1997), and in 1997 co-edited *Sociology: Australian Connections* (Allen & Unwin, 1997) with Ray Jureidini and Sue Kenny. She has also contributed a chapter to the book *Family Violence, Everybody's Business, Somebody's Life* (Federation Press, 1991).

Rosslyn Reed is a Senior Lecturer at the University of Technology, Sydney. Her teaching and research interests include gender and age. She has published widely in journals and edited collections as well as in monographs on aspects of women's employment including *Strategies of Regulation: Labour Market Segmentation in the Melbourne Newspaper Industry* and *The Invisibility of Older Women Workers: Women Aged 55 and Over in Retailing*. She is currently researching pay equity, professional careers and the media reporting of science.

Anne Riggs is a Research Fellow attached to the Centre for the Body and Society in the Faculty of Arts at Deakin University. Her research interests include social gerontology, intimacy and sexuality in ageing, and lifestyle and generational change. Anne has worked with Bryan Turner on several research projects in these areas.

Cherry Russell is a Senior Lecturer in the School of Community Health at the University of Sydney, where she teaches in gerontology, sociology of health and research methods. Her PhD thesis on the social construction of old age was published in 1981 as *The Aging Experience*. She is also the author of an introductory textbook on sociology for health workers. Her research in gerontology has spanned a range of topics, including media constructions of ageing, health needs and services, social isolation, and older people's experiences of living in different residential environments.

Bryan S. Turner is Professor of Sociology at Cambridge University. He is co-founding editor (with Mike Featherstone) of *Body and Society*, and is the author of many books and publications including *Medical Power and Social Knowledge* (Sage, 1995) and *The Body and Society* (Basil Blackwell, 1996).

Wendy Weeks is Associate Professor in Social Work at the University of Melbourne. Her research and practice focus on women's issues in social work and social policy, with a particular interest in women and work, and violence against women. She is co-editor of *Issues Facing Australian Families: Human Services Respond* (Addison Wesley Longman, 1991, 1995) and *Women Working Together: Lessons from feminist women's services* (Addison Wesley Longman, 1994).

preface

Over the past decade there has been a growing awareness in the community, in the media and in academic research, of the increasing numbers of older people and the changes to demographic profiles around the world.

This book was stimulated by some papers presented in the 'women and ageing' section of the 1996 Australian Sociological Association annual conference in Hobart. Participating in the lively discussions that followed convinced us that more work about women and their experiences of ageing should be undertaken.

We are especially grateful to the contributors for their patience and commitment to this project. In addition we wish to thank all the older women who participated in these research studies, and all our colleagues who have provided us with support and encouragement. We would like to thank Jane Yule for her keen editing skills.

Both of us have gained inspiration and first-hand knowledge of growing old from our mothers, Elsie Cresswell and Rose Foxman. Thank you!

Much of the work on women and ageing that has been undertaken over the past five years would not have been possible without the generous support and vision of Fleur Spitzer who founded the Alma Unit for Women and Ageing, University of Melbourne.

SUSAN FELDMAN
MARILYN POOLE

part one

positioning

one

positioning older women

SUSAN FELDMAN & MARILYN POOLE

'Old folk have ambitions and dreams just like everyone else', commented John Glenn on his return to earth after five days in space in 1998. The imagination of the world was captured by images of the 77-year-old astronaut, who made his second space mission after a gap of thirty-six years. Ageing in the strict sense means growing old. As an older man Glenn is a hero, an icon. But this book is not about valorising unusual and perhaps even dangerous and physically challenging pursuits undertaken by an older person; rather it is about the wide range of experiences of growing old and the multiplicity of positions on ageing, on getting on with life.

On a more personal note this book is a response to our own ageing as women. As feminists we are aware that ageing has not been a central concern of feminism. The more exciting battles it seems have been those concerning women's control over their bodies, the fight for equal pay, child-care provisions and breaking (or attempting to break) the 'glass ceiling' in management and the professions. Even as those people who worked for feminist goals in the 1970s themselves age and turn fifty-something, and more, few of them research and write about the ageing process and what it means for women. Why is this so? Is the thought of becoming an older woman (or an old woman) too terrible to contemplate? As one young woman said recently:

> I do wish older feminists would tackle ageing; we young feminists really are grateful for all the ground-breaking you have done

already, but matters such as reproduction rights and employment—these are for our generation. We are glad of your support of course but we would appreciate you going on and making some headway with the invisibility of older women, the ways in which they are stereotyped, the way they are treated . . .

This book is a small step in that direction.

Women are more likely to be penalised than men for ageing because, in Western culture, we are less tolerant of the ageing process and its physical manifestations in women (Kuhn & Gray Panthers 1974; Sontag 1972). The years beyond menopause have been viewed in a poor light, due in part to the dominance of the medically oriented, biological-decline model of ageing, and partly to the prevalence of derogatory stereotypes concerning the elderly generally, and women particularly. Menopause is 'a prominent biological marker for an aging process in cultures that extoll youthfulness' (Avis & McKinlay 1991: 65; Feldman & Netz 1997). The stereotypical view of the elderly as sickly and dependent has profound social and psychological effects. The reality is that, for the majority of older women, the later years are characterised by relative good health, activity and independence. Our society needs to provide cultural directions for older women beyond the stereotyped roles of submissive caregivers or frail recipients of care.

Who are 'older people' and how do we know who they are?

Ageing is a difficult concept and one that is hard to define. When we talk about ageing and older people do we mean those over sixty, over fifty, even over forty-five perhaps? Or do we mean people in the second half of their lives? Is the category of older person reserved for those retired from the paid workforce? The media are apt to label anyone over the age of fifty as 'elderly', and it is with a sense of shock that one reads in newspapers headlines like 'Elderly woman robbed' only to realise that this person is fifty-one! Indeed the media reflect the popular stereotypes of age—those of dependence, frailty, decay and decline: 'Ageing of the individual in the strict sense means growing old'. It can also signify 'life-long growth and development in physical, economic, psychological, cultural, spiritual and other ways', a concept encapsulated in the theme for the 1999

United Nations International Year of Older Persons which seeks to highlight the contributions to society made by older people.

'Chronological age is the simplest, most comparable, and most widely used measure of age' (Rowland 1991). It defines membership in an age cohort, adding a historical perspective to a person's life experiences. Using chronological age as a measure assists policy makers in terms of retirement and pension planning (Rowland 1991). The problem is that there is no 'true' point at which a person is considered to enter old age (Kerzner 1983). It can be argued that, as ageing is a process that begins at birth and ends at death, it is problematic to ask at what age one becomes older (Rossi 1994; Friedan 1993). Compared with the interest shown in the experiences of, and developmental patterns in, children and young people, little attention has been paid to the subtle distinctions between age categories for people over sixty years of age. Policy makers, clinicians and allied health practitioners need to bear in mind that there are many variations in people's experiences across age cohorts and within age cohorts. The experiences of a 65-year-old person will be very different from those of an 85-year-old. Not only are these people from different generations but they also have different experiences of, and perspectives on, ageing. As a simple but obvious example, we would be astonished if politicians, health professionals, educators and policy makers placed all people from newborn up to the age of thirty in the same category in terms of their health, accommodation, educational and income support needs; but we scarcely blink when the category of older people includes those aged from sixty to well over ninety years.

Why pay so much attention to ageing?

The ageing of the world's population is now recognised as a key issue, one that will have profound implications for our society from a global perspective. To date, population ageing has been a prominent issue largely in the industrialised nations of Europe, Asia, North America and Australia. In at least thirty of these countries 15 per cent or more of the entire population is aged sixty years or over and the elderly population is growing faster than the population as a whole. The rapid expansion in the numbers of older people in the population represents a social phenomenon without historical precedent. What is not as widely appreciated is that population ageing is occurring in developing countries as well, with the older populations growing much more rapidly than those in developed nations. Projections are that over the next twenty years the numbers of the world's people who are over the age of sixty years will grow to exceed 1 billion by the year 2020 (National Institute on Aging *et al.* 1991).

It is generally accepted that the increase in the ageing population is a consequence of a range of factors, particularly those related to women's health. These include the decreased fertility rates, reductions in infant and maternal mortality, reductions in infections and parasitic disease, and improvements in nutrition and education that have occurred, albeit unevenly, on a global scale. Because of the significant decline in the world's fertility rates over the past decades, particularly in the more developed regions, an increasing proportion of the population will fall into the older age groups. It is also estimated that the number of women in the world over the age of sixty years will increase from 188 million in 1990 to 320 million by the year 2015 (United Nations *et al.* 1991). With the average life expectancy in 1996 for women from developed countries being nearly eighty years (for Australian women the average is closer to eighty-two years)—seven years longer than for their male counterparts—single older women dominate the older age groups in the ageing population (Bonita 1996). Those people over eighty years old now constitute the fastest growing group among the elderly, with women as the majority in this age group. Population predictions point to this trend continuing beyond the year 2000 (Clare & Tulpule 1994). It has become conventional in gerontology to define people as 'young-old' (sixty-five–seventy-five years of age) or 'old-old' (seventy-five years of age and older) (Moody 1998: 6; Minichiello *et al.* 1992). Such categories do not consider gender differences nor do they take into account the fact that women live longer than men.

These demographic changes have important implications for social planning, delivery of health and support services, and policy development. There has been intense public debate over issues relating to ageing, including the socioeconomic costs, health-care provision and the education of professional practitioners. In the past, discussions concerned with ageing, and in particular with older women, have focused primarily on the negative aspects of ageing such as illness, physical and mental decline and increasing dependency.

At the same time, the growth of older populations poses challenges to national public policies because societies' needs change as the proportion of the elderly population increases.

Looking through the gender lens

Gender is one of those things that makes a difference in the way life is experienced (Arber & Ginn 1995). It has been argued that because social science research is not value-free the failure to incorporate a gender analysis of ageing into research is a reflection of the resistance to incorporating women into society, hence into sociological and psychological research. McDaniel (1986) emphasises that as women get older, the gender inequalities they experience at earlier stages in life become sharper and more visible. Arber and Ginn's research (1991, 1995) is concerned with examining whether social-structural factors are more relevant than chronological age; they consider that the issues of gender and class are prime influences in the well-being of people in later life.

As the Australian female population ages there are significant implications for social planners, policy makers and those involved in direct service delivery. It is important that research on women and ageing considers demographic changes within a broader social context. Coupled with these demographic shifts are significant changes that have taken place over recent decades in relation to beliefs and expectations about the role of women in Western society and their identities in the context of work, family and community. In both developed and developing countries alike, there is a need to achieve a more systematic recognition of older women's significant contributions in the family, in the home, in the fields, in both paid work and informal economic activities, and in the community.

The demographic reality is that there is a disproportionate and growing number of older women in communities around the world. While surviving to a greater age than men, women face a number of physical and social problems related to their longevity, including widowhood in older age. Experience of widowhood rises from 25 per cent of women aged between sixty and sixty-nine years to 75 per cent of women aged eighty years and over (National Institute on Aging et al. 1991). Women tend to outlive men and because women are usually younger than their male spouses the percentage of elderly women living alone is usually much higher than that of elderly men. The fact that many older women live alone is most often the result of having outlived a spouse, children or siblings.

While ageing is a life event that affects all human beings, it remains important to emphasise the inequalities suffered by many women over the life-course and to look at ageing through a 'gender lens'. Systemic inequalities have affected women over their life-course in the labour market, in education, in public programs for health and income security, in national legal systems, and in other institutional systems of society. More formalised gender inequalities are often reinforced by custom and tradition which combine to place women, particularly older women, at a distinct disadvantage. Focusing on gender is more than just including women as a demographic consideration—'add women and stir' (Glasse & Hendricks 1992)—rather, it involves a recognition that women's lives are subject to policies and ideologies that have been a major cause of their relative social and economic powerlessness.

When writers in the field of gerontology do focus on older women as subjects for discussion they often categorise them as a group who are considered to be 'at risk' in relation to their longevity. Wieneke *et al.* (1994) are critical of this approach and urge that research be undertaken with women who may be characterised by their independence and 'wellness'. This concern is also voiced by other writers who consider that women who live to very old ages could be viewed as survivors. As Moody (1993: xvii–xviii) points out, in recent decades we have seen the trend towards the 'biomedicalisation of gerontology' (Estes & Binney cited in Moody 1993)—that is, research interests and funding have focused on the 'biological and medical approaches to ageing'. As many governments in developed countries, including Australia, have moved to fiscal constraints in many aspects of public policy so the catchwords have become 'privatisation', 'means testing' and 'rationing'. A recent headline in *The Age* (7 November 1998: 3) read 'Young get Surgery before old', in an article that stated that 'discrimination against elderly surgical candidates had been taking place on an "unconscious level" in Victorian public hospitals for decades'. In Australia the current moves towards concepts of community care and the push for keeping the frail old in their own homes—while in some ways very positive—is also a cost-cutting measure throwing the care of the elderly on families.

A word of caution is appropriate at this point, as it can be argued that an overemphasis on gender inequalities experienced by some women may misrepresent the strengths of many older women and the very positive nature of their experiences as they age. There is the potential to reinforce the stereotype that all older women live out their years in ill-health, physical dependency and financial insecurity (Gibson 1993) and to do a grave disservice to the many older women who get on with their full, busy and useful lives.

Physical health and well-being

Everyone would agree that good physical health is the single most important contributor to quality of life for elderly women. The majority of older women maintain good health, although the incidence of ill-health increases in the last few years of life (Bonita 1993). Although experiences with acute illnesses are less common among older people than among younger persons, they may be more debilitating. Age-related and/or disease-related loss of sensory and neuromuscular capacities may be associated with a number of negative outcomes, including fractures suffered from falling, dependence on others, social isolation, hypokinetic disease, and depression. In contrast, the maintenance of certain physical abilities is associated with independence in daily living and other markers of functional health. In spite of the role of physical activity in promoting health, older women have the lowest rates of physical activity of any community group. It is the role of health practitioners and the general society (through media and educational programs) to develop strategies for promoting physical activity programs among older women.

An overriding concern of elderly women is to maintain independence for as long as possible and to avoid the loss of autonomy and self-respect that is often associated with a dependence on others. Although good health is a key determinant of being independent and autonomous it is incorrect to assume that some degree of ill-health will necessarily result in loss of independence or quality of life.

Ageing brings more realistic expectations about life and a greater knowledge of self and the world. Theories of life-course development have emphasised that an individual's life experiences greatly influence their attitude to, and experience of, ageing (Erikson *et al.* 1986; Heaven 1992). However, a limitation of life-stage theories is that many take very little account of social, environmental or cultural contexts and, therefore, the marked differences in both the private and public arenas in which people live out their lives (Bernard & Meade 1993). Age may also be defined culturally and socially by expectations for appropriate behaviour and by life events. Although Gutmann's (1987) cross-cultural studies show that women in older years become more adventurous, expansive and assertive, traditional developmental theories described old age as a time for gradual reduction in life involvement, as a time when there were no longer meaningful roles for the aged, much less for women. Friedan (1993) argues that these theorists have resisted confronting the fact that there is potential for further growth in old age and insists that this trend must be overcome before it is possible to envisage new possibilities for ourselves or for society.

Socioeconomic factors

In any discussion on women and ageing it is vital to consider that the pattern of women's work is often interrupted to raise children or to take up a role as a prime caregiver for children or an ageing spouse (Arber & Ginn 1991a; Bonita 1993). A crucial consideration for the current generation of women over sixty years old is that their lives may have followed the traditional pattern of working a few years before marriage, raising children and only re-entering the workforce once the children were older. Many women now in their mid-seventies and older would have become full-time home-makers once their children were born.

Because women are living longer they are particularly vulnerable to problems after retirement from the paid workforce (Bernard *et al.* in Arber & Ginn 1995). The biggest problem for women is that the benefits an individual gets from superannuation schemes and pension benefits are generally based on past continuous paid work and previous earnings (Donath 1994). In general, working women have lower incomes than men and their work patterns are often interrupted for child-rearing and other family responsibilities. For most women, marital status is the main factor that determines their income security.

Arber and Ginn (1991b) emphasise that personal income, or money over which the individual has direct command, is a primary source of independence, enabling the individual to express their own priorities in meeting physical and social needs.

This is particularly relevant for older women who are more likely to be involved in unpaid work. Unpaid work is a very large and important part of any economy and, most frequently, no economic value in measuring production and output is attached to women's many unpaid contributions. This is particularly the case for older women in developing countries, the majority of whom work in the informal sector and in agriculture. The vast majority of older women would not in fact even think of the many arduous tasks they perform daily as 'work'.

There exists at this time little research in Australia that explores whether the perceived inequalities in social and economic circumstances, in both rural and urban communities, lead to a reduction in the standard of, and access to, health care and other services for older women. Maintaining an adequate quality of life for many older women will greatly depend on the range of services that are provided publicly. These services include transport, housing and health. As Australia moves towards a user-pays system of health and welfare services it will become increasingly important for older people, and older women in particular, to have an adequate income of their own (Donath 1994).

Simone de Beauvoir (1972) wrote in *The Coming of Age* that ageing is a class struggle and, like race and gender, social class is a filter through which to see and understand differential life changes. In Australia more women than men received the age pension. Women are also more likely to be living alone and on limited incomes (Australian Bureau of Statistics 1998: 133). A number of writers draw attention to a major determinant of the ageing experience for both men and women alike as being the integral relationship between socioeconomic status and wellbeing. To have access to adequate nutrition and medical care throughout life is no guarantee against the physical changes experienced with age. 'While money does not bring happiness, it can be a hedge against misery and the daily worry about sheer survival that afflicts so many old people' (Hess 1976). In Western society, where money determines whether people can procure essential goods and services, the aged have very little or reduced financial capability. These circumstances may also deprive older people of power, status and autonomy.

Negative stereotypes versus positive images

There exists a dominant perception that the majority of older women will end their life bedridden or dying alone in nursing homes (Arber & Ginn 1991a). The reality, however, is somewhat different, with the majority of women remaining in their own homes and living relatively independent and active lives. We must be aware of the potential effects that negative stereotyping and ageist attitudes may have on older women. Ageism, encapsulated in statements like 'what do you expect at your age?', has the potential to reduce older women's ability to maintain control over their lives (Bonita 1993). For many women the future holds fears and it may be difficult to stay positive in the face of the unknown.

The role of the media is important in terms of constructing social views about older people. The *Weekend Australian Review* (7–8 November 1998: 31) says it succinctly and vividly: 'We regard our elderly as useless, toothless, hairless and sexless'. Media stereotyping should not be underestimated, as it often parodies societal stereotypes, reinforcing perceptions and misconceptions. Older women are often portrayed as a 'medical problem' and older women's longevity is portrayed as an indication of failure, not success (Millar 1994). For men, the physical aspects of ageing may be taken as a positive occurrence as they convey distinction, character and status or, alternatively, maturity, experience and power. For women in Western countries these physical changes are not valued and in fact may be viewed as undesirable.

There are very few positive images of older women in film, television and the media and there is a blatant double standard with regard to the age and body type of women (Millar 1994). A persistent view is that women's importance lies in youthfulness and the ability to procreate. Markson (1994) writes that dominant images of youthful and beautiful women in film reflect and reinforce the notion that older women have outlived their usefulness. In the main, older women cope well with the ageing process despite the physical, psychological and emotional changes associated with it. Older women are pooling their experiences and creativity to challenge negative images that affect the quality of their lives. They are increasingly becoming consumer advocates about older people's rights rather than allowing others to advocate on their behalf.

Demographic data show that an increasing number of older women in the population is used by the media to portray older women in a negative light. There is an assumption that the ageing population will put an intolerable financial burden on society with substantial increases in the cost of aged-care services. Older people are seen as a drain on health resources. However, analysis of Australian demographic data reveals that only a small proportion of women over sixty-five years of age require long-term institutionalisation or nursing home support, and this usually represents an acute intervention at the end of life rather than occurring at a chronic level. Most older women however— between 86 and 90 per cent—obtain assistance and support at an informal or community-based level. Indeed the media often contribute to the interesting concept of old age as a risk to society. The growing numbers of older people are portrayed as a drain on shrinking resources, as non-contributors who are siphoning off the hard-earned taxes of younger people through the escalating costs of their health-care needs. All this ignores, of course, the fact that older people are consumers of goods and services; that they contribute both financially and as carers to their families, often enabling the young dual-income family to function effectively; and that many remain in the workforce at least on a part-time basis well into their late sixties.

Conclusion

The biological process of ageing cannot be stopped or reversed, and human beings are engaged in the ageing process throughout the life-cycle. Ageing must be viewed as a continuation of, not as a separation from, the earlier phases of life. While the physical processes of ageing may be universal, the experience of ageing for many older women is coloured by the attitudes of the society in which they grow old and by the myths and stereotyping regarding women, particularly older women. For the majority of women, the final years of life have the potential to be experienced as a new evolving stage of human life—not merely as a decline from youth but as an open-ended development in its own terms (Friedan 1993: 38).

Whether the trends that confront older women now will continue as future generations age is unclear. The older women of the future may have experiences and problems very different from those encountered by their mothers and grandmothers today. What is clear is that older women want to contribute something positive to their community, to continue their responsibilities and obligations to family and community regardless of their age, and to be given the opportunity to develop new skills (Shanahan 1994) and fulfil their ambitions and dreams.

References

Allen, J. & Pifer, A. 1993 *Women on the Front Lines Meeting the Challenge of an Aging America* Urban Institute, Washington, DC
Arber, S. & Ginn, J. 1991a *Gender and Later Life* Sage, London
——1991b 'The Invisibility of Age: Gender and class in later life' *Sociological Review* vol. 39(2), pp. 260–91
——1991c 'Gender, Class and Income Inequalities in Later Life' *British Journal of Sociology* vol. 42(3), pp. 369–95
——1993 'Gender and Inequalities in Health in Later Life' *Social Science & Medicine* vol. 36(1), pp. 33–46
Avis, N. E. & McKinlay, S. M. 1991 'A Longitudinal Analysis of Women's Attitudes toward the Menopause: Results from the Massachusetts Women's Health Study' *Maturitas* vol. 13, pp. 65–79
Australian Bureau of Statistics 1998 *Australian Social Trends 1998* Catalogue no. 4102.0, AGPS, Canberra, p. 133
Bernard, M., Itzin, C., Phillipson, C. & Skucha, J. 1995 'Gendered Work, Gendered Retirement' in *Connecting Gender and Ageing: A Sociological Approach* eds S. Arber & J. Ginn, Open University Press, Buckinghamshire
Bernard, M. & Meade, K. (eds) 1993 *Women Come of Age: Perspectives on the Lives of Older Women* Edward Arnold, London
Bonita, R. 1993 'Older Women: A Growing Force' in *New Zealand's Ageing Society: The Implications* ed. P. Koopman-Boyden, Daphne Brasell, Wellington
——1996 *Women Aging & Health. Achieving Health Across the Life Span* World Health Organization, Geneva
Clare, R. & Tulpule, A. 1994 *Australia's Ageing Society* Background Paper no. 37, Office of EPAC, Commonwealth of Australia, Canberra
Davis, N., Cole, E. & Rothblum, E. (eds) 1993 *Faces of Women and Aging* Haworth, Harrington Park, New York
de Beauvoir, S. 1972 *The Coming of Age* Warner Books, New York
Donath, S. 1994 Is Women's Work Rewarded? Economic issues for older women, paper presented to Women and Ageing Seminar, University of Melbourne, Melbourne
Erikson, E., Erikson, J. & Kivnick, H. 1986 *Vital Involvement in Old Age—The Experience of Old Age in Our Time* Norton, New York
Feldman, S. & Netz, Y. 1997 'Beyond Menopause: Vulnerability versus hardiness' in *A Clinician's Guide to Menopause* eds Donna E. Stewart & Gail Erlick Robinson, American Psychiatric Press Inc., Washington, DC
Friedan, B. 1993 *The Fountain of Age* Random House, London

Garner, J. D. & Mercer, S. (eds) 1989 *Women As They Age: Challenge, Opportunity, and Triumph* Haworth, New York
Gee, E. & Kimball, M. 1987 *Women and Aging* Butterworths, Toronto
Gibson, D. 1993 Broken Down by Age and Sex: 'The Problem of Old Women' redefined, paper presented at RADGAG, Brisbane
Glasse, L. & Hendricks, J. (eds) 1992 *Gender and Aging* Baywood Publishing Company, Amityville, New York
Gouault, D. 1990 *Women and Aging in Canada* University of Ottawa, Ottawa
Gutmann, D. 1987 *Reclaimed Powers. Towards a New Psychology of Men and Women in Later Life* Basic Books, New York
Heaven, P. (ed.) 1992 *Life Span Development* Harcourt Brace Jovanovich, Sydney
Hess, B. B. (ed.) 1976 *Growing Old in America* Transaction Books, New Brunswick, New Jersey
Kendig, H. & McCallum, J. (eds) 1990 *Grey Policy—Australian Policies for an Ageing Society* Allen & Unwin, Sydney
Kerzner, L. J. 1983 'Physical Changes After Menopause' in *Older Women: Issues and Prospects* ed. E. Markson, Lexington Books, Massachusetts, pp. 299–314
Kuhn, M. & Gray Panthers 1974 *New Life for the Elderly: Liberation from Agism* Gray Panthers Tabernacle Church, Philadelphia
McDaniel, S. A. 1986 *Canada's Aging Population* Butterworths, Toronto
Markson, E. W. 1994 'Issues Affecting Older Women' *Promoting Successful Aging* Sage Publications, Belmont Hills, CA
Millar, M. 1994 The Lady Vanishes, paper presented to Women and Ageing Seminar, University of Melbourne, Melbourne
Minichiello, V., Alexander, L. & Jones, D. 1992 *Gerontology: A Multidisciplinary Approach* Prentice Hall, New York
Moody, Harry R. 1992 *Ethics in an Aging Society* The Johns Hopkins University Press, Baltimore
——1998 *Aging. Concepts & Controversies* (2nd edn) Pine Forge Press, Thousand Oaks, CA
Mott, S. & Riggs, A. 1993 *Elderly People—Their Needs for and Participation in Social Interactions* Research Monograph Series, vol. 5, Deakin University, Melbourne
National Institute on Aging, National Institute of Health and Public Health Service & Department of Health and Human Services 1991 *Research on Older Women. Highlights from the Baltimore Longitudinal Study of Aging* National Advisory Council on Aging, Baltimore
Older Persons' Planning Office 1990 *Looking Forward to an Older Victoria* Victorian Government Publication, Melbourne
Older Women's Network 1992 *Report of the Conference on Older Women, Feminism and Health* Older Women's Network, Sydney
Rossi, A. S. (ed.) 1994 *Gender and the Life Course* Aldine, Glenside, PA
Rowland, D. 1991 *Ageing in Australia—Population Trends and Social Issues* Longman Cheshire, Sydney
Russell, C. 1987 'Ageing as a Feminist Issue' *Women's Studies International Forum* vol. 10(2), pp. 125–32

Shanahan, P. 1994 *An Optimistic Future: Attitudes to Ageing and Well-being into the Next Century* vol. 13, AGPS, Canberra
Sontag, S. 1972 'The Double Standard of Aging' *Saturday Review of the Society* vol. 55(23), pp. 29–38
Thompson, P., Itzin, C. & Abendstern, M. 1990 *I Don't Feel Old—The Experience of Later Life* Oxford University Press, New York
United Nations & Department of International Economic and Social Affairs, S.O., Centre for Social Development and Humanitarian Affairs 1991 *The World's Women 1970–1990, Trends and Statistics* United Nations, New York
Wainrib, B. R. (ed.) 1992 *Gender Issues Across the Life Cycle* Springer, New York
Wieneke, C., Power, A., Bevington, L. & Rankins-Smith, D. 1994 *Separate Lives: Older Women, Connectedness and Well-being* Australian Research Council, Sydney

two

policy's black box: mass media, women and ageing

ANNE ELLISON

In 1964, 'J. J.' Campbell penned a letter to *The Australian* berating the press for its misrepresentation of women. Campbell argued that women wanted discussions on a range of issues broader than 'mere fashion and gossip'. Women wanted to see articles on important issues, such as jury service, contraceptives, middle-aged women, and religion ('Letters to the Editor', *The Australian*, 28 July 1964: 8). We do not know how old Campbell was, but assuming she was an adult, that would make her an 'older woman' today. Presumably, she would be doubly concerned that today, the media seem to consider her political views, as those of an older woman, quite irrelevant. In 1996, Mrs Carter from Melbourne wrote the following letter to *The Age*:

> During the 1996 Federal Election AGB McNair polled voters on twenty-one issues (*The Age*, 30 January 1996). The replies, published in *The Age* were logged by sex and age ranging from 18–54. Those value added citizens aged over sixty, and including the oldest of the World War II generation, were ignored. And now McNair and *The Age* have done it again, this time singling out women and their opinions. A whole week has been devoted to women's thoughts on identity, family, relationships, careers (self fulfilment?) and the future. But only four generations, again aged below sixty were deemed fit to be quizzed. Why, after the formal retirement age are you so contemptuously dismissed? Are you regarded as useless, brainless, lacking merit or interests?

The Age did not print Mrs Carter's letter, much to her annoyance. As we well know, in the media politics of the 1990s visibility is the path to political, social and economic success. For some wannabes, it is even 'to die for'. The importance of getting one's views in print or, even better, getting one's face on television makes mass media the vehicle *par excellence* of communication. Debates about the contradictory power for good or evil of mass media have been around for most of this century, but one of the issues that remains largely unexplored is the controversial relationship between mass media and the setting of public policy agendas. Analysts of public policy argue that mass media have little effect on government policy making. Media analysts strongly disagree, arguing that mass media exert considerable influence on government policy due to their ability to influence priorities in public opinion. They claim that although mass media might not tell the public what to think, they certainly set agendas concerning what is important.

Of course, these are the opinions of the experts, the elites in society. However, as Campbell and Carter want to remind us, the views of individuals in society are often ignored. Whatever elites may say, these two women certainly believe that mass media play an important role in silencing women's voices, especially those of older women. This sentiment is frequently articulated by other older women as a sense of 'becoming invisible'.

Campbell and Carter are not alone in their opinions. From 1996 to 1998, thirty-two women living in the Melbourne metropolitan district were interviewed as part of a project researching women, ageing and their progressive marginalisation from public life. Although mass media were not a primary focus of that study, newspapers and television were so frequently mentioned that it was impossible to ignore their role in women's experience of ageing. An analysis of these women's experiences provides insights into the contradictory statements concerning the influence of mass media in public policy making. A critical examination of the relationship between the media as organisers of social knowledge and the political culture of older women reveals points where older women's culture is at direct variance with market principles that undergird the symbiotic relationship between media and policy making. This 'deviance' on the part of older women results in them being 'media marginalised'.

Older women

A new view of the relationship between media and public policy agendas begins with talking to non-elites, that is, older women themselves, beginning with discussion of their views, experience and practices. Each woman who participated in this study was interviewed at least once, usually over a period ranging from several months to three years. Half of those who participated in interviews joined a focus group, which met monthly for eighteen months. These meetings were supplemented by follow-up telephone calls and personal contact over periods ranging from two months to two years, in order to build a profile of the women's lives over time and understand how issues that were important to them changed or remained the same over time. The participants were aged from fifty-five to eighty-two, and were of diverse political cultures, socioeconomic status and ethnic background. All were retired and primarily involved in family life or local community activities.

The participants were 'ordinary' grandmothers, mothers, wives, widows and single women. For twelve women, their main source of income was either the old age pension or a disability pension. Of these, three supplemented their income with some other investment. One woman worked as a cleaner, and another as a part-time teacher. At the other end of the economic spectrum, three regarded themselves as fortunate to have no financial worries. The remaining women—two of whom were single—were self-funded retirees. Although all the married women had worked in paid employment at some time during their marriage, only two of the participants, both single, considered themselves to have pursued careers and to have retired in much the same sense as men. With one exception, all worked in what are generally considered 'female' occupations, mostly as casual or part-time employees due to their family commitments. Seven women were widows; six had never married; two were divorced. The remainder were married and lived with their spouses. Three were 'homeless' in the sense that they were dependent upon either family or friends for a place to live. Two lived in public housing, six lived in a retirement village, and the remaining women lived in their own houses or units. All had been (and two still were) carers at some stage of their lives, even those who had been in full-time paid employment, and all performed informal voluntary work of some kind. Eight provided voluntary services in formal voluntary organisations.

Agenda setting in policy making

For policy makers, the diversity of these women's lives presents a challenge. Exactly what issues should be on the policy agenda? The ageing issues these women raised were broad ranging: from concerns about health, to those about transport, and issues of culture. Marianne (aged fifty-seven) explained her interest in good health as a desire to extend her middle age, her 'useful part of life'. The women recognised the importance of maintaining the health of their spouses and parents in addition to their own health. They expressed concerns over perceptions of poor standards of health care delivered to their aged parents. They were also anxious about economic insecurity in their later years and the problems associated with living on a fixed income. Another issue concerned transport, important as a lifeline in maintaining an active social life.

Less obvious issues included competition between pensioners and self-funded retirees for services and benefits; gender issues relating to the differential status of married versus single older women; and the devaluing of older women's knowledge, wisdom and skills. However, they were united in some areas. For instance, their disdain for and scepticism about political processes and politicians were unanimous, as was their feeling of exclusion from public life, which they believed was due to a combination of ageism, sexism and being caught in a culture warp. They believed that this culture warp was exacerbated by the media, whose values differed significantly from their own. However, the women's relationship with mass media was an ambivalent mix of interest and anger. On the one hand, they gleaned much of their information about current and international affairs from the media. On the other hand, they were dissatisfied with the way the media represented older people in general and older women in particular.

Returning to Mrs Carter's comments, her observation concerning media bias is representative of the views of other participants in the Melbourne project and aligns with the opinion of media analysts who argue that media attention is focused on younger women for commercial reasons (Cashmore 1994; Fiske 1996). Writing of the situation in Britain, Ellis Cashmore notes that:

> Women, especially young women, are the most sought-after group by programmers. As they have most control over disposable income and watch most television, they interest advertisers and by exten-

sion, programmers, who need advertisers' business . . . [S]ince researchers first identified the quintessential consumer as female and between the ages of 18 and 35, television has pandered to women, promoting a vision of the good life in which they play a key part and feeding an obsession with youth, affluence, beauty and glamour. (1994: 115 & 126)

This preference for young women is usually masked, so that discovery of the exclusion of older women occasionally occurs by accident. Mary, a 58-year-old participant, drew my attention to a newspaper article reporting the findings of a survey on the opinions of women approaching the new millennium, opinions with which she identified on several points. Later, to our surprise, we discovered that the company that conducted the survey had not actually interviewed any women over forty-five years of age, because their clients were only interested in the tastes of the target consumers, younger women. Media fascination with young women not only indicates a limited market imagination, it also is discriminatory and contributes to stigmatised images of women and ageing, which have important implications for policy decisions regarding the allocation of resources in a competitive market.

Communications technology and the circulation of social knowledge

The importance of communications technology, and especially mass media, in developing a working knowledge of contemporary society has been widely acknowledged in social theory. However, policy theorists generally argue that mass media have little influence on policy making. This view is premised on an understanding that policy making is an activity that occurs out of the public gaze, behind the closed doors of government. The view that government is the central authority in policy making is beginning to be challenged amid debates over the role of the state and whether it is in retreat (Strange 1996). Theorists who argue that we are witnessing the devolution of government authority to 'spheres of authority' recognise the growing importance of non-government organisations. In addition, planning for the changing needs of complex societies has given rise to a focus on the need for good models for consultation and participation in order to improve the interface and communications between policy makers and the general public. Policy making is becoming an increasingly complex system, with a range of policy actors struggling to get their interests on the policy agenda.

An important form of communication among these actors is mass media, and as stated earlier in this chapter there is a growing interest in the relationship between mass media and public policy agendas. Although there is disagreement over the nature of the dynamics of this relationship, some theorists argue that the media do influence policy agendas because they contribute to and circulate social knowledge among the public and policy actors. This social knowledge then becomes a set of premises which are reproduced throughout social systems within which public policy agendas are decided (Fiske 1996; Rosenau 1997).

The inverse is also true. An absence of knowledge, or misconceptions about the social world, can contribute to creating a gap through which certain groups of people disappear from public consciousness: in other words, what you 'see' becomes social reality and what you do not see falls out of public consciousness. In relation to older women, repetition of representations of them as frail, dependent, non-productive and even sometimes as ditherers constructs a social knowledge that is false. Two comments made by people during my own research illustrate this well. The first was made by an older woman who remarked with some degree of irony, 'is there anything more useless than an old woman?' The second comment was made by a young man who believed that 'old ladies just sit around and do nothing all day'.

Media representations of older women

This predicament concerning social knowledge of older women presents both dilemma and opportunity. On the occasions when older women are represented in the media, it is commonly through stigmatised images that devalue their wisdom, and their past and continuing contributions to society. The Older Women's Network argues that as women age, sexism operates in conjunction with ageism in negative stereotypical images:

> Age equals frail, passive, apathetic, confused, argumentative, dependent, ugly, stupid, frightened, rigid, obsolescent, unimportant, invisible, half-witted, sexless sex objects, asexual [and] apolitical . . . [S]tereotyping of older women is deeply rooted in our society and is reflected in the media in sins of omission and of commission.

The invisibility of older women and their denigration is so widespread as to be almost accepted throughout the whole community. (Older Women's Network 1995: 6–7)

Such stereotypical images disadvantage women in a political culture that privileges value measured in terms of profitability or investment potential. Market value is usually narrowly defined in aggressive, masculine terms, pitting winners against losers by using slogans such as 'attack life' or 'seize the day'. Add to this women's structural exclusion from public life due to caring responsibilities, declining socioeconomic status and decreasing mobility, and a situation emerges where negative images are likely to remain unchallenged. What remains intact is a world view oriented towards reducing costs, especially those associated with perceptions of dependency and need as well as declining productivity—images often associated with elderly women. It is not the need for efficiency that is criticised here, but the uncritical emphasis on cutting costs—at all costs—at the expense of a more challenging approach, which might instead tackle the creative task of reconceptualising the mutual dependency of Household and Gross Domestic Product (Ironmonger 1989, 1996). Within the current climate of compliance in accordance with the implementation of competition policy, older women are caught in an identity trap in which they become conceptualised as dependants or burdens on the system, rather than as valuable organisers of society.

The public sphere is one 'space' within which these issues might be debated, and the media, it has long been argued, provide an important interface between government and citizenry. However, the culture of mass media is at odds with that of older women, as we will see, while it increasingly converges with that of policy making, which is now oriented to the global market. The power relations by which the older woman's identity trap is constructed remain masked, especially if she is invisible or misrepresented. These power relations operate in the interests of the stakeholders in markets, and these include mass media and governments. In the interests of survival, none can afford to ignore the rules of the market where profit is the bottom line.

The challenge for women of all ages is to develop a critical understanding of how agendas of mass media and policy making converge to narrow the horizon of choices about what is considered valuable or productive in a society. While economic efficiency and choice are important, if the definition of consumer either excludes older women or, worse, can only conceive of them in terms of cost and dependency, the implications for all women are important. And while the clock cannot be turned back, issues of social justice, equity and fairness remain relevant for governments and society because these build the infrastructure for a truly wealthy society in the best sense of the word. Women are crucial to the building of wealth in society.

A clash of wisdoms

Women involved in this study often recognised negative representations of themselves in both media and policy. But what of the relationship between the two? Although there is some debate over the degree to which mass media influence public opinion, theorists do agree that the media 'prime' public opinion. The combination of negative or stigmatised images of dependency and burden, existing alongside repeated images and messages of the need for competition and productivity, can, over time, lead to the devaluing of older women. Women's groups, for example the Older Women's Network, challenge media representations of women, as did the Victorian State Government Inquiry into Ageing (Family & Community Development Committee 1997). The problem facing older women is that they must do battle with corporate ideology that valorises competition and maximisation of profits. Media and government policy converge as ideological forces that Douglas Kellner says promote 'transnational capitalism' (Kellner 1990). This ideology is exported internationally via the media network industry in a manner that Ellis Cashmore argues is a form of cultural imperialism (Cashmore 1994).

Older women did not discuss the contradictions this posed for them in such terminology, but they did recognise the underlying ideology as a clash of wisdoms. During one focus group the women spent half an hour airing their values and hotly debating the way they have been devalued by mass consumerist culture. They even went so far as to list this as the number one priority for policy making, arguing that if this were put right, then other policies would fall into place. If values were put right, they believed they would not have to justify access to health care, transport, housing and the like.

Older women recognised that they faced a tough battle with consumerism which promotes the values of competition, winning and status twenty-four hours a day through all forms of mass media, often using young, strong, sexy bodies to do so. They recognised that they were often left out altogether and that when they were included they were frequently misrepresented. These women's values were in conflict with, and sometimes subversive of, consumerism. Yet without these values, the women argued, they would never have been able to raise their families, survive immigration and post-war poverty or manage on low fixed incomes in old age. This achievement represents an enormous contribution to the national economy, which remains uncelebrated in contemporary market culture. In the following section, based on one of their group meetings, four women discuss the differences between their cultural and economic values and those they see disseminated through the media.

EXCERPT FROM A GROUP MEETING: OLDER WOMEN'S CULTURAL AND ECONOMIC VALUES

Janine is over seventy and a pensioner. She is proud of her achievements and her age, but says that values go beyond culture. She notes that older women draw upon a different culture and value system.

> *There is a question of difference in culture. The wisdom of old people is the wisdom of having lived for so long and had that much experience, and I think that's beyond culture.*

Maria, a pensioner who is also over seventy years of age, agrees with Janine but she argues that older women's wisdom is being lost.

> *The world is altering, and the young don't respect the old, because older people don't have the present stage of education or knowledge. The older people get very depressed . . . the old knowledge doesn't work any more. In the family generally, you've been trying to look after your family. Now they want it to change.*

Maria believes that women's knowledge is actually unpopular today. A first generation Australian-Italian, Maria regards her life as an achievement. She began life in Australia with nothing, but has raised a family of three children who are now married and successful professionals. In previous discussions, she revealed the various ways she scrimped and saved, recycled clothes and did all her own cooking so that her family would prosper.

In women's political culture, artefacts include such things as their clothes. Carmel, who has made no comment so far, speaks. She makes most of her clothes and always dresses neatly but simply. Plucking at her dress, she comments with pride that she 'made this little thing which cost $2'. Hers is not the wisdom of the advertisers who encourage women to spend hundreds of dollars on their clothes. For herself, a pensioner on a fixed income, such spending on clothes constitutes an astounding waste. Carmel declares that rather than spend that money on clothes, women 'could be putting clothes money towards their mortgages'.

Nancy, a divorced woman in her seventies, owns a small flat and lives on $200 per week. She picks up on this last point. In spite of her small income, she still manages to save enough money to provide for a 'little holiday each year'. But to do this, she must be inventive. Unfortunately, she laments, her inventiveness is regarded by some as 'quaint', out of sync with today's ideology. Such is the disparity between her political culture and that of commercialism. Undaunted, she defends her sense of exploration, which also gives her great satisfaction.

> *I work out how to do something rather than buy something and spend hundreds of dollars. I invent something. I create something. I've got the satisfaction . . . it's probably a bit quaint in modern day terms, but actually, it's very common sense . . . Supermarkets would go broke if they depended on me because I buy very little from them, maybe canned, processed foods. I make my own jams and things like that. But young people don't know how to do things like that. They don't know how to make their own spaghetti sauces.*

Each of these women articulates what Professor Duncan Ironmonger (1989, 1996) identifies as the contradiction that the household economy represents for capitalist economies. Because these women are non-conformist in their 'consumer' attitudes, and because they must budget carefully, they are resistant to the enticements of advertisers who would have them telephone during the evening news for a take-away pizza or chicken. Advertisers looking for easy markets will find little in these women to interest them. Consequently, older women are unlikely to see themselves reflected in the images relayed through a profit-driven commercial enterprise like the mass media. However, such an attitude is not good enough for government. While it may not matter to policy makers whether or not older women buy take-away food, their contribution to the economy does matter. Inasmuch as women successfully self-govern, they do what most of society has done for centuries: they allow the government to concentrate on other agendas (Kooiman 1993). This is no problem, unless older women's invisibility actually contributes to their receiving a smaller share of society's resources, or worse, to perceptions that they are a burden or an economic risk. The greater the convergence between government and market ideology, the more serious are the implications for groups who will be marginalised on arguments concerning profitability.

Women's constituencies

Much of women's social capital is produced and circulated within their own social circles, either through formal voluntary organisations or informal social contact. Eight of the participants contributed several hours to organisations in the voluntary (or 'third') sector. However, all participants made considerable contributions to informal voluntary work in the form of child minding, house cleaning and general caring when relatives, partners or friends were sick. In the light of demographic shifts in society and changing work patterns, a major issue for governments in the future will concern the harnessing of these social and economic resources.

But, in policy terms, voluntarism also represents massive savings to the public sector, as well as having a positive effect on the person providing the service and the recipient of the service (Family & Community Development Committee 1997; McCallum & Geiselhart 1996). As employment patterns change, the nature of work and remuneration in the third sector are set to become increasingly important and political over the next decade, as business and voluntary sectors compete for government benefits and business (Van Til 1988; Rifkin 1995; Rhodes 1995).

The voluntary sector also receives substantial funding from the government as part of the package of microeconomic reform and public sector restructuring. Changes in the nature of work and retirement will involve more complicated differentiation among older women, whose classification according to the male concept of retirement has never adequately described women's life-course. At this stage, little is known about the voluntary sector, apart from the fact that older women make a significant contribution as voluntary workers, to the tune of millions of dollars. In 1995 the Australian Bureau of Statistics Survey of Voluntary Work found that during the twelve months to June of that year, 641,500 people aged fifty-five years or over contributed 141.1 million hours of voluntary work, more than their share of the population's contribution. The question one might ask is why this 'other' picture is rarely, if ever, presented side by side with the messages of doom and gloom regarding the 'crisis' of ageing societies—in either policy literature or mass media. As the women participants asked, how much is enough? Surprisingly, women commonly did not regard such volunteering as 'work', and often rejected the idea of being paid.

However, these women did desire recognition for their contribution and some accountability towards them on the part of organisations they supported. Sometimes, they were angered when they saw a complete lack of accountability on the part of brokers who privatised organisations they had supported financially and through volunteer work. One participant recounted the hurt suffered over the handling of her own group's work. Over the course of fifteen years, her group had contributed $45,000 to two organisations. This money had been earmarked for specific purposes so they knew what the money had purchased. However, when the organisations were restructured or privatised, the group saw their voluntary contribution simply disappear. They had no idea what had happened, and were angry; but there appeared to be no forum for discussion of these issues.

Communicating conceptual knowledge

Central to understanding the conundrum of the media in agenda setting is an appreciation of the role of mass media as communicators of knowledge in a landscape where rapid transformation is normal. In this landscape non-government organisations are becoming increasingly important to government and the processes of public administration. One of the key problems in understanding the role of mass media in policy making concerns the strategic use of information and communication of that information. Many analyses of policy allude to the fact that the media are involved and are important in certain stages of policy making. However, rarely is there any elaboration of this role. Policy literature that draws on empirical analyses of agenda setting argues that mass media do not significantly influence government decision making (Kingdon 1984; Muller 1996; Considine 1998). Yet there are examples of analyses that demonstrate the influence of mass media on policy. Theda Skocpol's analysis of the failed Clinton Health Reform Bill is particularly illuminating in this respect. In *Boomerang*, a detailed analysis of the collapse of the Reform Bill, Skocpol argues that mass media played an important role in defeating a proposal for reform that had wide public support (Skocpol 1996).

Writing in the field of international relations theory, James Rosenau identifies mass media as increasingly influential for policy making. He argues that:

> Television and other media of communications not only provide first-hand information and short-term learning that keeps people and organisations up to date with the matters of concern to them, but through repetitive exposures they also contribute to the formation and sustenance of long-term working knowledge—that set of premises and understandings that enable individuals and organisations to categorise and evaluate any immediate situation that arises. *Working knowledge is not so much factual as conceptual.* (1997, emphasis added)

Communicating political culture of older women

The point that Rosenau makes is important. As do media analysts, Rosenau argues that it is the role of the media in shaping *conceptual knowledge* that is used as *working knowledge* which is important. Recognising this is crucial to understanding how older women become marginalised or, as one participant put it, 'invisible'. By repeating certain images of older women (their absence, irrelevance or non-productiveness), mass media contribute to a body of conceptual knowledge about older women (and thereby all women because we all grow older) that is not adequately challenged anywhere. But this representation runs in direct opposition to knowledge that would be obtained by observing the actual lives of older women at the grassroots, where they are busy organising their 'constituencies'.

When a particular conceptual knowledge is circulated by the media, and this knowledge converges with the interests of policy directives that stress a particular view of economic productivity, the implications for older women are dismal. What happens is that a particular conceptual working knowledge concerning older women is circulated in two spheres in such a way that women's work, productivity and value are denied. This message becomes particularly powerful when it is repeated in the absence of serious challenge from any quarter. In the case of older women, mass media and policy making work together to exclude older women, who cannot get their perspective on the agenda. In so doing, the media do influence policy agendas.

This problem is compounded by the assumption that mass media, policy makers and older women inhabit the same political culture—for they do not. An investigation into the political culture of women participants in this study revealed different political cultures, each with its own cultural artefacts. Those artefacts used by women are not currency in markets premised upon competition principles and profit. While we are well acquainted with the political culture of formal politics and, to some extent, of policy making, we are not so well informed about the political culture of older women.

This 'formal' political culture runs contrary to women's attempts to weave differences into some degree of harmony and to smooth out the ruptures associated with sudden transition. A common experience for participants was assisting husbands to make the transition from work to retirement, a task made more difficult if the husband was involuntarily retired. One female participant explained how she had tried to help her husband make this transition through utilising seemingly trivial, ordinary daily rituals—such as shopping and buying small gifts—in order to make him feel useful, important and valued. Another encouraged her husband to continue to rent office space and to visit his office each day, even if he only read the paper! Family ceremonies, including simple dinners, became times when people told and retold their stories, often bringing out photographs or other mementos, even old bottles of wine. One woman took me on a tour of the photographs adorning the walls of her home, not an uncommon rite of passage when entering someone's house for the first time. However, it became obvious that considerable thought had gone into decorating the house in order to keep these memories of the past and present together.

Over time, what became increasingly clear was the conscious planning and order that went into these rituals. This planning was no less than that which we normally associate with a board meeting or parliamentary session. Boardrooms have their artefacts—whiteboards, laptops, flow charts and statistics—while women have tapestries, needlework, photographs and so on. Homes can be conceptualised as representations of women's political culture, spaces within which meanings are invented and reinvented, where the echoes of the past are contained within the present. Often admired as beautiful pieces of artisanship for their own sake, or as examples of good home-making, artefacts also contain a rich set of meanings for these women and are, in a sense, their 'reports' or 'legislation' born of times of very difficult transition.

The problems women must solve are not uncommonly very private. Sometimes, they are 'secrets' contained within the inner sanctum of families undergoing dislocation. In this study women managed transition associated with migration, death, persecution, marriage breakdown and loss of employment, to name a few examples. When a woman responds to a compliment on her craft with the statement that it represents a very difficult time for her family, to deny the political underpinnings of her words is to deny this woman her form of political speech. To ignore her contribution is folly for policy, for the better she manages her constituency, the more she contributes to the public purse in expenditure saved, thereby enabling government to perform other work. Her political culture runs parallel with the interests of 'good governance', but, unfortunately for her, it counters the ideology associated with competition policy and the consumer ideology of television, both of which share a culture that devalues hers. When the interests of the media and policy making converge according to market principles, what happens is that one set of cultural artefacts—those associated with formal politics and market systems—is valorised, while another set disappears through repeated absences—and along with that, a group of people.

Women's political culture is of a type that facilitates acts of non-decision making at government level, an important consideration in understanding agenda setting (McClain 1990; Kooiman 1993). Women's ability to order their constituencies means that government services are not required in some areas, for example the in/voluntary work and caring often performed by women not officially designated as carers. But mass media preference for artefacts associated with a certain type of political-economic culture reinforces the invisibility of women, while simultaneously failing to acknowledge their productivity. Policy and the media uphold preferred types of productivity. Social theorists such as Anthony Giddens (1991) have argued that communications technologies have the capacity to act as a form of surveillance. Mass media appropriate this surveillance in what media literature describes as priming. Priming can be viewed as a form of gatekeeping as far as women are concerned, in that the media circulate symbols and meanings appropriate to a selective political culture associated with competitive markets. This dynamic keeps market culture or knowledge at the forefront of public consciousness while it absents another form of culture/knowledge. Inasmuch as women's political culture is absent in mass media, older women's stakes in the competition for allocation of shrinking resources are correspondingly lowered. Yet, their contributions to society remain undervalued. They become caught in an identity trap, which is reinforced by images circulated on television that do nothing to challenge viewers' basic assumptions about the facts of life concerning the world of older women around them (Gerbner & Gross 1986). In the world of mass media and markets, artefacts that are valued include consumer goods and abstract symbols of measurement—such as All Ordinaries Indices—not tapestries and meal rituals. What we do *not* see on our television screens concerning older women comes to represent social reality about older women. By this 'knowledge', older women are 'governed'.

The participants in this study did not articulate their dilemma in these terms. However, they did believe that their values were considered irrelevant, and they related this to policy decisions whereby they believed the elderly increasingly had to justify their 'right' to remain in society and to receive basic government services such as nursing home care in their old age. This was considered a basic right both for pensioners and self-funded retirees. The perceived challenge to justify their 'rights' provoked anger, but there was also an inability to identify the process by which this set of outcomes emerged. Consequently, these women did not know how to counter the developments taking place around them. The thought that remained in their minds, and which they expressed verbally, was that society wanted to get rid of them.

The complex relationship between communications technology and society illustrates a point that social theorist Manuel

Castells makes in his claim that, 'technology is society, and society cannot be understood or represented without its technological tools' (1996: 5). American media analyst John Fiske (1996) makes the same point in his analysis of television when he describes it as a discourse that can never be abstracted from the conditions of production and circulation. In other words, interacting via communications technology produces new forms of knowledge and new social and economic relationships.

The conditions of globalisation and the growth of communications technology make it imperative to understand the processes by which new social and economic relationships are formed. We are told that the challenges of complex and diverse societies and the growth of a global society have led to a type of policy making that stresses partnerships and interdependence, greater communication, consultation and increased participation by communities in planning their futures. According to the principles of new governance, governments increasingly share their authority with multiple actors—and this is often regarded as a process of democratisation. Communications technology and mass media are central to this new dynamic. Policy making should be a more inclusive process, but is it? Of communications technology, including mass media, the question to ask is: 'between whom and for whom do communications really occur'?

Castells points out that communications technology has certainly produced new ways of communicating, managing and living. But he does not believe that these are always fairer. He argues that, in America, those who led the way and who benefited economically in the steady march towards a brave new global economy were those sections of society who had access to information and communications technology (Castells 1996). In other words, interactivity and interdependence must not be taken at face value. Embedded within those concepts are sets of power relations and therefore inequality. Those power relations pull the levers of the communications technology by which knowledge is circulated. This interaction can be positive if it is inclusive of 'other' images. But, if it is not, it excludes or stigmatises the 'other'. Then it reproduces inequality. It is in this environment that the relationship between the media and policy making becomes much more difficult to analyse. In a sense, mass media are what has been called a black box of policy processes. Mass media play a crucial role in shaping and mapping the social and conceptual fabric within which policy making takes shape as it is continually made and remade. Policy emerges from a web of political, social and economic forces of which mass media form an integral part (McWilliam 1997).

The problem in analysing the influence of mass media on policy making concerns recognition of the status of mass media as one of the spheres of authority involved in new governance. From a cultural and political perspective, inasmuch as mass media act as a social institution disseminating information and helping to create public opinion, they should be identified as influential in policy processes. However, unless the power of television and other media communications in the construction of working conceptual knowledge is recognised, mass media will continue to be regarded as unimportant in policy making. This merely perpetuates an uncritical acceptance of a culture that marginalises older women. The analytical problem concerns adapting policy theoretical frameworks to include media in policy analyses. One fruitful approach is to consider the role of mass media in the communication of some cultures but not others. It is essential to understand the dynamics whereby media culture converges with the political culture of policy making to marginalise older women. Critical analyses that expose the way mass media mask relations of power—by only circulating certain types of public knowledge and by valorising the cultural currency of the market—are necessary in developing strategies to counter both the images circulated and the power relations inherent in these. It is a necessary step for women in regaining their visibility.

References

Cashmore, Ellis 1994 . . . *and there was televIsIon* Routledge, London
Castells, Manuel 1996 *The Rise of the Network Society* Blackwell Publishers, Cambridge, MA
Considine, Mark 1998 'Making up the Government's Mind: Agenda Setting in a Parliamentary System' *Governance: An International Journal of Policy and Administration* vol. 11(3), July 1998, pp. 297–317
Family & Community Development Committee 1997 *Report upon the Inquiry into Planning for Positive Ageing* Family & Community Development Committee, Melbourne
Fiske, John 1996 *Media Matters: Race and Gender in US Politics* University of Minnesota Press, Minneapolis
Gerbner, G. & Gross, L. 1986 'Living with Television: The dynamics of the cultivation process' in *World Perspectives on Media Effects* eds J. Bryant & D. Zillman, Lawrence Erlbaum, Hillsdale, NJ

Giddens, Anthony 1991 *Modernity and Self-Identity* Stanford University Press, Stanford, CA
Ironmonger, D. S. 1989 *Australian Households: A $90 Billion Industry* Centre for Applied Research on the Future, Parkville, Vic.
——1996 'Counting Outputs, Capital Inputs and Caring Labor: Estimating gross household product' *Feminist Economics* vol. 2(3), pp. 37–64
Kellner, Douglas 1990 *Television and the Crisis of Democracy* Westview Press, Boulder
Kingdon, John W. 1984 *Agendas, Alternatives and Public Policies* HarperCollins Publishers, Boston
Kooiman, Jan (ed.) 1993 'Social-Political Governance: Introduction' *Modern Governance: New Government—Society Interactions* Sage Publications Ltd, London
McCallum, John & Geiselhart, Karin 1996 *Australia's New Aged: Issues for Young & Old* Allen & Unwin, Sydney
McClain, P. D. 1990 'Agenda Setting, Public Policy, and Minority Group Influence: An introduction' *Policy Studies Review* vol. 9, pp. 215–18
McWilliam, Carol L. 1997 'Using a Participatory Research Process to Make a Difference in Policy on Aging' *Canadian Journal on Aging/Canadian Public Policy/Supplement*, pp. 70–89
Muller, Denis 1996 'Policy Elites and Agendas in Victoria' University of Melbourne, Melbourne
Older Women's Network 1995 *Policies and Statements* Older Women's Network, Sydney
Rhodes, Rod 1995 'Looking Beyond Managerialism' *Australian Journal of Public Administration* vol. 55, pp. 106–9
Rifkin, Jeremy 1995 *The End of Work* G. P. Putnam's Sons, New York
Rosenau, James N. 1997 *Along the Domestic-Foreign Frontier: Exploring Governance in a Turbulent World* vol. 53, Cambridge University Press, Cambridge
Skocpol, Theda 1996 *Boomerang: Clinton's Health Security Effort and the Turn against Government in US Politics* W. W. Norton & Co., New York
Strange, Susan 1996 *The Retreat of the State* Cambridge University Press, Cambridge
Van Til, John 1988 *Mapping the Third Sector* The Foundation Center, New York

three

meanings of home in the lives of older women (and men)

CHERRY RUSSELL

Discussion of the private world of older women inevitably centres on the home. As people age, their activities become more home-centred (Howe & Manning 1987; Social Policy Directorate, NSW & ABS, NSW 1995). Women of all ages, and especially older women, generally spend a greater amount of time than men in this private sphere (Gibson 1998: 138). With the onset of age-related disability, more women than men will find that home becomes not only the centre but also the boundary of their social world.

Most of what we know about older people comes to us in the form of generalisations, often statistically based, about patterns within and between large groupings of these people. Surveys, for example, show that the vast majority of older people are 'satisfied' with their homes and want to stay there. Public aged-care policy is geared towards maximising the numbers who can remain 'living independently' at home, a goal that is both cost-effective for government and desired by older people. While these kinds of data are useful for many purposes, they fail to capture the complexity and uniqueness of individual, private lives.

Qualitative research aims to fill out this dimension, and the study of ageing has a long tradition of this kind of investigation. It has shown that personal meanings often 'defy the patterns and regularities identified by social scientists' (Jerrome 1996: 99).

Researchers with an interest in older women, particularly those who approach the issue from a feminist perspective, have made a substantial contribution to our understanding of the personal experiences of being or becoming an older woman. They have concluded that ageing is a gendered phenomenon which has special meanings for women.

In this chapter I draw on one of my own recent research projects.[1] This involved in-depth interviews with community-dwelling older people in which they were asked to talk, in their own words, about the meaning and significance of home in their lives. My findings suggest that the meaning of home to older cohorts of Australian women and men is complex and multi-layered. I begin by summarising the picture that emerges from research of older Australians' homes as private places, paying particular attention to what is known—or assumed—to be 'special' about the home for older women. I explain why, in a book about older women, I am also talking about older men. Then, drawing on theories from sociology and phenomenology (the study of 'lived experience'), I outline a conceptual framework that allows us to think systematically about the meaning of home in later life. I use this framework to present and analyse what my interviewees had to say about their homes.

Background

We know a great deal about the public issues that surround the housing of older Australians. From extensive work on housing policy, for example, we know that older home owners are substantially better off financially than non-home owners (Kendig & Gardner 1997) and that non-married older women pay particularly high housing costs (Kendig 1990; Rowland 1991; Giles 1993). We know that more older women than older men live alone in their homes and more of them risk having to leave home for ongoing care.

Thanks to some in-depth qualitative studies (for example, Thorne 1986; Davison *et al.* 1993; Russell 1995; Russell *et al.* 1996, 1998), we also know something about the objective features of older people's homes and how older people make practical, everyday use of their domestic and local environment. These studies tell us that the objective 'spaces' that older people negotiate vary widely. While some homes are comfortable, pleasant and safe, others are not; they might be inconvenient, deteriorating, noisy, smelly, dark, damp or downright dangerous. Nonetheless all the available evidence, including more extensive surveys (see, for example, Rowland 1991; Fine 1992; Gibson 1998), shows that the vast majority of older people are 'satisfied' with their homes and strongly committed to staying at home, even in the face of substantial environmental and other practical difficulties.

This apparent contradiction has often been remarked upon. It suggests that we need to look beyond the objective characteristics of housing—the 'spaces' older people occupy—for a full understanding of home in the lives of older people. We need to grasp what is the subjective dimension of home—its meaning— for older people themselves. Given the centrality of home to older women, it is especially important to explore ways in which gender might shape the meaning of home in later life.

Few Australian studies have investigated older people's homes in relation to culture and personal meaning. In their report *'It's My Place': Older People Talk about their Homes*, Davison and her associates are mainly concerned with practical issues of daily household management. They do, however, offer the observation that:

> The home has special meaning for older people. It is a familiar place that houses possessions gathered over a lifetime and is a place where they are in control. Emotional ties to the memories of people and events long gone are hard to sever. (Davison *et al.* 1993: xii)

One image that consistently emerges from the gerontological literature is that of the home as the domain of the older woman. 'Men are constructed . . . as newcomers to the home' (Hearn 1995: 101) who, if still married, may represent nuisance value for their wives; if widowed, they are depicted as somewhat pathetic, powerless figures. It is often suggested, for instance, that widowed men find household tasks 'unfamiliar and daunting' (Davison *et al.* 1993: 103).

In some sociological literature, on the other hand, the home is described as a site for the continuation into old age of gendered and exploitative social relations. Despite the fact that retired men report increased levels of domestic activity, this is not apparently accompanied by significant change in the organisation of domestic tasks, with older wives continuing to assume the main role in, and responsibility for, domestic labour

(Fennell *et al.* 1988: 95; Matras & Caiden 1994; Dempsey 1989; Gibson 1998: 74).

It has also been suggested that men usually have the final say in an older couple's decision to move home, and that this 'may reflect long-established patterns of power in the marriage' (Davison *et al.* 1993: 181). While this might appear logical on *a priori* grounds, empirical evidence for it is lacking (Madigan *et al.* 1990: 643).

Finally, there has been some exploratory research suggesting that the home has a particular psychosocial significance for women, especially for widows. From interviews with a small number of older rural Australian women, Gattuso (1996: 175) supports such a view, arguing that it reflects important relations between gender, home and identity:

> Older women struggle to keep their freedom—or risk a spoiled identity. In their struggle home can be, and is for many, a buffer. To lose home is to lose self . . . For women who experience home as a site of connectedness, and as a refuge in which they feel powerful, relocation may be traumatic.

Similarly, an American study of the psychological significance of home to older women speculated that the home 'may take on new meanings for widows as they reflect on earlier family experiences or as they discover that they can competently manage an independent lifestyle for themselves' (O'Bryant & Nocera 1985: 403).

Clearly, only a partial picture of home in later life emerges from this work. One of the limitations of much feminist research on later life comes from its exclusive empirical focus on women and, to a considerable extent, on particular kinds of women, especially widows. This is understandable, since it has been part of an attempt to redress the gender neutrality of previous work, and to document the circumstances of an important subpopulation of older women (but see Gibson 1996). But such an approach inevitably leaves some important questions unanswered. In relation to meanings of home, for instance, are there differences between older women and men? If meanings of home are gendered, how are these expressed in the daily lives of women who share their homes (or not) with men? What are the implications of gendered 'private places' for public issues of resource allocation in relation, for instance, to housing and care policies?

Further, the dominant image of home's 'special meaning' is essentially static and homogeneous. It depicts older people 'at home' as if they have always been there, or at least have occupied their present dwelling long enough to accumulate cherished memories and possessions. What of those who have moved home, perhaps a number of times, during their lives? Does the 'special meaning' of home only derive from long occupation and familiarity? If this is the case, how do we account for the high levels of satisfaction reported by many people who have moved to retirement villages (see, for example, Russell & Sauran 1995)? Conversely, does familiarity automatically generate 'special meaning'? Should we be cautious of an apparent view of older people as essentially passive repositories of their past lives, with neither agency in the present nor capacity for change in the future?

From a feminist perspective, the home appears to be a contradictory place for women. For widows, somewhat romantically, it appears able to embody their identities as independent and even powerful persons. Older wives, on the other hand, are said to experience home as a place of exploitation and lack of power. What might be the implications of this for their identities and attachment to home?

For a better understanding of meanings of home in later life, we need to move beyond cultural stereotypes and *a priori* commitment to an ideological position. We need data on how older people themselves—women and men, living alone or with others—interpret the significance of home. But first we need a conceptual framework for analysing the home as a place with multiple dimensions of meaning.

Personal meanings of home: a conceptual framework

Australian and international researchers (for example, Davison *et al.* 1993; Gurney & Means 1993) have concluded that the home assumes special symbolic and personal significance in later life. As I noted earlier, most studies of the home in later life have emphasised its objective dimensions, that is, the home as 'space' (Rubinstein & Parmalee 1992: 151). Some researchers, however, have explored the meaning of home as 'place'. Sandra Howell (1983) proposes that the meaning of place in later life needs to be thought of as a fluid, dynamic and contextual process, which is centrally concerned with questions of identity. In this approach, attention is focused on describing the processes by which older persons form and maintain 'attachments to home'. Rubinstein and Parmalee (1992: 139) define attachment to place as

> a set of feelings about a geographic location that emotionally binds a person to that place as a function of its role as a setting for experience . . . For older people in particular, place attachment is related to experience of the life course and themes of self-identity that span that life course.

Echoing a frequently made observation in studies of ageing, they suggest that 'the effort to maintain an acceptable degree of autonomy is a primary theme of identity in old age' (Rubinstein & Parmalee 1992: 147). From this perspective, the most salient aspect of a particular locale is not simply what environmental amenities (or deficits) it directly provides, but how compatible these are with one's identity as an 'independent' person. If an individual perceives a given place as more supportive of an independent identity than is an alternative environment, she develops a sense of attachment to it (Rubinstein & Parmalee 1992: 146). According to Howell (1983: 103–4), this helps to explain why 'objective impoverishment or affluence are not always perceived as a deprivation or advantage, nor are they truly reflected in satisfaction–dissatisfaction reports'.

These and other authors see individuals as expressing a range of psychological involvements with the home environment. The lowest degree of involvement amounts to little more than experiential familiarity with a space. At the other extreme, the boundaries between the self and home may be blurred to such an extent that the home 'becomes' or 'embodies' the person (Rubinstein & Parmalee 1992: 152).

As Rubinstein and Parmalee (1992: 143) note, the lived experience of home is neither static nor uni-dimensional: 'one can form any number of bonds with place over the course of a lifetime; these bonds may continue even as new ones are formed, and one may become attached to new places at any point in life'.

What do older Australians say?

Beginning in 1993, I undertook an interview study of sixty-six people over the age of sixty years living at home in suburban

Sydney. The research design and recruitment procedures have been described in more detail elsewhere (Russell 1995). Briefly, the overall aim was to find out how older people living at home perceived the meaning of 'home' and 'independence'. About half the sample (thirty-three people) were relatively active and mobile outside the home. The others received some level of assistance from community services; only a minority of these retained sufficient mobility to move about the neighbourhood without help and some rarely left home at all. The ratio of female to male interviewees was approximately 2:1. The interviews were semi-structured, guided by three main topic areas: dimensions of satisfaction/dissatisfaction with the dwelling and local environment; the meaning of 'home' to the individual; and the meaning and significance of 'independence'.

Without exception, all interviewees emphasised—and usually spontaneously—the importance of independence to them, and they saw 'living at home' as synonymous with independence. In their perception, alternatives to home were undesirable because they were associated with negative impacts on one's capacity for independence. Most frequently mentioned in this regard were the loss of privacy and the imposition of rules and regulations, characteristics that were universally ascribed to 'institutions'.

This commitment to home was largely unaffected by objective characteristics of the dwelling and neighbourhood; that is, people's desire to 'stay put' was not always linked to the material condition of the home. Only a small proportion expressed any dissatisfaction with their homes at all. The concerns of these people (such as noise, smells, absence of light, spartan furniture, general deterioration of the dwelling) could rarely be remedied other than by moving to another dwelling. Some of these people were not, in fact, averse to relocation in principle, although very few were prepared to contemplate moving to a 'retirement place'. They reported a range of obstacles, especially financial constraints. One frail couple in a dark, damp Department of Housing unit would have welcomed something better with open arms but saw themselves as having no other option. Similarly, a divorced seventy-year-old woman, also a public housing tenant, would have been happy to move to 'a better suburb'. For others in failing health, the 'hassles' of moving home were too daunting to contemplate. In other words, for some older people a commitment to living 'at home' does not necessarily entail a sentimental or emotional commitment to living in their current home. Structural constraints, such as lack of economic resources or personal health problems, simply limit opportunities to change their circumstances.

Nor was commitment to staying put related to the individual's functional health status and capacity for self-reliance in activities of daily living. Among many frail old people, living at home might appear to an observer to be associated with excessively high costs in terms of quality of life. For instance, access to the 'world outside' was often confined to limited local shopping and entailed little if any social interaction. These were cases where outings without assistance were not possible because of a health problem. Some respondents relied on family, neighbours and/or community services for shopping, banking, taking out the garbage and other chores.

Two interviews from women in very different circumstances illustrate these themes. Eighty-one-year-old Mrs B's dark flat is in an old dilapidated building. She 'lives' in the front room, which opens onto a gloomy covered passageway leading to the half-dozen other flats on the first floor. Near her armchair is a low table with the telephone, a dish for the expected 'Meals on Wheels' delivery, some magazines and the television remote control. She has her legs up on a stool. She has an ulcerated toe and is recovering from shingles. She is completely housebound. A neighbour takes out her garbage and calls in daily to see if she wants anything. She receives occasional visits from family members and regular assistance from Home Care. But, she says:

> I don't want to go to a hostel, full stop . . . I can't see why I should. I can do what I like here. I get up when I want to and get to bed when I want to, sit down when I want to. It's a big difference being in your own home, doing what you want. A home run by other people is not for me, and while I can manage in my own flat, why should I go into a home? I would lose a lot of my independence.

Similar views were expressed by Mrs S, the 79-year-old widow of a professional man and herself a retired social worker. She lives alone in a luxurious apartment overlooking the harbour. She has severe mobility problems, but has the financial means to pay her own housekeeper to come in for several hours each day:

> *People are better in their own home, if it is any way possible . . . I would hate to live in a village . . . I'll try to keep living by myself as long as possible . . . You see, I have always worked all my life . . . and I feel that my generation of women did not do that . . . I feel I've got different ideas from people of my generation. I probably wouldn't find anyone congenial in an old people's home . . . A lot of my friends are telling me, 'You ought to go into some sort of care', but I don't want to! I just couldn't bear the thought of living with a lot of dull people . . . I pay Katherine $120 a week to come . . . She does all the things I can't do . . . Independence is doing what I think is best for me, not taking too seriously the well-intended advice of other people. I've always looked after myself, I've looked after other people . . . I suppose it's because I like to be in control. I suppose old age means that you are dependent on other people to a certain extent and I am not very fond of that. Why should I move to an old people's home if I can possibly stay here?*

There were no differences between men and women in relation to this meaning of home. Both men and women explicitly linked the maintenance of an independent identity with being 'at home', regardless of either the objective characteristics of their dwelling or their own functional capacities. In terms of the conceptual framework outlined above, they emphasised 'place' over 'space'. Alternatives to home were rejected because, in their view, they were less supportive of an independent identity. Importantly, what they meant by 'independence' was not necessarily self-reliance. Formal help with activities of daily living was acceptable as long as it was not seen to compromise autonomy, or being in control of decisions affecting one's life. As a married man in his early seventies explained in answer to the question 'What is independence to you?':

> *My freedom! I just like to do my own thing and make my own rules, not let anyone dictate to me. I don't know how to describe it in any other way.*

Gender differences did, however, emerge in other ways. Both women and men perceived the home as having special meaning and significance for women. It was, in particular respects, a different 'place' for women and men. Some interviewees were quite explicit about these differences, and offered explanations for them. These centred on a number of key themes: the fact that women have typically spent more time in the home, that the social worlds of women have been more locality-bound than men's, that women have been more involved in the domestic and emotional work of 'making' a home, and that such work has been central to their identity and power as women. Here are some examples of the things they said:

> *During my working life I used to travel overseas. When I was in Sydney I came home every night, but often quite late. My wife would have spent more time in the home than I ever did when our children grew up.* (A 72-year-old man, explaining why he felt less committed than his wife to remaining in the family home)

> *Men don't get as involved as women do in the community in which they live, because they don't make friends like women do, and when they lose their wives they can move on . . . When your husband dies or you separate, a woman loses everything.* (Widow, 70)

> *Women have been pretty powerless in many areas of their lives. Often a home is a place where they have power. And as you get older, it is the repository of your possessions.* (Divorced woman, 72)

All interviewees were asked if they were emotionally or sentimentally attached to their homes. Many, though by no means all, replied that they were. However, both the reasons given for this attachment and the kinds of feelings people displayed when they talked about it varied widely, reflecting the range of psychological involvements with the home environment described in the conceptual framework.

Here there were clear associations with gender. Strongly attached women often showed considerable emotion when they spoke about their homes, a passion that was largely absent from the accounts of those men who reported themselves as 'attached'. One married woman expressed such feelings of 'embodiment':

> *Every time I come home from a holiday I think I don't want to go away ever again, it feels so good to be home. You belong to the place in which you have lived for so long as much as the place belongs to you. I mean, you own the place, but in*

fact it owns you. You are it's thing, if you see what I mean. It is part of you.

The reasons these women put forward to account for the strength of their feelings about their homes varied. They included such things as pride of ownership, associations with family life and security, and some responses identified several factors at once. For example:

This home is everything to me . . . I can do anything I want, because it's mine. I love looking after it, because it's ours . . . I had to work while the children were growing up, but I hated it . . . Our home meant so much to us, our family life was in the home. (Married woman, 67)

Home becomes something important to me at this stage in my life because I am dealing with a childhood of illness and insecurity . . . My own home now means an awful lot to me . . . I moved into this one about twenty-four years ago and put up with a lot to keep it. I've gone without a lot of other things because I like it, it suits me . . . It is very precious to me. (Divorced woman, 68)

Others, perhaps unable or unwilling to elaborate, offered more straightforward observations:

I moved here in 1928. That's sixty-six years ago. I am very attached to this place. I wouldn't want to move from here. (Widow, 94)

I wouldn't want to be anywhere else but where I am because I have lived there for forty-three years. (Widow, 77)

Men who felt bound to a particular home, on the other hand, typically emphasised their role in building or renovating it as the source of their attachment. To this extent, they seemed to be identifying an attachment to 'space' over 'place'. For example, the question 'Are you emotionally attached to your home?' elicited the following responses:

I am attached to it because I created it and all the things I have done to make it very livable. (Widowed man, 76)

I built this place fifty years ago . . . I love it because I designed it. (Never-married man, 84)

> *In fact, there is some satisfaction in restoring a place as I did here. I almost feel as if I built it. Building a place is a very satisfying project.* (Divorced man, mid-80s)

> *In a way, yes. I have done everything myself in this place. I spent years renovating it . . . It is not the same as when you buy these things or pay someone to do it for you.* (Married man, 73)

Even 92-year-old Mr R, a widower who has lived in a spartan Department of Housing bed-sitter for fourteen years, says he is attached to it 'because I cleaned and painted it myself'.

This difference between attached men and women was also reflected in varying degrees of willingness to contemplate moving from one's existing dwelling. Whereas 'attached' women reported considerable difficulty in contemplating such a move, this was not the case for the 'attached' men. Most of the latter approached the prospect in a decidedly pragmatic fashion. Some had already given thought to the matter and reported a readiness to move on, either out of preference for an alternative (such as for a smaller, more manageable property), to realise potential capital gain, or to relocate to an environment with more recreational opportunities. Others could envisage relocation—even, if necessary, to a retirement village—with equanimity 'if the need arose'. Consider the following questions and answers from two 'attached' men:

> Are you in any way emotionally attached to this place? *That's a funny question! I suppose I am in a way, but I could live somewhere else if it were as convenient for me as this one, in size and location. If I had to move, for health reasons or some other reasons, so you move. I could move, certainly I would not want to because moving is a pain. I don't intend to move, but if it had to be, I could.* (Separated man, 85)

> Would you find it difficult to move to another place? *Probably not. I am a reasonably pragmatic sort of a person. If I had to leave the house, I would probably take an apartment close to the city.* (Widowed man, 76)

At the same time as noting these gendered responses, it is important to emphasise that not all women (or men) said they felt emotionally attached to their homes at all. Despite, in some cases, very long periods of residence, some women did not show evidence of strong feelings one way or the other, like this 87-year-old widow:

I've been in this flat for forty-one years. That's a long time. So what does this place mean to you? My husband died six or seven years ago . . . I've been here half of my life. I manage.

Yet other women made it clear that they did not feel at all 'sentimentally attached' to their current homes, as the following responses (all from female home owners) reveal:

Are you sentimentally attached to this place? *No, I'm not. I have only lived here for eight years. I think I moved fourteen times in my married life . . . I have no roots anywhere, except that I like Sydney.*

I can make practically every place a home, because I've got this in me . . . So that's no problem . . . For me, a home is . . . no more than a roof over my head.

Are you attached to this home sentimentally? *No, no . . . I have been here for nine years. When my husband died, I couldn't stay there . . . I attach no sentiment to the house. It's practical, that's all.*

You've lived here for a long time? *Twenty years.* So you may be quite attached to this place? *No, not that I am attached to it. It's just that it suits me . . . I never did like it very much.*

It's not that I am particularly fond of this place . . . I came here thirty-three years ago . . . You said that you are not really emotionally attached to this place? *No. I moved about such a lot in my life that I don't become attached to anything.*

I am not attached to that place as the 'home beautiful'. I am not into that any more.

Overall, there were no clear, systematic relationships between women's subjective feelings of attachment to their homes and specific sociodemographic characteristics such as marital status, housing tenure or length of residence. Thus, for example, the home owners quoted above were not attached, while some public housing tenants, such as this 77-year-old widow, were:

I don't want to lose my home. That's why I make sure I always pay my rent on time . . . I really feel I belong to that street.

Interestingly, some women who had previously been employed outside the home believed that their working histories made them different from women who had only been 'housewives'. They suggested that the identities of such women were far more extensively bound up with their homes than was the case for themselves. They said things like:

> *Women who have not had careers and jobs and nothing except that home, so their feeling is, if I let it go, my whole person goes.*
>
> *Single women find it much easier to move to other dwellings, because they've always had to plan and decide for themselves.*
>
> *Women who have always done what their husbands told them to, they never had to make their own decisions. They only decided whether they'd read the* Women's Weekly *or* New Idea. *So they find it very difficult to make a decision to sell their home.*
>
> *My sister . . . made a career of her marriage and husband and that is their [housewives'] life . . . [She] still regards her home as her creation and she is terribly attached to her furniture [that] she dragged with her from place to place.*

My data, however, did not convincingly support this view. Some previously employed women were passionately attached to 'home', while some 'housewives' were not.

Finally, some of the interviews with married couples provided insight into the largely unexplored topic of marital decision-making in later life. As I pointed out earlier, there is empirical evidence to show that an unequal division of domestic labour continues into old age. Some commentators have assumed that key decisions in an older couple's life, such as whether or not to move home, will similarly reflect these lifelong patterns of gendered power relations and that, if there are different opinions about where 'home' should be, the husband's preferences will prevail. In my interviews, there were several examples where couples attached very different meanings to their current home. In all these cases, the wives were strongly attached to home as 'place'. While some of the men expressed the kind of perspective I have described above as attachment to 'space', all of them would have preferred to live somewhere else. For example, Mrs W's home:

> means a lot to me. I was only six when my family moved into this house and I have never moved since . . . I like home! . . . Home is a bit like a security blanket to me . . . this is my little part of the world.

Her husband on the other hand said that he was not at all sentimentally attached to it:

> Oh no! I could pack up and go tomorrow. It would not worry me two hoots . . . I don't attach any sentimental value to anything physical, I mean material. Once a thing has been used, I have no use for it any longer. I can discard it easily. My wife is not like that. She finds it very difficult to relinquish anything . . . As for me, I could walk out of this place right now and it would not worry me one little bit.

Another couple expressed similar differences. As far as the husband was concerned:

> There is no sentimental attachment. It is just a nice house. If I move out from one house, it goes completely out of my mind. I don't turn back at all. Never have.

His wife on the other hand said that she

> would find it more difficult than Jim to pack and go. I worked a lot to make the garden what it is and I spend more time in the home than he does. He goes out every day. I rarely go out other than to the shops nearby . . . I want to look after my home. I am a homey person. I don't care if I never go out. I like home. I like cleaning the house myself.

These men, along with some other married men, would, in fact, have preferred to move for a variety of reasons. But they described a situation quite the opposite to that assumed in the literature: they deferred to their wives' preferences. Some, like the 72-year-old married man quoted below, were 'not unhappy' with where they were, but saw considerable practical benefits in relocating at this stage in their lives. In his account of the reasons for staying put, he echoes the construction of home as the 'woman's domain':

> Yes, I have [contemplated moving to a smaller place], but my wife hasn't! She likes where she is. I would like to move closer to the water . . . It's no use moving unless we both want to move, because I am not unhappy where we are. But moving

would give us much more independence financially, because we'd get a lot of money for the place we are living in. We could buy a cheaper house and have that bit of capital. But she likes the area generally and she likes the garden . . . Would she be more emotionally attached to that home than you are? *I don't know. I've never thought of it that way. She just likes to be there.* And how attached are you to that place? *Oh, I like the place and I like the area, but to me it's a house in a dormitory suburb. I'd prefer to move to a resort-type suburb . . . I feel that it would be wise for us to relocate now, but I feel it is not worth making an issue of it with my wife.* Would you find it difficult to leave that house behind? *No, I don't think so. If we move, I'll be able to make a clean break. I have no great passion invested in that house. We moved in in 1971 when it was a derelict place . . . we renovated every room. It would hurt me if someone took it over and did not look after it the way we did—to that extent it would irk me—but even if they did, I would not lose any sleep.*

Similarly, an unhappily married man:

Do you like the house? *Not particularly. It's just a place to live. I'm not sentimental about it. A house is just like a car, just like a tool, nothing more. A car moves you from A to B, a house is a roof over your head. I don't go in for all that sentimental goo about 'home sweet home' . . . The house is too big, just like the garden.* Why don't you move to something smaller that takes less energy to keep tidy? *Because my wife wouldn't move in a fit. She is too insecure. If she had to move she would die.* Have you ever considered a retirement village as an option? *Actually, we have discussed it, but you can guess what the answer was! I wouldn't mind. I could go into a retirement village and settle in very well. [The wife] will find one excuse after the other for not leaving this place. You can't reason her fears. She's got her roots here and that's that.*

Conclusion

These findings show that there are many meanings of home in the lives of older Australian women (and men). The most important of these from the perspective of older people themselves is the association between home and independence. In terms of the conceptual framework I have adopted, older people are attached to home as the 'place' that best supports an independent identity. This meaning of home as the 'place' for independent living has little to do with the objective advantages or disadvantages of a particular, concrete 'space'. Some older people who express dissatisfaction with uncongenial aspects of their current dwelling are not necessarily committed to 'staying put' in this particular home. Often they are constrained by limited financial resources to seek out anything better.

While both men and women share this identification of home with independence, there appear to be other, gendered meanings of home as 'place'. Older cohorts of women and men ascribe certain meanings to the home as a 'woman's place'. More so than for men, the home is seen to have particular significance for the formation and maintenance of a woman's identity as a woman over the life-course.

Men do not seem to have the kind of passionate sentimental attachment that (some) women express when they talk about the roots that bind them to a particular home and the sense of identity they derive from 'belonging' to it. Men who say they are attached to their homes more often talk about it as the product of their role in building or renovating the physical environment. Somewhat speculatively, we could see in these men's manipulation of home as 'space' an expression of masculine self-identity that has spanned their life-course; namely, the cultural representation of men as active 'doers' and 'makers' of things or objects in the world. However, such identification of self with home as a practical male accomplishment (if that is what it is) does not seem to be as thoroughgoing or central to older men's identities as some women's 'places' are to theirs. Certainly they say they could move on without as much difficulty.

At the same time, it is important to bear in mind that not all women feel the same. For some, home is simply a roof over their heads that is (more or less) practical or convenient at this stage in their lives. Some say they have never felt 'sentimental' about any home, while others have chosen to leave a loved home in order to escape (now painful) memories.

An interesting finding was the discrepancy between what these older people said about who has the final say in decisions about where 'home' will be, and the assumption in some of the literature that control over such a key decision will reflect the 'usual' direction of gendered power relations. Relatively little is known about the ways in which men's retirement from work and their reduced involvement with the public world impact on the private social relations of home. My own data do not permit me to do more than speculate about the possible connections here between the dominant construction of home as a 'woman's place', and the everyday negotiation of power between older husbands and wives. It may be that women's continuing control over, and identification with, the domestic sphere—including, paradoxically, their disproportionate contribution to the work it entails—becomes a source of power for wives when their husbands lose alternative 'places' to be.

Overall, an account of older people's own perspectives alerts us to the risk of constructing an overly romanticised view of home. Those who study old age and those who make policies or design services for older people should not assume that 'staying put' represents an existential as well as cost-effective solution to the problems of ageing. Older people's expressed commitment to 'staying at home' does not necessarily reflect a single, uniform set of personal meanings that they confer on their present home; what we might loosely describe as 'pull factors' that 'attach' them to a specific point in time and space.

While this appears to be the case for many people, and especially for women, we need also bear in mind the absence or inadequacy for others of meaningful alternatives. Failure to recognise the structured inequalities that render some older people's dwelling 'spaces' more comfortable and secure than those of others, coupled with a romantic image of the meaning of home, lends credence to minimalist strategies of intervention in 'big ticket' budget items, such as adequate and affordable housing—one of the key resources to which disadvantaged older women are known to have unequal access.

References

Baldwin, N., Harris, J. & Kelly, D. 1993 'Institutionalisation: Why blame the institution?' *Ageing and Society* vol. 13(1), pp. 69–81

Davison, B., Kendig, H., Stephens, F. & Merrill, V. 1993 *'It's My Place': Older People Talk about their Homes* AGPS, Canberra

Dempsey, K. 1989 'Gender Exploitation and the Domestic Division of Labour Among the Elderly: An Australian case study' *Australian Journal on Ageing* vol. 8(3), pp. 3–10

Fennell, G., Phillipson, C. & Evers, H. 1988 *The Sociology of Old Age* Open University Press, Milton Keynes

Fine, M. 1992 *Community Support Services and their Users: The First*

Eighteen Months SPRC Reports & Proceedings no. 100, Social Policy Research Centre, University of New South Wales, Sydney
Gattuso, S. 1996 'The Meaning of Home for Older Women in Rural Australia' *Australian Journal on Ageing* vol. 15(4), pp. 172–6
Gibson, D. 1996 'Broken Down by Age and Gender: "The problem of old women" redefined' in *Sociology of Aging: International Perspectives* eds V. Minichiello, N. Chappell, H. Kendig & A. Walker, International Sociological Association Research Committee on Aging, Melbourne, pp. 16–30
—— 1998 *Aged Care: Old Policies, New Problems* Cambridge University Press, Melbourne
Giles, P. 1993 'Ageing in Australia 1982–1992: A decade of action' *Australian Journal on Ageing* vol. 12(2), pp. 4–13
Gurney, C. & Means, R. 1993 'The Meaning of Home in Later Life' in *Ageing, Independence and the Life Course* eds S. Arber & M. Evandrou, Jessica Kingsley Publishers, London, pp. 119–31
Hearn, J. 1995 'Imaging the Aging of Men' in *Images of Aging: Cultural Representations of Later Life* eds M. Featherstone & A. Wernick, Routledge, London, pp. 97–115
Howe, A. L. & Manning, I. 1987 'Retirement in Australia' in *Retirement in Industrialized Societies: Social, Psychological and Health Factors* eds K. S. Markides & C. L. Cooper, John Wiley & Sons, Chichester, pp. 287–326
Howell, S. C. 1983 'The Meaning of Place in Old Age' in *Aging and Milieu* eds G. D. Rowles & R. J. Ohta, Academic Press, New York, pp. 97–107
Jerrome, D. 1996 'Continuity and Change in the Study of Family Relationships' *Ageing and Society* vol. 16(1), pp. 93–104
Kendig, H. 1990 'Ageing and Housing Policies' in *Grey Policy: Australian Policies for an Ageing Society* eds H. Kendig & J. McCallum, Allen & Unwin, Sydney, pp. 92–109
Kendig, H. & Gardner, I. L. 1997 'Unravelling Housing Policy for Older People' in *Ageing and Social Policy in Australia* eds A. Borowski, S. Encel & E. Ozanne, Cambridge University Press, Melbourne, pp. 174–93
Madigan, R., Munro, M. & Smith, S. J. 1990 'Gender and the Meaning of the Home' *International Journal of Urban and Regional Research* vol. 14, pp. 625–47
Matras, J. & Caiden, M. 1994 'Effects of Spouses' Characteristics on the Social Roles and Activities of Married Elderly Persons in Israel' *Ageing and Society* vol. 14(4), pp. 537–74
O'Bryant, S. L. & Nocera, D. 1985 'The Psychological Significance of "Home" to Older Widows' *Psychology of Women Quarterly* vol. 9(3), pp. 403–12
Rowland, D. T. 1991 *Ageing in Australia* Longman Cheshire, Melbourne
Rubinstein, R. L. & Parmalee, P. A. 1992 'Attachment to Place and the Representation of the Life Course by the Elderly' in *Place Attachment* eds I. Altman & S. M. Low, Plenum Press, New York & London, pp. 139–63
Russell, C. 1995 'Older People's Construction of Dependency: Some

implications for aged care policy' *Dependency, the Life Course and Social Policy, 118* ed. S. Graham, Social Policy Research Centre, University of New South Wales, Sydney, pp. 85–105

Russell, C. & Sauran, V. 1995 'Challenging Assumptions about Residential Care: Frail older people in two contrasting environments' *Lincoln Papers in Gerontology, 31* Lincoln Gerontology Centre, Melbourne

Russell, C., Hill, B. & Basser, M. 1996 'Identifying Needs among "At Risk" Older People: Does anyone here speak health promotion?' in *Sociology of Aging: International Perspectives* eds V. Minichiello, N. Chappell, H. Kendig & A. Walker, International Sociological Association, Melbourne, pp. 378–93

——1998 'Older People's Lives in the Inner City: Hazardous or rewarding?' *Australian and New Zealand Journal of Public Health* vol. 22(1), pp. 1–9

Social Policy Directorate, NSW & Australian Bureau of Statistics, NSW 1995 *Older People in New South Wales: A Profile* ABS Catalogue No. 4108.1

Thorne, R. (ed.) 1986 *The Housing and Living Environment for Retired People in Australia* Hale & Iremonger, Sydney

---

[1] The research described in this paper was supported by a grant from the Research and Development Grants Advisory Committee. Vera Sauran conducted the interviews and carried out a preliminary analysis of the data.

four

mauve is an old woman's colour: women's visual representations of menopause

MARILYS GUILLEMIN

'Draw what comes into your head when you think of menopause', I asked them. Most giggled nervously and claimed that they could not draw. After one and sometimes two or three hours with each woman, asking them about their experiences of seeking help during menopause, this request to draw usually came as a surprise. Hesitantly, the women drew; some in silence, others embellishing their drawings with explanatory narratives. The women chose colours carefully, intent on portraying their individual images of menopause. What emerged were simple, yet potent and vivid, representations of women's menopause.

Asking women to draw menopause began as an interesting adjunct to a larger research study examining understandings of menopause. I was specifically interested in exploring how the notion of menopause as hormone deficiency came to be established and how it continues to be so staunchly reinforced today. Australian menopause clinics were a fascinating site in which to situate such a study. As I visited the five participating menopause clinics, I was struck by the largely medicalised setting in which menopause was being managed. Menopause clinics function as specialist sites often within, or associated with, large tertiary hospitals. The clinics bring together a large collective of specialists—gynaecologists, endocrinologists, physicians, and very occasionally a psychologist—and a huge array of medical technologies, such as hormone replacement therapy (HRT) in its various forms, bone densitometry, mammography and ultrasound as well as their various operators and diagnosticians. This was clearly white coat territory. How then has menopause, widely considered to be a normal passage in a woman's life, come to inhabit these medical quarters? This was my guiding question.

Fifty-three women participated in the study, with the majority involved in in-depth interviews (eight women participated in a pilot group interview). The only criteria for inclusion in the study were women's attendance at a menopause clinic and their willingness to participate. It was important that women were not excluded on the basis of age. Although statistics claim that the average menopausal age in Australia is fifty years, there is great disparity about when, and how, women in Australia experience menopause (Daly 1997). This variation is well illustrated by the range of ages of women from the participating menopause clinics: from thirty-four to sixty-eight years, with half of the participants being over fifty years.

The majority of women were attending a menopause clinic to seek help for menopause-related problems. This may seem an obvious statement but it conceals the complexity and uncertainty of problems that many women experience at this stage of their lives. For most women, their first visit to the menopause clinic was preceded by many unsuccessful attempts to seek help from a variety of health-care practitioners. For most of these women menopause was not an occasional hot flush or night sweat. More commonly, the women's problems were a combination of irregular heavy bleeding, constant tiredness, joint pains, depression, panic attacks and extreme anxiety. These problems were a complex assortment of physical, psychological and emotional upheavals. Compounding this situation were the everyday problems of balancing work and family, and the responsibilities of teenage children and ageing parents, together with planning for the next thirty-something years of life. These problems were complex and difficult, and it needs to be stressed that these women were a biased group. Most studies show that only a small number of women experience serious problems during menopause, and that not all women going through menopause seek medical advice (Abraham *et al.* 1995).

The primary mode of treatment in menopause clinics for menopause-related problems is HRT. Of forty-five women attending the five participating menopause clinics, 71 per cent were currently using HRT (Guillemin 1996). This figure is validated by an earlier Australian study that showed that of seventy-nine women attending a Sydney menopause clinic, 73 per cent were currently using HRT (Wren & Brown 1991). However, these figures are not just interesting statistics but rather are testimony to the primacy of the medicalised processes of the menopause clinic. A woman who has been prescribed HRT enters into a complex arena of constant monitoring and surveillance. HRT is associated with increased cancer risks and side effects. Women on long-term HRT must be monitored for increased risks of breast cancer and endometrial cancer using a number of surveillance technologies. Side effects, such as bleeding and breast pain, must be investigated and managed. All this contributes to the construction of the menopause clinic as a largely medicalised site.

The medicalised process of managing menopause is interesting in the context of the women's drawings. Here were a group of women experiencing serious problems for which they were seeking help. However, the representations of menopause in the women's drawings stood in sharp contrast to their medicalised lived experience.

Menopause as a life transition

In asking women to draw menopause I was interested in how they understood menopause, particularly in relation to their management practices. The drawings revealed the multiplicities of women's menopause. Unlike the dominant notion of menopause as hormone deficiency that inhabits menopause clinics, women's drawings highlighted not one singular menopause, but multiple notions of menopause.

Three themes emerged from the analysis of the women's drawings. The first of these focused on menopause as a life transition and, significantly, almost half the women's drawings fitted this theme. Predominant in this group of drawings were sketches of trees, symbolic of seasonal change and ecological harmony. Helen, whose menopause was initiated early following a total hysterectomy, explained her drawing of a full and healthy tree, growing on a bed of grass and surrounded by soaring birds:

> It's like a tree of life—family and branches. Also, menopause is something you expect to get to when you're older and retired and sitting down under a tree and relaxing and living life at a quieter pace. When you're younger you're busy and

women's visual representations of menopause

running around; when you're older you can sit under a tree and relax. I love landscape photography so I love trees anyhow. It's an image I had before I had the hysterectomy that one day I would be old and retired and relax under a tree and enjoy it. I thought menopause would be like that. (Helen)

Images of seasonal change and positive growth were dominant in many of the drawings in this group. Cate was looking forward to menopause, to no longer having periods and to no longer having to think about contraception. Cate's drawing was of a tall, vibrant tree positioned beside a large, smiling face.

I think of it as a lovely leafy tree and as a happy time. My childbearing days are over which is a relief. This is the second period of my life. (Cate)

Nina represented menopause with a bright drawing of a yellow, green-leafed daisy.

Menopause—well, I suppose I see it as a daisy. That sounds silly doesn't it but I see that I've got a whole lot of living to do yet and I suppose I'm not ready for it to be a droopy daisy. I want to be in full flower so when you talk about it I see it as . . . I'm in the bloom of my life and I want to get on and enjoy it. I look at my life and I think I've raised four lovely children and I've got so much to do, so much living to do; I don't want to be burdened with all this. So I see it . . . yes, a daisy growing in a green field. I don't know what other women would tell you but I certainly don't see it as anything dreary. I see it as something there in your life; it's possibly a symptom of your life that . . . should be helped along to be . . . not overbearing or anything like that. It should be something that's there. It passes, it's gone; it's a phase in your life. It's a bit like pimples when you're a teenager. They're awful old things while you've got them but it's only a phase, it passes and there are products on the market now to help you with them. You've got help to cope with these awful phases you go through in life and I guess I feel my life is just like a daisy. I don't want to be all droopy, I want to be in full bloom.

I just feel I've got so much living to do. I'm at the peak of my career. As I said to you before, I'm a woman with limited education. I'm now bringing in over $40,000 a year and I think to myself I'm at the peak of my career, what am

I doing feeling like this. I want to get on and do things. I want to travel; I want to go overseas; I want to do things; I want to see what the other side of the world looks like and I want to feel great about myself again. (Nina)

Although some women chose not to draw, like Vera, they described potent images of how they thought of menopause.

I can't draw but I can describe to you what I would draw. It would be a sun setting and the moon coming up. Something finishing but something marvellous is happening. One thing is ending but another is beginning. New sets of relationships opening up. It is a transition—a rite of passage. It's a new life. It's different in that now I can't have children but that's not a concern—I had my children before I was twenty-eight, in another time. (Vera)

Mary reinforced the theme of seasonal transition with this statement:

Having reached middle age I think of it as autumn. Spring was as a teenager, summer in my thirties and winter will be my old age.

Women used phrases like 'autumn of my life' and 'three-quarter point of my life' to describe their drawings, conjuring up representations of life transitions. One woman drew her life as a series of steps starting with birth and ending with death, with menopause as just one of these many steps. In addition to these symbolic representations, women often discussed other significant life stages—their own puberty, child-bearing or their mother's menopause. These representations typically organised women's lives in terms of reproductive stages. For these women, old age was a new phase, categorised not in terms of reproduction, but as one season of their lives.

Recall that most of the women who drew these positive, vibrant images of seasonal growth and life transition were experiencing serious menopause-related problems, regularly attending menopause clinics, and that most were taking HRT. Women's everyday experience of this highly medicalised process was in sharp contrast to their visual representations of menopause. Despite their often serious problems, women in this group consistently represented menopause as a positive stage of their lives and something to look forward to. Women like Cate and Nina saw menopause as symbolising the end of their reproductive lives. Moreover, menopause was an opportunity to experience the positive facets of their lives, previously hampered by family and financial commitments or lack of time. For most women, menopause was a transition towards older age, a period of life they looked forward to with positive anticipation.

Menopause as lived experience

For a smaller group of women, the drawings reflected their current lived experience of menopause. These drawings belonged to one of two categories. The first category was straightforward and consistent, and reflected women's joyous anticipation of menopause with largely written statements such as 'no more periods', and 'end of monthly periods, great!'. Such statements clearly reflected women's anticipation of the end of a monthly routine that had plagued them since menarche. All women in this category spoke of the cessation of menstruation in terms of relief and jubilant expectation. The second category of drawings also reflected menopause as lived experience, but depicted the immediate lived experiences of problems that had brought the women to the menopause clinic. Many women in this group felt unable to draw but often systematically listed their problems in the language of symptoms. These symptoms included pain, headaches, fluid retention, mood swings, embarrassment, discomfort, tiredness, fatigue and, notably, hot flushes.

Of this group, over half the women described their problems of depression, confusion, loss of confidence and anxiety. These descriptions often accompanied drawings depicting black clouds or black blobs. Camilla was so overwhelmed by her experiences of menopause that she had contemplated suicide on more than one occasion. Consumed by fear, panic and severe depression, Camilla represented menopause in the following way:

> *A big, black blob; just a black blob. Who can understand a black blob? You can't . . . I used to write poems about how I felt. Still sometimes in the morning, look I'm so very, very well now, but when I get up in the morning it's still a little bit dark.* (Camilla)

Kathy's feeling of vulnerability and confusion was characterised by the forceful, black scribbles that filled the page.

I see it as being chaotic and messy. It's not been an easy stage of my life. It's been fraught with being put off by doctors and being dismissed and causing me to go around and around looking and seeking information and treatment for myself. So I see it as being something which has been quite chaotic and messy instead of being a natural process. Women should be able to go and see a doctor who should give her some honest straight answers and to head her off in a direction where she can get information instead of having to go around and around in circles trying to get information and get help. I think that it's poor that today when women are so far advanced than twenty years ago that they are still treated this way about a natural process, a natural part of our lives, such an important part of our lives. It's the grief, we're moving from being middle aged to old age; it's just such a vital important part of our lives and it's treated so badly. That's what that means to me—chaotic, confusing, messy time that should not be like that. It's a time of our lives when we need to be nurtured and be helped through this transition because that's what it's all about—a transition period from fertility to reproduction ceasing and we should be treated with respect. I don't think we are. At the time when we are very vulnerable, at this time of change from young to old, that's how we're treated; we're treated without respect and as if we should just be able to take it in our stride. (Kathy)

The drawings of this group of women were indicative of the often overwhelming problems they were experiencing. Unlike the first group of women who were able to reflect on menopause as the seasonal passing from one life phase to the next, these women were consumed by their current problems. In reflecting upon menopause they were not able to look beyond their immediate physiological and emotional problems. For these women the drawings captured a particularly difficult moment in their menopause.

Menopause as loss and grief

The understanding of menopause in terms of loss and grief was first extensively developed in the early 1900s. Psychoanalysts in the 1920s promoted the notion of menopause as a depressive disorder (Delaney *et al.* 1988). The depressive signs of menopause were read as a symbol of grief and loss. Women were said to be grieving over the loss of reproduction with the cessation of menstruation, and in an interpretation with strong essentialist overtones, loss of reproduction equalled loss of femininity. Having lost the capability of producing life, women were considered to be left only with impending death (Swartzman & Leiblum 1987). This analysis of menopause in terms of loss and grief has persisted since the 1920s and reappears in current texts on menopause.

In light of this notion of menopause as loss and grief, it is interesting that only a small number of women represented menopause this way. Although most of the women in this group said they were unable to draw pictures, most gave vivid descriptions of their images of menopause. Women described images of a 'wrinkly, old lady' or 'a matron gone fat; an old grandma'. Only two women spoke specifically of loss of child-bearing ability. One of these women had unsuccessfully tried IVF in order to have a child and then found that she was going through early menopause. The second woman, Rose, was in her sixties and spoke of the sadness she felt when she reached menopause and realised that she would no longer be able to have children:

> *I have six children and I felt so sad to think that I wouldn't have any more children. My child-bearing days were over. It makes you wonder just what use you are after your child-bearing days are over, especially at our age when you had bigger families. I didn't linger on it but I remember having those feelings.* (Rose)

It should be noted that this comment expressed in a group discussion was met with some amazement from most of the other women present, who exclaimed that they were overjoyed that child-bearing was over and that contraception would no longer have to be a concern for them.

Menopause as loss was expressed in different ways. Marg discussed how she hated the word menopause and regarded menopause as something she preferred to keep private. She clearly associated it with old age, a period of her life she was dreading, and described menopause as:

> *Finish of life. The end of it all. Beginning of the end. Getting ready for the scrap heap—that's how I feel. I'm always saying that I wish I was twenty years younger. I don't feel younger*

[on HRT] but I do feel better. I don't think I'm old for my age. I went on a trip with friends my age and younger and I thought that I look better than them. (Marg)

This negative association of menopause with deterioration and ageing was evident in the comments of a small number of other women. Ruth talked of her reasons for considering taking HRT.

What started me thinking about HRT was my doctor saying that once you finish your child-bearing years, every organ in a woman's body starts to deteriorate. I always thought that menopause was normal and you don't have to take anything. He said that once you have your babies your body starts to break down. He then gave me the leaflets that HRT can really reduce the risks of osteoporosis, and, being a bit vain I thought your skin is a pretty big organ in your body and it might stop me getting wrinkles. All in all I think it's really great so that's the reason why I'm here.

We tend to think that it's all natural because people are living longer. Before, they died younger because their bodies did start to close down. Some people have nasty little lines and I think I'm not going to end up like that. You don't want to grow old. (Ruth)

Nancy talked about menopause as something private, best kept to oneself or perhaps to be discussed only with close women friends. Nancy was advised to seek the advice of menopause clinic practitioners following a total hysterectomy. She was pre-scribed HRT. When asked to draw menopause, Nancy drew a copy of Germaine Greer's book *The Change*, and added beside her drawing the words 'negative' and 'old'.

The book, that's the first thing I think about; that's very negative to me. The discussion in Australia about it was very negative. The other thing is menopause is getting old and that's quite negative. That's probably why I don't want to make too much of it. It's not a positive thing for me at all. I can't imagine anyone thinking it's a positive thing. (Nancy)

When asked to draw menopause, Kath wrote one word—grief. Kath felt unable to draw what for her was a very complex emotion. Kath had led a turbulent life and spoke of her sadness, suffering and of her utter despair. Kath had been married three times, had five children, and many failed pregnancies. She had been physically abused by two of her husbands and experienced many emotional upheavals, resulting in several nervous breakdowns. The word grief was, for Kath, symbolic of the constant ache she had felt for most of her life. There were other women, like Kath, whose lives had been marred by abuse, incest and tragic circumstances. It appears that for many of these women, menopause was a time where they felt that they must confront their past, kept submerged over the years under the daily routines of child-rearing, work and daily living. Grief, for many women like Kath, was not due to a vain attempt to hold on to one's youth, but was a process of dealing with past pain. I asked Kath what she felt she was grieving for and she replied:

The babies. I was not allowed to cry. I was beaten for it. If I started crying, I was beaten, so you don't cry. You bottle it all up. It's all got to come out sooner or later and it came out through the menopause problems, so there were two parts that had to be mended. There was the menopause side and the emotional side.

Women like Kath were grieving for the lost years that were spent in despair. For many of these women menopause was a cathartic episode where, for the first time, they had sought help and had to confront past injustices. Rhonda described this emergent process.

The trouble with women is you put up with so much for so long that when people say to you well, you know, what's it like, you say it's nothing and just put up with it. You put up and shut up so you don't talk about it. So when you ask me all these questions, well how do you express that, because I've just put up with it and shut up for so long . . . Now I realise you don't have to put up with it.

The representation of menopause as loss and grief is complex. It is not a simple and straightforward reading of menopause as lost youth and beauty, or as loss of reproductive ability. Although these notions exist for some women, for others menopause is associated with a fear of ageing influenced by the devaluing of older women in our society. For other women menopause represents a different kind of loss and grief: the grief of lost years consumed by emotional pain and despair. These multiple representations are indicative of the richness of the visual images produced. Menopause is a complex, multi-layered phenomenon. The methodology of interpreting visual representations enables some of these many layers to be revealed.

Choosing colours

The women's visual representations of menopause were particularly marked by their use of colour. When asked to draw menopause, the women were given a blank card and an assortment of coloured felt pens. Many deliberated for some time over their choice of colour until satisfied that their choice would best represent the way they understood menopause. The most popular colour was, not surprisingly, red. However, the chosen colour did not necessarily realistically represent what was being drawn. For example, women who drew trees used red, as did those who drew the tunnels they felt they were passing through. Red was a significant marker for these women, symbolic of their lived experiences of menopause. Those women depicting depression or confusion in their lived experience of menopause characteristically used black, opting for thick, dense drawings. Women who listed symptoms chose to use red or a neutral colour, or else totally discarded the coloured felt pens and used a biro.

The choice of colour in the representations of menopause was important for the women participating. Upon contemplation of their drawings, many women reflexively commented on their use of colour. After earlier describing menopause disparagingly as a time when women start wearing pink or beige, Helen exclaimed with some concern about her choice of colour for her drawing, 'That's beige, menopausal beige'. Nancy deliberated carefully over her choice of colour for her drawing of Germaine Greer's *The Change*. 'I can't use mauve,' she cried, 'that's an old woman's colour.'

Analysis of colour is a significant part of the methodological interpretation of visual images. Colour is an important metaphor and signifier of emotion and meaning. In the drawings of menopause, women's use of certain colours was noteworthy. Colour was not always used as a representation of reality but rather was used as a metaphor for women's understanding and experience of menopause: red for heat, blood, and anger; black for fear, depression and despair; and beige for the neutral, drab, colourless older women they wanted to avoid becoming.

Analysing drawings as data

The use of visual representations in social research is a much neglected source of data (Harper 1989; Silverman 1993). My decision to ask women to draw menopause was triggered after reading Emily Martin's research on the understanding of the immune system (Martin 1994). In this study Martin carried out extended conversations with different community groups about how they understood their immune system. As part of these conversations, participants were asked to comment on media images of the immune system, after which some participants offered to draw how they perceived their own immune system. This use of drawings as data is infrequent in social research. Within anthropology, the use of photographs to document physical characteristics of different social groups and their environments is well recognised (Ball & Smith 1992). The use of film and video in ethnographic research has increased as technical difficulties with these media have been largely overcome (Prosser 1998). Within psychology, children's drawings have been used in various ways, from investigation of possible child abuse, to health promotion and prevention (Wakefield & Underwager 1998; Wherton & McWhirter 1998). However, the use of drawings as data in social research remains limited.

There has been considerable attention drawn to the problems involved in the analysis and interpretation of visual images, in particular with photographs and film. Prosser (1998) highlights that images are ambiguous; it is this very ambiguity that poses problems in interpretation. It is for this reason that I asked the women who drew images of menopause to interpret and describe their representations. In this way, the images went through several steps of interpretation: first, they were interpreted by the women themselves; second, they were interpreted by me, in relation to the women's interview data; and third, the images were analysed comparatively to generate common themes. In analysing the visual images of menopause, it was not my aim to unearth a singular, true representation of menopause. Rather, I used the visual images as a source of data additional to the spoken narratives to understand women's different ways of knowing menopause.

Conclusion

All the women participating in this study were regular attendees of menopause clinics; most were experiencing serious menopause-related problems for which the majority were receiving HRT. The women's management of menopause was dominated by hormone therapy, treatment by medical practitioners, and the various surveillance technologies associated with menopause. In contrast to this medicalised process, the women's drawings were in most cases far removed from the medical domain. Although women's visual representations of menopause varied, there were significantly no drawings of depleted hormones or HRT. Menopause as a transitional phase dominated the drawings, together with the joyous anticipation of the end of women's reproductive lives and the beginning of a positive and more relaxed older age.

How is one to account for this 'discrepancy' between women's lived experiences, dominated by a notion of menopause as hormone deficiency, and their visual representations of menopause? It is clear from women's spoken narratives and their visual representations that there is no singular menopause but, rather, multiple ways of knowing and living menopause. Just as there is not one notion of old age, there is similarly not one menopause. Menopause is not determined solely by age, nor by hormone level or any other single determinant. Furthermore, women's experiences and ways of knowing menopause are not uniform. Women's menopausal lives are fraught with complexities, of which their physiological responses are only a small yet integral part.

As qualitative researchers, we are predominantly word oriented. Our analyses centre on spoken narratives and written material. In this work, we often deceive ourselves that we can capture some kind of singular 'truth'. However, all we can ever really hope for is to catch brief glimpses of the complex lives of those who participate in our work. In concentrating on word-oriented methodologies, we neglect the use of other kinds of methods such as the analysis of visual images. The use of drawings in combination with other methods offers an additional way of understanding these multiple ways of knowing. Menopause is riddled with complexities. Using drawings as representations of the ways women understand menopause offers a rich and fruitful approach to exploring the multiplicities of menopause.

References

Abraham, S., Llewellyn-Jones, D. & Perz, J. 1995 'Changes in Australian Women's Perception of the Menopause and Menopausal Symptoms Before and After the Climacteric' *Maturitas* vol. 20, pp. 121–8

Ball, M. & Smith, G. 1992 *Analyzing Visual Data* Sage, Newbury Park, CA

Daly, J. 1997 'Facing Change: Women speaking about midlife' in *Reinterpreting Menopause. Cultural and Philosophical Issues* eds P. Komesaroff, P. Rothfield & J. Daly, Routledge, New York

Delaney, J., Lupton, M. J. & Toth, E. 1988 *The Curse. A Cultural History of Menstruation* University of Illinois Press, Urbana & Chicago

Guillemin, M. 1996 Unravelling the account of menopause as hormone deficiency: working practices of the menopause clinic, unpub. PhD thesis, University of Melbourne, Melbourne

Harper, D. 1989 'Visual Sociology: Expanding sociological vision' in *New Technology in Sociology. Practical Applications in Research and Work* eds G. Blank, J. McCartney & E. Brent, Transaction Publishers, New Brunswick, NJ

Martin, E. 1994 *Flexible bodies. Tracking Immunity in American Culture—from the Days of Polio to the Age of AIDS* Beacon Press, Boston

Prosser, J. 1998 'The Status of Image-Based Research' in *Image-Based Research. A Sourcebook for Qualitative Researchers* ed. J. Prosser, Falmer Press, London, pp. 97–112

Silverman, D. 1993 *Interpreting Qualitative Data. Methods for Analysing Talk, Text and Interaction* Sage, London

Swartzman, L. C. & Leiblum, S. 1987 'Changing Perspectives on the Menopause' *Journal of Psychosomatic Obstetrics & Gynaecology* vol. 6, pp. 11–24

Wakefield, H. & Underwager, R. 1998 'The Application of Images in Child Abuse Investigations' in *Image-Based Research. A Sourcebook for Qualitative Researchers* ed. J. Prosser, Falmer Press, London, pp. 176–94

Wherton, N. & McWhirter, J. 1998 'Images and Curriculum Development in Health Education' in *Image-Based Research. A Sourcebook for Qualitative Researchers* ed. J. Prosser, Falmer Press, London, pp. 263–83

Wren, B. G. & Brown, L. 1991 'Compliance with Hormonal Replacement Therapy' *Maturitas* vol. 13, pp. 17–21

part two

participating

five

learning at the end of your life: a pedagogy of relocation

BARBARA KAMLER

In a recent discussion with women aged sixty-five to ninety, I asked how a university might cater for their needs. What, I asked, did they want as learners? One recurring answer was that they wanted to be taken seriously. Many of the women were enrolled in University of the Third Age courses, which by reciprocal agreement entitled them to audit selected units at their local university. While they were appreciative of the opportunity they did not, they said, simply want to audit. They wanted to do the hard work—assignments, essays, reading, tutorial presentations—in short, they wanted to be assessed and judged in terms of their output, like their younger associates. They wanted to be taken seriously as learners rather than treated as dilettantes who taste from the smorgasbord of educational offerings, like ladies who lunch.

The women were participants in a collaborative research project called 'Stories of Ageing', where their knowledge and experience as older women were the object of our study. The purpose of the project was to provide an opportunity for women to explore how their own life stories might challenge conventional storylines of women and ageing. Their comments alerted me to the profound ways in which our educational practices marginalise older women as learners. When we don't think of ageing itself as a process of change and possible growth, it is difficult to embrace the idea that older women might want to engage in serious study.

Part of the difficulty in taking older women seriously as

learners is that our notion of learning itself appears to be shaped by ageist discourses. Do we believe, for example, that mental and creative facilities necessarily decline with age? Do we see the post-retirement years as the end of productive learning and contributing? Certainly we have seen a proliferation of new spaces where older people can come together as learners, through courses sponsored by the Council of Adult Education, University of the Third Age and a variety of community-based groups committed to agendas of positive ageing. But the crucial question to ask, I think, is: how do we think of these spaces? Do we see them as places for companionship and 'keeping mum busy', or as new opportunities for sustained growth and challenge?

In recent years, the phrase 'lifelong learning' has crept into our vocabulary, suggesting that as a culture we are committed to learning as a lifelong project. Lifelong learning is written into the mission statements of most Australian universities and is centrally on the agenda of the Organization for Economic Cooperation and Development with its firm commitment to 'strengthening the foundations for lifelong learning'. Current emphases, however, seem to focus on preparing young learners to see themselves as lifelong learners, rather than on making provision for older learners. If lifelong learning is seen simply as a perspective to be adopted within existing curriculum structures, young people never see models of older women and men learning, thus compounding the older learners' invisibility. To be somewhat disruptive I would ask: how old do we think the lifelong learner can be? As old as sixty or seventy? Do we think there is a stage when lifelong learning stops? What about at age eighty? Or ninety?

To explore such questions this chapter will examine an instance of lifelong learning—the 'Stories of Ageing' writing workshops[1]—where older women demonstrated their determined and passionate engagement as learners. Particular attention will be given to what I call a 'pedagogy of relocation' (Kamler, in preparation), to creating a learning space where older learners are positioned as knowledgable producers of text. A text is any meaningful use of language that is written or spoken by the women. In the workshop space, the women's texts are read and critiqued, and their sense of dislocation from a culture that reveres youth is transformed and rewritten. In this space, older women demonstrate they have a great deal to teach a culture that reveres youth, idolises the taut, lean body and fears death.

Creating a critical/collaborative space for learning

It is difficult to tell stories of ageing outside the dominant discourses of loss and pain. Discourses can be defined as a range of social attitudes, values and beliefs which have for a long time been understood as natural and proper ways of seeing, knowing and talking about things (Bradkey, 1992). Western cultures conceal loss, yet ageing inevitably involves loss: the loss of loved ones, partners, friends; the loss of beauty, youthful appearance; the loss of position in the workforce, of power and influence. Loss was certainly a central part of the lives of the women we worked with in the 'Stories of Ageing' research project, but loss was not self-defining. The challenge of the project was to create a pedagogical space that would allow women to rewrite the narrow range of discourses—which defined ageing as loss and deterioration.

Those of us involved in the project were particularly interested in the ways that dominant narratives prevent certain stories from being told and in how, by interrupting dominant narratives, it is possible for older women to tell other stories. The stories we tell are significant in providing the frameworks through which we act (Lyotard 1984). They are interpretive resources that we use for dealing with the everyday world and for understanding ourselves within the cultural storylines available to us (Gilbert 1993). Such notions are useful in providing a way to theorise ageing as a changing, contradictory and gendered process, and the ageing woman as positioned within the categories our dominant narratives have provided.

To disrupt these narratives, we aimed to construct what Bronwyn Davies (1994) calls 'collective biography': stories that speak of each woman's experience but which also speak to larger cultural and social issues shared by women engaged in the process of ageing. Through the writing women can, according to Davies (1994: 83–4), 'examine the construction of their own biography as something at the same time experienced as personal and their own—woven out of their body/minds—and yet visibly made out of, even determined by, materials and practices not originating from them'.

Our research method called on memory work as developed by Frigga Haug (1987), a method of inquiry that is collective and deconstructive, where the subjects become co-researchers, producing data in the form of written stories and subjecting these stories to a progressive critical process of reading, theorising and rewriting. Our work differed from Haug's in that we worked for a much shorter period of time with women who did not identify as academic or feminist, and sometimes set writing topics on particular themes that emerged from our discussions.

In this chapter I call on the work of three writing workshops. The first two groups met weekly for two hours in Melbourne over a six-week period, from May to June and August to September 1994 (see also Kamler & Feldman 1995). The third group met for an intensive four-day workshop in Perth, Western Australia, in March 1995. There were thirty-eight participants in all—eleven in the first group, seven in the second, and twenty in the third—representing a predominantly white middle class to lower middle class population from a range of Eastern European and Anglo-Celtic origins. Many of the women had a strong interest in writing—sometimes out of an interest in documenting their family histories—and had attended other workshops under the banner of 'creative writing'. Like these writing workshops, we taught strategies to make writing more powerful. This was part of our collaborative exchange: we would share new writing techniques with the women, they would share their experiences of ageing with us. We were also interested in creating a learning community where writers could see that they had something significant to say.

The learning space we created, however, differed significantly from other workshops in its critical orientation and its creation of a space for disrupting dominant discourses of ageing. We adopted a number of strategies for creating distance between the writer and her text through what I call a 'pedagogy of relocation'. Through the act of writing, of transforming experience into text, we created a space for women to construct new positions outside the stereotypes. Once separated from the body/mind of the writer, the text could be viewed again with other participants in the workshops, for patterns, omissions, absences and contradictions. In this chapter I document three aspects of the pedagogy we developed—in particular its focus on power, representation and critique—and present stories written by Rowena, Mary and

Bella to illustrate the dynamic, multiple representations of ageing produced in the workshops.

Writing as a political project

A crucial component of the workshop was the research team's commitment to a set of political purposes that encompassed the individual but went beyond her. Our political purposes were feminist and transformative and we were explicit about these. Such purposes are often absent in writing workshops where language is treated as neutral or as an expression of the writer's inner self. But for us, it was crucial to have a social, cultural and political reference point outside the self in order to locate women's personal experience in larger sociocultural patterns of power.

Issues of power and powerlessness are central for older women who have become 'invisible' to their culture. We adopted the practice of foregrounding such questions as they arose in our discussions and developed an exercise where we asked women to write about a time when they felt both powerful and powerless. This framing allowed writers such as Rowena to play with the personal/political interface. In particular, it enabled Rowena to reconstruct the experience of taking her husband home to die as a VICTORY of discourses of dignity over discourses of medicine.

I just want to go home!: A story about feeling powerful
or
The Day We Marched to Peter's Tune . . .
Dah, Dah A Dumpty Dee
(n.b. hum refrain to the tune of 'Peter and the Wolf')

'If you go home Mr Brown, you'll be dead within six weeks.'

'I just want to go home!'

'Mr Brown, if you go home you won't have access to our life-saving machines. You will be dead within six weeks.'

'I just want to go home!'

'If you go home, Mr Brown, it may not be possible for you to be admitted to hospital. You will be dead within six weeks.'

Are my heart beats breaking the silence? What will happen if I burst into tears?

What if Harvey caves in? He hung his head even lower.

'I just want to go home!!!'

Overnight the news of Harvey's decision must have reached some of his friends who were employed at the hospital. So, imagine the procession.

First, came HARVEY in a wheel chair,
then a couple of social workers,
after them a wardsman, walking beside a nursing aide,
next came a doctor in his white coat
An occupational therapist joined in and soon after
a physio student,
And I was trailing the rear,
HUMMING

A dah, dah a dumpty dee, a dumpty dumpty dumpty dee, A dah dumpty dah, dumpty dee . . .
Dah dah a dumpty dee, Harvey's coming home with me!
For one whole month we will be free . . . a dah dumpty dah dumpty dee . . .

But what if he had said 'I don't want to die, let me stay in hospital,' what then?

DAH, DAH, A DUMPTY DEE!! HARVEY'S COMING HOME WITH ME!! A DAH DUMPTY DAH.

Rowena's text is poignant. The staging, the procession out of the hospital, the use of song as triumphal march work powerfully as a dramatic construct—as a social critique of the politics of death and dying. The genre of the children's story is invoked, as the procession of storybook-like characters—the social worker, the nursing aide, the occupational therapist, the physiotherapist—marches out of the hospital with Harvey leading the way. This playfulness undercuts the fact that within weeks Rowena will be a widow and face the loss of her life partner.

Her personal pain and fear are always there—but understated, distanced. She and her husband have asserted their rights over the hospital hierarchy; this is a time when Rowena felt powerful. Her grief is not given prominence in this counternarrative, although the fear sits at the edges—('But what if he had said, "I don't want to die, let me stay in hospital"')—as she carefully crafts the personal for the purposes of social action and critique.

While many of the women did not take such an overtly politicised stance as Rowena, they did use the resources of the workshop (conversations, critiques, other women's writing) to disrupt 'cultural common sense' and build a politics of their own. That is, the researchers' sense of purpose was taken up by group members but transformed by them. It was the women, for example, who taught us that ageing is a continuum, characterised by diversity and difference. Through their writing and discussion, they refused the cultural construction of the older woman as an undifferentiated category. Furthermore, they challenged our romantic tendency as workshop leaders to valorise the positive aspects of ageing, to replace images of weakness with images of courage, hopelessness with optimism, powerlessness with power. They refused to create new dualisms of super-ageing, where storylines of fit, creative, physically active, adventurous ageing become the new oppression. Ageing was not one thing or the other; it encompassed a multiplicity of positions, some of which were not pleasant.

Writing as representation not as truth

A second important component of the workshop was our focus on selection and representation; on the fact that the details a writer selects are a construct which give greater power (vividness, engagement) to a narrative, but not necessarily greater truth. One way we tried to interrupt the women's practised ways of telling about their experience as truth was to follow Haug's (1987) procedure of writing in the third person, as if the story were about someone else. We asked the women to write with detail and without judgment and kept the workshop focus on textuality and crafting. It then became possible to ask questions about what was represented, and imagine other possibilities rather than be glued to the details. These were not the facts that told the truth about older women, but rather *a* truth, a particular way of representing their experience.

This was not a simple matter, as the women faced the difficulty of finding language and metaphor for talking about ageing outside such binary oppositions as loss/gain, death/life. Initially, they talked about not being old, of what was *not* rather than what was. In talking about the word 'old', Baba Copper (1986: 48) says: 'Old was without hope, ignored, invisible, trivialized, patronized, limited, powerless. If I didn't want to embrace all that, how was I to speak of myself'.

One exercise we developed to explore imagined positions and unfamiliar ways of speaking, was to ask women to write on the topic, 'She let herself go'. We found this a rich phrase because it encompassed not only the damning cultural judgment of not caring for one's appearance, but the possibility of moving beyond the boundaries that constrain a woman's life. Mary's playful response positions the ageing woman's desire centre stage.

> Boy, did she let herself go in her sixty-ninth year. She left family, friends, husband, hobbies, house and mindless domesticity . . . Removing the mask of wife and mother, she danced every day in the streets to the jazzed up music of Bach. Along with the broom, she threw out the morality makers' restrictions on women's sexual behaviour. With regret for missed past joys, and with no sense of guilt, she made love to every sensuous, clean, intelligent, responsive, perceptive, delicious man who crossed her path. She noted there were not too many of them.
>
> In time she joined every choir in the land and sang her heart out whether they said she could sing in tune or not. She left behind her watch, her proper behaviour, her high heel shoes and a long list of shoulds. She laughed, drank and ate only mangoes, home made bread and lemon curd and talked with anyone nourishing who came her way. She had surely let herself go. And for the first time in her life, her age collided with her youth and she felt truly free.

Mary constructs a text of great energy and vitality. The image of collision is powerful in smashing the young/old dualism and allowing it to break apart. Here the aged body disrupts what is thought to be the right of the young—celebration and joy, music and sex, food and drink, a pleasuring of all bodily senses. In this space the woman asserts her right to reclaim passion and freedom and not simply define herself in relation to others. She takes off the mask of wife and mother. Here she may move beyond the constraints of her youth and celebrate their loss.

While it is possible to dismiss this text as unreal or silly, such a judgment says more about the taboos operating around older women's sexuality than about the inadequacy of the text. In a culture that valorises youth and beauty, where are the love stories of old age? Where are the bodies being pleasured by one another? Mary's text refuses the silence. The ageing woman is not a desiccated, sexless creature, and ageing need not bring loss of loving and sensual pleasure. The celebration has a critical edge which comes as a result of the writing; the writing in turn brings into existence a different understanding.

Writing as critique

The workshops were structured so that each week the women brought a piece of writing which they read aloud to the group for response and critique. Reading aloud gives the writer distance from the experience being written about. Asking critical questions helps the writer see that her text is a representation of experience—not the same thing as the experience itself.

To foster this distancing, this relocation, we developed a number of critical questions. We did not ask, Which part did you like best? or What person did you identify with? or How did you feel about the writing? as might occur in 'creative' writing workshops. Instead we placed the focus on the textual practice, on the writing as a representation. We asked, what image or metaphor in the text is powerful? What aspects of the experience have you selected? And what have you left out?

The focus on image or metaphor makes the reading of the text self-conscious with regard to structure, and also creates a space to affirm what writers have achieved. Once the women in the workshops began to look for images, these became productive points for our discussions of ageing: grey hair as a symbol for mushy brains, tightrope walking as an image to represent retirement, or a compass as a metaphor for finding one's way at the end of a life.

The questions that focused on absence, on what was not said, were particularly powerful in helping the women to disrupt dominant narratives of ageing and make a space for cultural critique. Seeking out the 'unnamed, the silent and the absent' (Haug 1987: 65) demonstrated that what is not said is as interesting as what is said; that silence also works powerfully on the body and mind of older women. Once addressed, absences have the potential to transform understandings and to reposition the writer, so that the stories she brings to the workshop are extended, questioned, rewritten.

This can be illustrated by Bella's story. Bella entered the writing workshop a woman in grief. Her husband had died thirteen months earlier and each week she cried easily. After three weeks of working together, I suggested she might consider writing about her husband's death, as the writing would probably be no more difficult than her present pain. To confront death by making it textual, to construct a narrative of dying, is to break a cultural silence that refuses death as part of life.

When Bella returned the following week with her text, she seemed physically transformed. The black circles ingrained in her cheekbones had lifted; her eyes were alive, her white streaked hair was pushed back from her face with a dramatic flair as she read the text aloud to the group.

It was late Friday afternoon and the sun was going down. I set the table for Shabbat. The white tablecloth, the candles, the Israeli Shabbat plate Irene gave us, the velvet cover for the challot. Sam watched as I went through the ritual of lighting the candles and we wished each other Shabbat Shalom. I knew he was pleased.

We started our last meal. He ate the fish our friend Sula had cooked his favourite way. He enjoyed eating it and had to ring to thank her. For the rest of his last conscious evening he was his usual sweet self. We sat at the table and talked. He was sorry for losing his patience earlier and apologised. He was frightened of losing his mind and please would I forgive him. I hugged him and reassured him I was with him in whatever he did.

He went to bed. I gave him his sleeping pill and as every night before falling asleep he said, 'Darling another day together—thank you'. We kissed and soon he was asleep. I read for a while and went to sleep next to Sam.

When I woke up some time later, Sam was laying across my bed—he could not move or talk, he just looked at me with wide opened eyes. I tried to shift him but could not do it. A nurse arrived and we put him back in his bed. He was conscious and restless. The doctor ordered a Valium injection which calmed him down and he fell asleep.

When he awoke on Saturday morning, he was conscious and responded to requests, but did not speak any more . . . I knew that he was dying and that I could not do more than stay with him. I was calm. I knew that this was the end and that these moments would stay with me as long as I lived. I needed to remember every one of them, every breath, every change. I lay next to him fully dressed and watched him. I called his name. He opened his eyes—he could hear me. His mouth was dry and I put some soothing lotion on it. I listened to his breath, felt his pulse, touched his body. I lost sense of time and space. I felt removed from everything and everybody. There was only Sam and I. I remember his breath becoming slower, the silences becoming longer and then it stopped. Sam was dead.

I touched his face and kissed him. He was warm and soft. I do not remember crying. I stayed alone in the room until he was taken away. The last I saw of Sam was the long plastic black bag in which he was carried out. Somebody tore the blouse I was wearing. I was left alone. There was nothing for me to do, Sam had arranged all the formalities ahead of time. I vaguely remember the funeral. I felt and still feel that part of me died with Sam.

Bella's story constructs the passing of her husband's life as an intimacy within a loving marriage. This is not simply the anguished howl of a grieving widow. Like Rowena, Bella crafts her experience of loss to disrupt dominant discourses of death and dying. She positions the reader on the bed with her—she forces us to watch Sam's last breath—to see the end of a life.

The images are soft and romantic there is a tenderness in lying beside Sam, a sensuousness in applying the soothing lotion to his lips, in touching his soft skin and in the final kisses.

The group was moved by Bella's writing and inspired by her courage at writing about this time of grief. Her text, however, presented a challenge to our goal of separating the writer's personal life from its textual representation, for Bella was, so to speak, enmeshed in her text and indistinguishable from it. Without being insensitive to Bella's pain and to the memories of loss engendered in the group, I was also looking for a space to move forward, a space where we might view her text as a particular way of representing her experience of Sam's death.

I was struck by a number of absences that we might address—in particular, the text's primary focus on the husband's goodness and the lack of naming of the wife's love and generosity in providing her husband with a 'good death'. The move I made was to ask Bella if she also wanted to treat this writing as text, as an object that we could ask questions of and interact with critically. I was surprised when Bella said yes. The writing was therapeutic, she said, but she wanted more. In subsequent weeks Bella made a few changes, but the most interesting of these was the addition of a final line to the very end of the text.

> If there is anything that lessens my pain, it is the feeling that my being with him 'til the end gave him the strength he needed and that he died surrounded by love and care.

This revision is significant, it seems to me, in accomplishing a slightly more significant place for Bella—a different understanding of her agency in accomplishing a peaceful death for her husband. By creating a discursive space for her to explore her loss, she was freed in subsequent weeks to construct a variety of positionings in text other than that of grieving widow. Importantly, the text also accomplished a repositioning of Bella within the group and empowered her to become a more energetic group member and authoritative reader of others' texts—less consumed with her own pain and more attuned to others.

Stories that teach: A postscript

Ageing women's engagement in a rigorous intellectual community—in critical processes of writing, talking, rewriting—

positioned them as powerful. It was the workshop pedagogy that enabled the women to produce counternarratives of older women's sexuality, courtship, solitude, family relationships, and experiences of death. Creating a cultural space where older women tell narratives of ageing from their own perspective produces a richer sense both of what they have accomplished and what lies ahead. Such stories have a material effect on older women's well-being and survival. They also have a great deal to teach a culture obsessed with youth and fearful of ageing.

Importantly, the workshops were more than hobby or pastime, more than a chat group. They asked women to confront challenging questions of power and representation and examine the way cultural storylines shape their lives. The women's work, within a collaborative community of other learners, enabled them both to find new locations from which to speak, and to produce stories that confront, amuse and shake up our 'ageist' assumptions.

Clearly there are implications in this work for those concerned with providing opportunities for lifelong learning. At the very least, we need to think more seriously about the learning spaces we provide for older learners, and the time frame for productive learning. Further, we need to extend our understanding of what the lifelong learner may be capable of. To this end, I conclude with a story by Leila Joan Strachan, a woman committed to learning to the end of her life. Joan was a member of our writing workshop in 1994. At a literary lunch during Senior Citizens Week 1997, Joan's daughter approached us and told the following story, which I reconstruct here from memory.

> You don't know me. My mother was Joan Strachan. She died six months ago. She received an invitation to this lunch and I just had to tell you how important your writing workshops were for my mother. We knew she was happy to attend and she loved writing. But we didn't know what she was writing. She never showed us and we never asked. We had no idea what she was capable of. When she died we went into her computer and found her stories. We were amazed.

The following story was read aloud at Joan's funeral by her children, as part of the elegy service. I offer it here as a tribute to her memory and to the power of stories to teach us about growing older.

She looked in the mirror and what did she see?
Leila Joan Strachan

It was a flesh and blood reflection—the head, neck and shoulders of a wrinkled old woman. She could see it all too clearly. It was all very well for her husband to have put an extra bright light over the bathroom mirror so he could see to shave and trim his moustache, but that light did show up every wrinkle, spot and blemish.

The head was not big, only 21 inches; such trouble she used to have buying hats when hats were an essential item of one's wardrobe. Hats would fall down over her eyes which was embarrassing in front of superior sales ladies. She hopes that a small head does not mean she is narrow minded.

Brown eyes like her father's, maybe a bit faded now but still basically brown. The colour doesn't matter when she remembers what her lucky eyes have seen—new born babies, gorgeous sunsets, Uluru and the Red Centre, the fern gullies of Tarra Valley. They have seen famous people—the Duke and Duchess of York in 1927, Kingsford Smith, Mother Teresa; acts of artistic and athletic brilliance—the Russian Ballet, Don Bradman, Billie Jean King, Imran Khan, Gary Ablett.

Her ears are not big and have tiny lobes so that screw on earrings are horribly uncomfortable to wear, but the thought of having holes punched in her ears was even more horrible, so she never succumbed to fashion . . . She is full of gratitude for what those ears have heard: music, the song of magpies and blackbirds, words of wisdom, poetry recited by Richard Burton, the humour of the Goons and of course, conversations with family and friends.

The nose—the family nose. 'Oh grandma what a big nose you have.' It's a funny thing that although the nose seems to get bigger, the sense of smell seems to be fading, but what memories are recalled by that nose: Boronia, her mother's favourite flower, the smell of the wet earth after rain, coffee and spice in an old fashioned grocer's shop, and the terrifying smell of bushfires.

The mouth—from the mouth comes speech and also song. There are many happy memories of singing four part harmonies to the *Hallelujah Chorus* with her sisters and brothers when driving in the car. Solo singing was always confined to songs over washtubs in the laundry or singing nursery rhymes to children and grandchildren.

The neck, oh dear, it looks even longer and scraggier than ever, like an emaciated emu, but no matter, that's what skivvies, high-necked shirts and scarves are for.

Well, all in all, it's no thing of beauty, but it has lived, it shows signs of having lived and she can be grateful for how it has lived. There is still a lot of living to be done, so don't just stand there gazing into the mirror. Straighten those shoulders and go out and do something.

References

Bradkey, L. 1992 'Articulating Poststructuralist Theory in Research on Literacy' in *Multidisciplinary Perspectives on Literary Research* eds R. Beach, J. L. Green, M. L. Kamil & T. Shanahan, NCRE & NCTE, Urbana, ILL, pp. 293–318

Copper, B. 1986 *Voices: On Becoming Old Women* Calyx, 9(2&3), Winter, p. 48

Davies, B. 1994 *Poststructuralist Theory and Classroom Practice* Deakin University Press, Geelong, Vic.

Gilbert, P. 1993 *Gender Stories and the Language Classroom* Deakin University Press, Geelong, Vic.

Haug, F. (ed.) 1987 *Female Sexualization: A Collective Work of Memory* Verso, London

Kamler, B. (in preparation) *Relocating the Personal: A Critical Writing Pedagogy* SUNY Press, Albany, NY

Kamler, B. & Feldman, S. 1995 'Mirror Mirror on the Wall: Reflections of ageing' in *Australian Cultural History: Ageing* vol. 14, pp. 1–22

Lyotard, J. F. 1984 'The Postmodern Condition: A report on knowledge' (trans G. Bennington & B. Massumi) in *Theory and History of Literature* vol. 10, Manchester University Press, Manchester

[1] The 'Stories of Ageing' research project reported in this chapter was conducted between 1994 and 1997 with my co-researcher Susan Feldman, Director of the Alma Unit on Women and Ageing, University of Melbourne.

This work served as a pilot project for a large three-year Australian Research Council Grant (1997–99) in which Terry Threadgold (Monash University), Susan Feldman (University of Melbourne) and myself (Deakin University) are working with women aged seventy to eighty-five in both writing and video workshops. One of the major conceptual shifts has been to frame the ARC project as a longitudinal study of women's self-representation. While it is common to examine change in the lives of young people, so entrenched is the cultural expectation that age is about decline or death, that longitudinal studies of the social and cultural aspects of ageing are rare. By studying the written texts and video diaries the women produce over the three years, we hope to learn more about issues of identity and representation in growing older.

six

it's a lovely feeling: older women's fitness programs

MARILYN POOLE

Browsing through a family photograph album, I found a picture of a small, wrinkled old lady wearing the black bonnet and gown of widowhood. This photograph of my great-grandmother was taken a few years before she died in her late fifties at the beginning of this century. Growing old for her, in her fifties, was signalled by her clothing, the way her hair was scraped back tightly into a bun and, according to family folklore, by her seclusion and withdrawal from social life except for contact with family and close friends. Featherstone (1991) points out that the role of photographs in our lives is to remind us of what we once looked like. We have our before and after pictures at home with us the whole time. In the case of older people the row of framed photographs and the family albums with photographs of weddings, children and holidays all mark the passage of time; they also mark ageing and the decay and decline of the body. Photographs of our relatives when old not only remind us of our own mortality but provide some intimation of what we, too, might look like when old. Turner (1995: 252) comments that the photograph has 'become an essential feature, therefore, not only of individual images of ageing, but of collective, generational ageing'.

How much have times changed for older women since my great-grandmother's photograph was taken? Hareven (1995: 131) comments that 'the characterization of the aged as "useless", "inefficient", "unattractive", "temperamental" and "senile" accompanied the gradual ousting of people from the labour force at age sixty-five since the beginning of the twentieth century'. For older women, what Goffman termed 'spoiled identity' was emerging in the literature of the late nineteenth century (in Hareven 1995: 131). Frueh (1997: 202) notes:

> Ageing women's visible differences and the changed psychic and physiological ground from which they manifest, disgust and frighten society to such a degree that in an effort to secure its members against ugliness and death which society uses the old woman to symbolize, no socially active defined role exists for the post menopausal woman and she sinks into invisibility.

Is growing older still a period that places women in double jeopardy—not only because they grow older but also because they become old women? Do they still face being subject to the stereotypes of frailty and dependence, and also loss of their attractiveness as women as their bodies and appearance undergo inevitable decline? It is useful to consider here Foucault's (1977: 137–8) argument that power is exerted on the body by means of disciplinary practices producing what he termed 'docile bodies'. Each individual internalises control mechanisms through bodily disciplines. In this way individuals are governed not so much by repressive power mechanisms but by themselves. Individuals recognise that the presentation of self is important to their sense of identity, and this individuation of society has facilitated control and surveillance of its members: people may be rewarded for their appearance or their lifestyles—'you don't look a day over forty!'—or marginalised by the negative connotations associated with those who 'let themselves go'.

Featherstone and Hepworth (1993: 250–75) report on a growing trend towards positive images of ageing and retirement in Britain—and as Encel (1997: 5) points out, the slogan 'healthy ageing' may indicate a new policy paradigm in Australia. While in the past notions of age often invoked decay, frailty and loss of independence, in a postmodern and consumer culture a deconstruction of the life-course is occurring. Featherstone and Hepworth (1995: 31) believe that since the 1960s the 'construction of positive ageing' has spread and that discourses on ageing 'have become a significant feature of popular and consumer culture', an important force behind these being the emergence of the 'ageing industry'.

This chapter is a study of a group of older women fitness instructors, who themselves exercised on a regular basis several times a week. Regular exercise did not include activities such as household duties and light gardening. The study will explore whether the women's commitment to exercise is a reflection of a new climate of empowerment and enablement, and will examine the ways in which the body is managed and controlled and constructed discursively. The chapter will highlight the importance of participating in exercise classes for older women in terms of enhancing feelings of independence and social connectedness.

The study

I used a number of methods in order to reconstruct the discourses of older women's commitment to exercise. I participated regularly in aerobics classes in a private health club that catered to a wide age range, from teens to late seventies, and I also joined classes for the over-fifties on an irregular basis in community centres, church halls and centres such as the YMCA. In addition, I based this chapter on a study of seventeen women fitness instructors who had trained in a Vicfit program (no previous qualifications required) sponsored by the Victorian Department of Sport and Recreation.[1] They had done so in order to work with 'mature' (over-fifties) groups in exercise programs that ranged from low-impact aerobics and aquarobics to armchair exercises for the frail aged. The women in the study were themselves all over the age of fifty and the age range of the sample was fifty-two to seventy-three. All of the women in the study exercised frequently: their methods of exercise ranged from conducting exercise classes twice a week plus playing eighteen holes of golf, to playing tennis, swimming or taking regular long walks (Poole *et al.* 1997). The women were all middle class (though not necessarily affluent), and living in the eastern suburbs of Melbourne. The majority were Anglo-Celtic but some were from European migrant families.

One of the main questions driving the study was, why do some older women exercise so often—what do they get out of it? Is frequent exercise an attempt to retain the slender, taut body of youth and stave off the ravages of age, or is the reason rather more complex—a means of taking control of one's body in order to lead a healthy lifestyle? According to Featherstone (1991), the two reasons are intertwined—the internal body needs to be maintained in good health in order to better promote the external body as being desirable in appearance. For the participating fitness instructors, in responding to questions about the benefits of exercise and why they thought women attended their classes so regularly and so enthusiastically over the years, the discourses of health, fitness and body shape were clearly important. However, responses regarding social interactions, group support and general social benefits also emerged, to the point that one could speculate that for many women the real reason for attending fitness classes is to find friendship, fun and support as well as a healthy lifestyle.

Interpretation of the data from the exercise instructors, based on questionnaires and in-depth interviews, attempts to position the women within the discourses of the body and health, but also seeks to explore the social benefits that accrue from participation in exercise programs. The interviews were a means of discovering not only what the women in the study thought about the benefits of exercise, but also what their views were on the older women who participated in their classes.

All the women in the study conducted at least one fitness class per week. These were held in a variety of settings, such as community halls, aged-care hostels or centres such as the YMCA. None of them, with the exception of two women who ran classes at aged-care hostels, had men participating in their classes.

The ideal of feminine beauty

Feminist writers (Bordo 1990; Bartky 1988; Spitzack 1990; Wolf 1990) have written extensively on norms of feminine beauty that consign women to what Chernin (1981) terms 'the tyranny of slenderness', which leads them to engage in the disciplinary practices of diet and exercise. Many of these accounts place the dominant norms of women's femininity in a wider sociocultural context, and challenge the image that appears in many women's magazines of the 'perfect' Size 10. These magazines devote pages to the body-beautiful: in advertisements for 'age-defying' cosmetics; in discussions of the relative merits of the nips and tucks of cosmetic surgery; and in stories about diet, exercise and healthy lifestyle. Only occasionally, such as in *New Woman*'s April 1997 issue on body image entitled 'The Big Issue', do they try to encourage debate and feature women with differing sizes, shapes and looks. The former editor of *New Woman,* Cyndi Tebble, wrote in *The Age* (4 December 1997: A11) following her resignation over this issue, that 'management was adamant that this focus on "fat" was not to continue, and that I should instead concentrate on articles designed to help women "find a man and keep him"'. She continued to say how saddened she was that the owner of the magazine likened using 'real women in women's magazines to featuring used cars in an automotive magazine', and how *Vogue*'s publisher asserted 'when you pick up a copy of *Vogue* you don't want to look at a run-down house with furniture in it'. So pervasive are the discourses on reconstruction and representation that, according to Tebble, advertisers representing the beauty and health industries do not support editorial content that contradicts their advertisements for products.

While it can be argued that dominant norms of feminine beauty may be culturally specific, a shift has been noted from the 1950s when the ideal was the curvaceousness of Marilyn Monroe and Jane Russell, to today with the taut, slender and sculpted bodies of Claudia Schiffer and Naomi Campbell (Lloyd 1996: 80). Despite these changes the ideal body portrayed by the media is still the youthful body. Featherstone (1991) argues that in a postmodern consumer culture youthful body shape can be achieved by means of the use of hard work. As women age they must work all the harder to achieve the ideal figure (Markula 1995: 442). The *Jane Fonda Workout Book* launched in 1981 was significant not so much for being one of the first such manuals for popular consumption, but because it 'purveys the notion that it is possible to achieve the "right" body' (Lloyd 1996: 83–4). In spite of Fonda's confessions in its opening chapters that she pursued unhealthy means to attain the body-beautiful through the use of diuretics, Dexedrine and bulimia, in this manual she sees 'selling exercise to music as a legitimate, medically sanctioned way to achieve slenderness, her earlier objection to the imperialistic norm having all but vanished' (Lloyd 1996: 84). Whether it is promoted by aerobics classes, or by workout videos and the plethora of articles in the media, the message to women of all ages is clear: you can have the body you want if you are prepared to work at it.

Feeling good: health and fitness

The women in this study clearly were conscious of images of body shape. One 66-year-old said, 'I think women always worry about how they look even when they are older; I don't think it is as important as when you are younger but it is still important'. Older women now have examples of how to achieve a more youthful appearance. The successful marketing of exercise videos and of Jane Fonda herself, now over fifty, demonstrates the effectiveness of a vigorous exercise program (and more recently cosmetic surgery). As Markula (1995: 443) points out, Fonda's body could be seen by older women very positively in that they, like her, can retain a 'good body'. On the other hand it means that they must continue to monitor their appearance and work on a positive image well past their middle years.

While appearance matters to these women, it is not the most important reason for attending fitness classes. One instructor in her early fifties commented about her class:

> *I think they want to feel good rather than look good, but [that] certainly comes in [to it]. When we are starting and I say, 'These exercises will help the loose flabby bits under your arm', they say, 'Well, how many should I do before I start to tone?'. So what else, tummies. Most older women have developed a bit of a tummy and often they will say, 'Can you give me exercises that will help me tone up my tummy muscles?'. Posture, I guess, again they want to know if they are walking correctly. So appearance factors, yes, but it's not the most important thing.*

Not all, however, were convinced that regular exercise could help reduce weight or even assist in toning flabby arms and slack stomach muscles. One 62-year-old instructor said:

> *I think when they get past a certain age the much older ones don't care, but the ones around the mid-forties to their sixties are a bit embarrassed if they are a bit overweight. I have had a couple—not many, mind—[who] didn't come back, and I felt that they weren't coping, that they looked awful . . . I have this particular woman who is Spanish and doesn't understand much English at all, but she has been coming regularly. She's quite huge and she can hardly [participate] . . . her legs are so big . . . but she is trying and I think that is good.*

Another commented:

> *. . . if people think they are going to lose weight by exercising it doesn't work . . . Well, I've got this here, [my upper arms],*

and that drives me mad. I've tried everything and it does not really work, because it is more loose flesh than being overweight and getting old, so I've given up worrying about it. I've got some weights, and my son gave me some new ones for Christmas, but I forget to use them.

Another instructor felt that many women over fifty do not participate in exercise classes because of the pervasive, negative images of older people in Australia. On participation in exercise, one 68-year-old woman comments:

Whether it actually stops the ageing process I don't know, but I do think it's a terrific help. I think mainly [that a lot of] people give in so quickly . . . [when] they get to a [certain] stage . . . Because unfortunately the way things are . . . [from] 50 onwards you are called elderly sometimes here in Australia . . . It's very hard on people especially if they haven't got very much feeling for themselves. So I think this is why a lot of people just won't come along to do things, because they've been told they're now in the age bracket. So therefore, 'I couldn't do it, people will laugh at me', or 'People will think I'm silly', or you know 'I can't do it'.

The view that exercise improved self-confidence was supported by an instructor in her early fifties:

They feel much better about themselves because they have a different image of themselves. I think when they have exercised they feel good about themselves and it sort of carries on. And perhaps through exercising a little they feel more confident to expand, like they might like to play tennis or golf or feel confident to try other activities.

Another 62-year-old instructor was much more up-beat, however:

The rewards are tremendous. All ages, figures the body shape changes. I like to see them all after they have done a few classes. I have an 82-year-old. She wears bike shorts and it is amazing what she can do. I would really like to see them in leotards but they wear big T shirts. They love it. I see the sparkle and energy in their faces; [I] see it as they are doing their classes.

As Turner (1995: 256) points out, in contemporary societies 'the body has become a site of regulative practices and as a consequence of these regulative practices the body has become a project'. All the women in this study had been regular participants in fitness programs for some years, and from their comments it would seem that many also attended such classes over a long period of time. Lloyd (1996: 92) comments that women who perceive their body to be 'out of condition, lacking in muscle tone, in need of correction and reshaping' through their participation in fitness programs, have become 'self-committed to relentless self-surveillance'.

Health

Spitzack (1990) believes the key to understanding women's situation is the 'aesthetics of health'. The healthy and natural look is now fashionable, with the healthy body being promoted as a beautiful body (Markula 1995). Spitzack (1990) sees traits, such as increased self-esteem and self-confidence, as measures of the 'healthy look'. Certainly the women in this study commented on the feel-good factor as a positive spin-off from attending fitness classes.

> *[Exercise] improves your health, so if your health is improved your physical fitness is improved and you feel better yourself, probably your digestion is better, your whole lifestyle is better. I haven't time to sit down and think, 'I'm growing old'.*

> *That is the one big thing. People say, 'I FEEL so good after my exercises. And I feel good when I go home—I might be tired but the next day [I] feel good'. Their muscles are stronger, they can cope better with everyday work. Feeling good and feeling fit is, I think, the most important thing they get out of it.*

Prior to being interviewed, one instructor in her early sixties talked about this study and asked her class some of the reasons why they participated.

> *I asked the girls this morning. There were varying answers. One woman was telling me her back is nowhere as sore as it used to be, another who had very painful legs at night is not getting that any more so her circulation has improved. Another reasonably fit lady, [who] has always done exercise, says she gets mental stimulation from it, and yet another said*

the social contact was very important. I have a few widows in my class and they seem to find the social thing very beneficial . . . Personally I think people need a hug every now and then and they get that in our classes. We do partner work and everything. Oh, a lot of them enjoy the outings we have, so there are lots of different things coming out. One of them said 'general well being', she just feels a lot better. In fact, three of them said that. Self-esteem came through, too.

These comments sound very encouraging and very empowering. The women attending these classes feel they are getting a number of benefits—they feel good, their self-esteem is improved, physically they may feel stronger, and exercise can assist their mobility. As one participant in her early sixties commented:

I can remember when I first started and I thought, 'Gee, I can do a little extra today' . . . Then you look around and you think, 'Well, I am exercising and I feel better. I'll start to make myself look better.'

Even those in retirement hostels engaging in armchair aerobics are seen to benefit, according to this 61-year-old instructor:

And the rewards for them are their joints are going to be a little bit more mobile. They aren't going to jump up and run round the block, but they will be able to dress themselves with a little more ease than they would [have before]. And just a little exertion helps their cardiovascular performance; they breathe better.

Spitzack (1990) argues that such liberating discourses are illusory. The feminist argument of Spitzack and others is that fitness classes, such as aerobics and the like, simply serve masculine ideology by improving appearance (Markula 1995: 426). In fact, fitness classes that take place in public areas ensure that women's bodies are scrutinised more carefully and that regulatory mechanisms are the more powerful. Using the Foucauldian (Foucault 1977) concept of disciplinary practices that produce 'docile bodies', it could be argued that these women are being persuaded to control their own bodies and thus contribute to their own oppression. Rather than seeing them as taking responsibility for their own health and body shape, these writers would regard women as being enmeshed in a complex power network, oppressed not only by patriarchal ideology but also by the powerful discourses of the beauty and health industries.

The discourses on taking responsibility for one's own health are powerful. Many health promotion and health education schemes urge people to watch their diets and to exercise, a number implying that through these regimens the scourges of old age—such as heart disease and cancer—might be prevented. As one of the women in her early seventies said:

> *Well, they start thinking . . . They see their friends dropping by the way with all sorts of ailments and they think, well, you read it in the papers all the time. I mean the doctors are telling us all the time—in magazines and newspapers—to exercise. And you have a much better quality of life.*

However, the arguments about oppressive discourses take into account neither individual agency, nor the well-established connections between regular exercise and psychological and physical well-being in older adults (Ruuskanen & Ruoppila 1995; McPherson 1995). The women in this study were not passive consumers dedicated to bodily reconstruction. They enjoyed the classes, they were animated and had fun. Many of them both laughed about and questioned the efficacy of claims that exercise could tone and firm underarm flab and unwanted bulges. However, the fitness classes made them feel better able to cope, and energised them. The women in this study did not participate in their classes simply to improve their bodies and their health. There were other more powerful reasons such as making friends, belonging to a social network, encountering other caring women of a similar age, and finding some space for themselves.

Social networks and sociability

All the women in the study supported the view that getting out and about and mixing with other people in the class was very important. They also facilitated a sense of group membership and worked hard at developing group cohesion not only by facilitating sociability when their classes met but by organising a follow-up if someone failed to attend for a while.

> *Like if somebody's not there. We have what we call a buddy system. And if somebody's not here and they're in your group*

> *of buddies, say six or seven names and phone numbers, well someone from that group will ring and see if there's anything they can do, follow up . . .* (Age 61)

> *And, you know, if anyone is sick, I always ring up and check up on them. And I always send them cards if they're, you know, in hospital, or [send them] something from the class.* (Age 73)

Except for those who ran classes at venues that usually have a coffee shop, such as the local YMCA or in aged-care hostels, all of the instructors ensured that both tea and coffee were available for the women who attended their classes. They encouraged the participants to stay for a cuppa, to talk and get to know one another. Many of the women talked of how the women in their classes often went out to lunch together on a regular basis or met to see a film. One of the instructors, aged sixty, commented:

> *I get lots of widows in their late sixties, seventies. For them it is looking forward to Monday morning, and looking forward to Thursday for another walk or meeting her friends again, so I feel that is a very important part. I don't know whether the exercise is in the foreground, or whether it's balanced out [by] socialising and meeting others, [and] getting out of the house. I think some of them meet afterwards or they meet [at] other times and [that's] fantastic, and what it's all about. Because women outlive men on the whole and the chances are they will be by themselves. And even if they have husbands [at] home, they [might not] want to do anything . . .*

Another, also in her sixties, said:

> *The rewards are social support and friendship, and this comes from time spent together before and after the class and from sharing activities. People attending gradually learn about the lives of the others in the group, and while they may not share their lives by spending time together, they do become very supportive when things go wrong, even if only by telephone.*

One of the more interesting issues that emerged from the interviews was that while some older women, especially widows, came to classes to socialise, make friends and get out of the house, there were others with husbands at home who also attended classes for the same reasons. Women with retired husbands also used the classes as a way of making some time and space for themselves. One of the older instructors, herself in her seventies, felt that attendance at fitness classes gave the women in her classes confidence to cope with difficulties in their lives.

> *It's amazing to see these women blossom, [as] really some are in a little shell. Their families are all gone, their husbands have died, they're on their own and in a little shell, and then they come [here]. Some of [the others] find it extremely difficult coping with husbands when they retire. Now we all laugh about it. No one's complaining really, no one is weeping and talking about their problems, but they are off-loading it. And they get a sort of confidence again. It's fantastic.*

However, the selfishness and demands of some family members was noted:

> *Yes, the Italian ladies. I understand because my husband is Italian. They have a problem with them, [as] they have to be home to cook a hot dinner for their husbands. It makes me mad, honestly! And they are always worried about their husbands. A lot of them don't drive so their husbands pick them up [and] they have to be on time. They can't go [even] a few minutes over class at eleven, [as] that is too late. Their husbands want them home at a certain time.* (Age 62)

> *Their daughters are sometimes extremely selfish. And they ring up their mother, just as she's ready to come to the class and say, 'Will you BABYSIT?'. And they drop everything and go. I suppose you can understand it. They would do that. But I think it's a pity they couldn't say to the daughters, 'Now these are the days I will help you but I can't on these days'.* (Age 73)

Conclusion

One of the key questions asked of the women in this study was why they exercised so much themselves, and why they thought the women in their classes participated so regularly in fitness classes over a number of years. The answer was:

> *Well, fitness for a start . . . that's really the top benefit. And the people you meet . . . the friends that you make. It's a lovely feeling of meeting new people, and getting to know*

new people and learning about them. It's definitely the friendship, I suppose. (Age 55)

Body image was important, as was strength and mobility. But what mattered to these women was fitness, feeling good about themselves, spending time on themselves, and making friends. Seen this way their stories of participation in exercise can be empowering and liberating, increasing self-confidence and enabling them to participate in social networks. On the other hand, one might argue that the stories the women told about their reasons for exercising demonstrate their positioning within powerful discourses associated with positive ageing, and that their commitment to exercise is an example of the regulatory practices associated with such discourses. This commitment can be seen as their collusion in their own oppression, and as something that enmeshes them in constant surveillance and bodily discipline. However, such explanations reduce women; they ignore the meanings invested in the women's narratives and fail to provide adequate explanations for the ways their lives are lived with such zest.

The discourses have changed over the years, as have the regulatory practices. Women earlier this century, such as my great-grandmother, were expected to become secluded and withdrawn from the world as they aged and became widowed. My great-grandmother's bowed, wrinkled and somewhat shrunken body is perhaps some reflection of this. Turner (1995: 254) points out that ageing takes place within the cohort of one's own generation, it is culture-specific, and therefore 'the actual bodies of cohorts are recognizably different from other generations'. Healthy ageing today can be viewed as a process 'endlessly open to construction and reconstruction' (Featherstone & Hepworth 1995: 46). For the women in this study this involves keeping in shape, maintaining a healthy lifestyle, keeping active and being part of social networks.

References

Bartky, S. L. 1988 'Foucault, Femininity and the Modernization of Patriarchal Power' in *Feminism and Foucault: Reflections on Resistance* eds I. Diamond & L. Quinby, Northeastern University Press, Boston, pp. 61–80

Bordo, S. 1990 'Reading the Slender Body' in *Body/Politics: Women and the Discourse of Science* eds M. Jacobus, E. Fox Keller & S. Shuttleworth, Routledge, New York, pp. 83–112

Chernin, K. 1981 *Womansize: The Tyranny of Slenderness* The Women's Press, London

Encel, S. 1997 'Healthy Ageing: New paradigm or new buzzword?' *Social Policy Research Centre Newsletter* # 67 SPCC, University of New South Wales, November, pp. 1, 4–5, 10

Featherstone, M. 1991 'The body in consumer culture' in *The Body: Social Process and Cultural Theory* eds M. Featherstone, M. Hepworth & B. S. Turner, Sage, London, pp. 170–96

Featherstone, M. & Hepworth, M. 1993 'Images of Ageing' in *Ageing in Society: An Introduction to Social Gerontology* eds J. Bond & P. Coleman, Sage, London, pp. 250–75

——1995 'Images of Positive Aging: A case study of *Retirement Choice* magazine' in *Images of Aging: Cultural Representations of Later Life* eds M. Featherstone & A. Wernick, Routledge, London, pp. 29–47

Fonda, J. 1981 *Jane Fonda's Workout Book* Simon & Schuster, New York

Foucault, M. 1977 *Discipline and Punish: The Birth of the Prison* Vintage Books, New York

Frueh, J. 1997 'Visible Difference: Women, artists and ageing' in *The Other Within Us: Feminist Explorations of Women and Ageing* ed. M. Pearsall, Westview Press, Boulder, Colorado, pp. 197–220

Hareven, T. K. 1995 'Changing Images of Aging and the Social Construction of the Life Course' in *Images of Aging: Cultural Representations of Later Life* eds M. Featherstone & A. Wernick, Routledge, London, pp. 119–34

Lloyd, M. 1996 'Feminism, Aerobics and the Politics of the Body' *Body & Society* vol. 2, pp. 2, 79–98

McPherson, B. D. 1995 'Ageing and Active Life Styles: A cross-cultural analysis of factors influencing the participation of middle-aged and elderly cohorts' in *Physical Activity, Ageing and Sport, Vol. IV,* eds S. Harris, E. Heikkinen & W. S. Harris, Centre for Study of Ageing, Albany, NY, pp. 293–308

Markula, P. 1995 'Firm but Shapely, Fit but Sexy, Strong but Thin: The postmodern aerobicizing female bodies' *Sociology of Sport Journal* no. 12, pp. 424–43

Poole, M., Isaacs, D. & Jones, J. A. 1997 'Disciplinary Practices? Older women and exercise' in *Desperately Seeking Sisterhood: Still Challenging and Building* eds M. Ang-Lygate, C. Corrin & M. S. Henry, Taylor & Francis, London, pp. 94–115

Ruuskanen, J. M. & Ruoppila, I. 1995 'Physical Activity and Psychological Well-being Among People Aged 65–84 Years' *Age and Ageing* vol. 24(4), pp. 292–6

Spitzack, C. 1990 *Confessing Excess: Women and the Politics of Body Reduction* State University of New York Press, Albany, NY

Turner, B. S. 1995 'Aging and Identity: Some reflections on the somatization of the self' in *Images of Aging: Cultural Representations of Later Life* eds M. Featherstone & A. Wernick, Routledge, London, pp. 245–62

Wolf, N. 1990 *The Beauty Myth* Vintage Books, London

---

[1] This study was funded by a grant from the School of Social Inquiry, Deakin University. My thanks to my colleague Dr Judy Anne Jones of Deakin University for her work on the project.

seven

pebbles and hugs: older women in small business

HEATHER HORROCKS

'I wanted to be my own boss': four out of seventeen small businesswomen, all in their late forties or early fifties and all new entrants to the small business sector, used this phrase in response to the question 'why did you do it?'.

They took part in a survey about older women entrepreneurs where responses were sought from women aged between forty-five and fifty-five who had recently started their own business. All were involved in service-oriented businesses. Five mentioned their previous work history in the context of losing a job or being made redundant. Mostly their answers were quick and precise, sometimes funny, sometimes poignant, but each woman was very sure she had chosen the right course.

The phrase 'I wanted to be my own boss' sums up what many women feel in their middle years. They want to take back control of their lives, test out skills learnt over a lifetime in the paid workforce and, if these women are any guide, exercise the new feelings of strength and self-confidence that maturity brings.

The women's responses revealed an interesting element, hard to define, of a new sense of self-interest and a degree of edginess. It was not quite anger, but it bordered on resentment—of time passing and needs not met. It was expressed in comments like: 'I thought it was time I made things happen instead of waiting for my partner to do it for me', or 'It's my turn now', and 'The first fifty years is gone, the next fifty is mine'.

One of the most illuminating, and representative, set of reasons came from a woman who had enjoyed a period in public life. It reflected the duality in women's lives. She wanted to continue to be active in her community, so had opted to open her home as a bed-and-breakfast. An important factor in determining this choice of business was the need to give priority to her caring roles; she has responsibility for an elderly mother and two young grandchildren. She said, 'I didn't want to become invisible. I wanted to keep contributing in the community'. Then she said, 'And it makes me do the housework'.

Stereotypes

As we move towards the new millennium older women make up more than half the population of so-called 'baby boomers'—a group of people who dominate the demographic statistics and have done so since they were born. New schools were built to accommodate them in the 1950s. New markets were created to exploit them in the 1960s—in music, film and television, food, fashion. For women, new political paradigms developed in the 1970s and 1980s in response to their activism: equal opportunity laws, affirmative action programs, consultative processes at the highest levels of government. And it's likely that new ways of dealing with old age will have to be developed to cope with them in the future.

Stereotypes of old women are common. In the past, the choice for women as they approached old age was stark: sharp-tongued old witch or gentle, white-haired grandmother; thin and whiskery or plump and soft; opinionated and caustic or loving and caring. Today's women have few role models for a graceful old age. Most media images of women in their fifties show them going to extraordinary lengths to look more like their daughters.

As women age they undergo a plethora of change—to their bodies, their lifestyles, their feelings about themselves, and their attitudes to their own and their families' future. They become aware of changing attitudes towards them: no longer young and attractive, they face the choice of accepting a degree of invisibility or beginning new and strenuous efforts to combat the effects of ageing. Or do they? One woman said, 'As an older woman in business you are not a threat. You are sought for your experience'. Perhaps there is another choice for older women: ignore the stereotypes, value yourself and get on with life.

But before dismissing the stereotypes out of hand, they should be explored further. In searching for a way to illustrate how older women have been—and might still be—viewed, I recalled a story read in childhood: Charles Kingsley's *The Waterbabies*, sub-titled *A Fairytale for a Young Land-Baby*, first published in 1863. In this morality tale Kingsley introduces two old fairies who have evocative, self-explanatory names: Mrs Doasyouwouldbedoneby and Mrs Bedonebyasyoudid.

The latter is described as follows:

> [Mrs Bedonebyasyoudid] had on a black bonnet, and a black shawl and no crinoline at all; and a pair of large green spectacles, and a great hooked nose, hooked so much that the bridge of it stood quite up above her eyebrows; and under her arm she carried a great birch rod. (p. 180)

One can only speculate about the equivalent, in today's terms, to the sin of 'and no crinoline at all'. No bra? No stockings? Tracksuit pants and T-shirt? Kingsley implies that old age brings on a disdain for the prevailing fashions. More likely, old age brings on poverty, and this, more than anything else, leads to the appearance he describes.

Although only two of the seventeen respondents to the survey cited money as a reason for starting a small business, none of the women would have embarked on this course to become poor.

Charles Kingsley's stereotypes of old age for women are played out to the full. Mrs Bedonebyasyoudid teaches the main character a lesson. Instead of popping a lolly into his mouth as she had done with the other water-babies, she gave him 'a nasty, cold, hard, pebble'.

> 'You are a very cruel woman,' said he, and began to whimper.
> 'And you are a very cruel boy, who puts pebbles into the sea-anemones' mouths to take them in, and make them fancy that they had caught a good dinner! As you did to them, so I must do to you.' (p. 182)

But Mrs Bedonebyasyoudid has a cure for her ugliness:

> I am the ugliest fairy in the world, and I shall be till people behave themselves as they ought to do. And then I shall grow as handsome as my sister, who is the loveliest fairy in the world, and her name is Mrs Doasyouwouldbedoneby. So she begins where I end, and I

begin where she ends; and those who will not listen to her must listen to me. (p. 184)

Mrs Doasyouwouldbedoneby, who spends her time cuddling the water-babies and telling them stories, is introduced thus:

. . . for when anyone looks at her, all they can think of is that she has the sweetest, kindest, tenderest, funniest, merriest face they ever saw, or want to see. (p. 190)

There are no sharp edges to Mrs D. She is all softness and warmth, the ideal grandmother. Everybody loves her, and she loves everybody. She needs no description because her looks are unimportant. No judgments are made about her tastes, her opinions or her needs because she only evokes feelings.

The two fairies provide a perfect example of the extremes of stereotypical behaviour patterns attributed to older women: witches and bitches or grey-haired grannies, whisky and soda or tea and scones, Joan Collins or the Queen Mum. Movies and television reinforce the options. My thesis is that this generation of women deal with these options as they have dealt with the many life choices they have faced: rather than an either/or choice, they want a little of both.

The important point to make is that Mrs Doasyouwouldbedoneby and Mrs Bedonebyasyoudid are a continuum: one can change into the other. It's a handy skill.

Change, of course, has been a constant in the lives of women approaching their middle years at the end of the millennium. Women now aged forty-five to fifty-five have faced more change and more choices than any other generation of women. These are the daughters of women who wore corsets to keep their bodies stiff, had permanent waves to keep their hair stiff and went to church on Sundays to keep their morals much the same. Growing up in the 1960s, women now in their middle years experienced more freedom than any generation before them. Safe, cheap and reliable contraception was available first to this generation. Unlike their mothers, these women no longer had to choose between an active sex life but multiple pregnancies, or no sex life but the prospect of improved living standards. Even Catholics barred from using the pill by the Vatican opted for it anyway.

The 1970s saw the women's movement fight for equality of opportunity—in the workplace, in the home and in women's personal lives. Not all women became feminists. In fact, few of the women in this study would call themselves that—but the broader choices opened up by the women's movement permeated their lives nonetheless. It's hardly surprising that this cohort of women should choose to pursue new challenges, and yet more change, in their later years.

The ticking clock

Time is our most valuable resource. Barry Jones, federal politician, broadcaster and futurist, talks about time in *Sleepers, Wake! Technology and the Future of Work* (1995: 213):

> The traditional work ethic asserts that work means income and the power to make choices, and that free time means impotence and rejection. Often the reverse is true and free time represents power to make choices whereas work means response to economic necessity—perhaps performing tasks set by someone else . . . The question of life after death has always occupied human thoughts. Basic changes in human working patterns may stimulate interest in the possibility of life before death.

The women in this study seem to have discovered that already. The classic signals of approaching middle age—a spreading girth, forgetfulness and aching feet—can be positive, providing a timely excuse to start retiring from those aspects of the competitive outside world that cause stress and anxiety. There are other compensations: as eyesight fails it's harder to examine what we see reflected in the mirror—wrinkles, hairs and sunspots. Even hot flushes have their advantages. As one woman put it, 'Last year I had a great winter!'.

Mothers and grandmothers of today's middle-aged women rarely thought of, or could afford, such anti-ageing remedies as plastic surgery, specialty cosmetics, or superannuated retirement. They accepted the downside of ageing, just as they accepted the burden of care for grandchildren and ageing parents. The baby boomers can choose all, or none, or both.

When the seventeen businesswomen interviewed were asked why they entered small business, the next most common response after 'I wanted to be my own boss' had to do with time: 'I wanted more time for myself', and 'I felt I was wasting my time working for someone else'.

This is not to say that nurturing and caring for others ceases. Like the bed-and-breakfast proprietor already mentioned, another woman expressed the view that, as a small businessperson, she could manage her time better and balance the competing demands of family and work. 'Before, I couldn't do things, like going to a family friend's funeral. I couldn't support people.' Mrs Doasyouwouldbedoneby would understand.

Work, work, work

Women have always worked: in paid employment, in the home, and at maintaining and nurturing relationships. But women's work patterns have changed markedly over the lifetime of the women in this study. In the 1950s it was common for women to be compulsorily retired from the workforce when they married. In the 1960s, women, even in the professions, were regarded as short-term workers, not expected to take a career seriously and unlikely to ever make a contribution at management level.

Women's Lib not only expanded choices, it gave women permission to negotiate their own path through life. Many women found they enjoyed working outside the home. They enjoyed the company of adults—it balanced the constant demands of home and children. They found they had as much talent as their male colleagues. They learnt that if they honed and developed their skills they could compete for new positions and new jobs.

In *Sleepers, Wake* . . . (1995: 121), Barry Jones describes some of the changes to work patterns in the past thirty years:

> . . . there has been a dramatic shift in employment, from physical to mental, from male to female, a shorter working lifetime, fewer youths and aged workers, unusually high levels of recorded unemployment and unusually high participation rates . . .

He calls this 'the employment revolution' and goes on to elaborate on the patterns of employment for women:

> In the period 1975–95 when female wage rates moved 30 per cent toward parity with male rates, female employment increased rapidly, contrary to the conventional wisdom that increasing wages decreases labour demand. A high proportion of part-time jobs are held by females: in 1994 women took 47 per cent of 289,200 jobs created in Australia, almost half of their work (48 per cent) being part-time. (p. 134)

In fact, women have quietly but effectively shaped their own entry into the workforce. Despite the opposition of the trade union movement in the 1960s and 1970s to part-time work, women voted with their feet and part-time employment opportunities exploded. It suited women's lifestyles, allowing them to care for their children and their homes, while still meeting their need for an income and a career. No longer is part-time work stigmatised in the workplace. Job-sharing is common. In the *Financial Review* of 20 February 1998, a law correspondent reported that when a woman was appointed as a partner in a large Sydney law firm she received calls from all over the city congratulating her. 'Female partners are rare enough, but the thing that makes Ms Cahalan's appointment almost unique [*sic*] is that she has become her firm's first part-time partner.'

Social researcher Hugh Mackay, in *Reinventing Australia: the Mind and Mood of Australia in the 90s* (1993: 27), describes the process that women went through:

> The social and cultural pressure on married women to use work outside the home as a means of acquiring a clearer and more independent sense of identity was almost irresistible. And so was born one of the most significant socio-cultural changes of the last 50 years: the emergence of the working mother as a mainstream phenomenon.
>
> But women who had embraced the new values of Women's Lib had not abandoned the traditional home-and-family, wife-and-mother values which they had inherited from their mothers and grandmothers. So although they were busily constructing a new framework for their lives, they were continuing to operate within an existing framework as well. Needless to say, this created enormous complications and difficulties for the women involved.

The women's movement, often blamed for pressuring women to enter the paid workforce and denigrating the role of wife and mother, argued cogently, forcefully and successfully for policy changes to allow women to participate equally in the workforce, and in particular for quality, affordable child care. The battle for recognition of permanent part-time work was also taken up.

Anne Summers, in a new Introduction to her book *Damned Whores and God's Police* (1994: 9) argues that 'Australia had become an inadvertent pioneer on status of women policies'. Australian women were able to convince government, as well as unions and the business community, to accommodate their demands for equality and flexibility in workplace practices.

But having achieved some measure of job satisfaction, perhaps reaching middle and upper management level, baby boomers find the rug being pulled from under them. In the 1990s jobs are less secure. Managers are under pressure to improve productivity without increasing overheads, so hours actually worked are stretching out. Bosses are anxious and harder to get along with. As one woman said about her own retrenchment: 'If the glass ceiling doesn't get you, downsizing will'.

The 'boss' factor

In an article in the *Financial Review* (25 July 1995), Robin Robertson summarises a study by Breen and Calvert produced for Victoria University of Technology's Small Business Research Unit:

> Of the 169 women who supplied answers to the questions about why they had started their own businesses, most did so for negative reasons. Forty per cent were generally disappointed with their previous employment, but the lack of promotional opportunities took the backseat for 18 per cent. Twelve per cent had been made redundant and 14 per cent saw it as an alternative to unemployment.

After a lifetime of work opportunities, older women are looking at their options again and seeing advantages in taking a further step in controlling their working conditions: 'being their own boss'. But the phrase may imply more than just an attempt to take back control over their lives. It is a statement about power or the lack of it. It suggests resentment about years of loyal service to bosses—without adequate reward. It reveals frustration at never having been a boss.

One respondent, who maintains a part-time job while also operating a small marketing and publicity consultancy, said: 'I've worked for some dreadful people and worked very hard. Now I have two satisfying jobs that I love'. She has the security of a wage plus the chance to try her skills in the marketplace.

Another respondent, who operates a cleaning business and has just taken the big step of appointing her first employee, said that after working in the same area for local government for many years she wanted to do the job better and help her clients more. Being her own boss, to her, means she can explore the possibility of being a good boss by looking after her workers as well as looking after her clients better. Not that she is prepared to take any risks with employing labour. Her experience in the industry with previous work colleagues and poor work standards led her to be less trustful. She has designed a form of agreement with her new employee to enforce a strict work ethic and ensure that the good name of her business is protected. Her primary concern is caring for her clients but, like Mrs Bedonebyasyoudid, she is prepared to keep a few pebbles handy, should she need it, to pop into the mouths of those who need to be taught a lesson or two.

In other words, there is a sharp edge to the notion of being a 'boss'. Women have something to prove. They have spent their lives managing the competing pressures of work and family, juggling their own needs with those of their families and often putting themselves second. The ageing process brings awareness that time is running out. Being a boss means they can reward themselves for their efforts, in the knowledge that if they don't, no one else will. As one respondent put it: 'It was now or never'.

As old as you feel

Participants in this survey were asked their date of birth, and then 'how old do you actually feel?'. The average age of the respondents was forty-eight, but the average age they felt was thirty-six. One woman said she felt anything between seven and 107, but most gave a figure about ten years younger than the one appearing on their birth certificate. This group of women does not feel old. One woman said she didn't feel middle-aged: 'Middle-aged is anyone ten years older than me'.

The survey demonstrates that women are aware of the changes happening to them, and can use them as a stimulus for reordering their priorities. None of the respondents complained about symptoms of menopause. Despite unwelcome bodily changes and the shock of losing familiar body rhythms, women are still capable of reacting positively. One woman said, 'I'm concentrating on moving into another stage of my life'. Finally able to spend time and energy on their own needs, women can use their middle years to explore new ways of behaving. One woman surveyed said, 'I now live life for myself'. Another said, 'I am having trouble knowing how powerful I can be. I'm fighting the beliefs that it's not OK to be powerful'.

Most of the women interviewed reported a new sense of confidence, more energy and a greater focus on, and belief in, their own capacities. One said, 'I'm old enough to know that I can do business doing what I love doing and this makes me feel good about myself'. Here, being 'old enough to know' implies confidence born of experience. It also speaks of a comfort level about the consequences of decision making—good or bad.

This woman might have made mistakes in the past, but now she is prepared to trust her own judgment, and nobody else's, about what is good for her.

Germaine Greer in the introduction to her book *The Change* (1992: 8) says of it:

> This book suggests other role models for the ageing woman . . . If the world has dubbed you crone, you might as well be one. There is no point in growing old unless you can be a witch, and accumulate spiritual power in place of the political and economic power that has been denied you as a woman.

Shades of Mrs Bedonebyasyoudid. Greer (1992: 115), no doubt describing her own experience, says:

> Many women feel during the climacteric that they are changing personality; . . . The most unnerving, even terrifying, change is a sudden horrible propensity to blind rage . . . This is the reality behind what doctors refer to rather prissily as 'irritability'.

For the women who responded to the survey, the possibility of using new feelings like these to their own advantage is being exercised. The symptoms of menopause can be disturbing, but none of the women surveyed complained of anything debilitating. One woman referred to hot flushes as 'power surges'. Another said: 'I'm grumpier, less patient, and more critical of those around me. But that's a good thing. It means I now assert myself more'.

Establishing a small business is exciting, but risky and stressful. These women have all decided to do it in mid-life. Far from accepting a lesser role, they are seeking new status, perhaps better status, and the chance to prove they can take on a whole new role by becoming their own boss.

There's no business like small business

Are the respondents to this survey typical? Are women taking on small business in greater numbers? Is this likely to be a continuing trend? The evidence would suggest that the answers are yes, yes and yes.

Definitions of small business are wide. According to the report of the Employment & Skills Formation Council, *Making it Work: Women in Small Business* (1994: 2):

> A number of different definitions are current for characterising or defining small business. These generally focus on operational characteristics (for example, owner/manager decision-making,

control and operation) or on employment size. The Australian Bureau of Statistics adopts a definition based on employment size for statistical purposes.

Included in the definition are businesses employing up to one hundred people. The women surveyed are operating businesses more accurately described as micro-business; sole proprietors or partnerships employing fewer than five employees.

Figures on the age of women in small business are available, but because they include businesses employing up to one hundred people, and partnerships where the woman is a silent partner (often for tax purposes, since women on average earn less than men), extracting meaningful data is difficult. However, Australian Bureau of Statistics (ABS) figures show that there is an overall decline in women's participation rate with age. While it is true that most small business owners are aged between thirty and fifty years of age, indicating a higher propensity to maintain a position in this sector by mature operators, the percentage of women small business operators aged over fifty was 28 per cent, compared with 31 per cent between thirty and fifty years of age, and 37 per cent aged less than thirty years (ABS 1995).

More work needs to be done on disaggregating statistics on small business ownership to determine the contribution of women to the small business sector. Even if the overall participation of women declines with age, start-ups may increase. This survey indicates that it could be a fruitful avenue for research.

In a *Financial Review* article (25 January 1995) entitled 'Women Opt to Run Their Own Show', Robin Robertson writes:

> Statistics on women in small business are few and scattered, but the trend of growing female ownership is becoming clear. According to the Yellow Pages Small Business Index, July 1994, while just 26 per cent of small businesses started more than five years ago are managed by women, 31 per cent of new (last five years) small businesses are female operated . . . If this trend continues, by the year 2000, half of all small businesses will be owned, managed and operated by women.

The attrition rate for small businesses is acknowledged to be very high. Many do not survive their first two years let alone their first five. According to *Making it Work: Women in Small Business*:

> Available research . . . suggests that small businesses operated by women have significantly higher survival rates due to better preparation prior to start-up—including research into financial and

management advice, and keeping debt and overheads low. Evidence also suggests that women are more likely than men to adopt a deliberate strategy to remain small rather than pursue a high growth strategy. (1994: 3)

In addition:

Women are often not seen as 'real' business operators. Women generally tend to establish or operate small businesses in areas where they have worked and gained expertise as employees. More women small business operators are therefore found in the services sector with fewer in areas such as manufacturing. (1994: 17)

One respondent, an operator of two large country guest houses, agreed, saying about success in small business: 'It's an extension of the skills you've learnt: networking, and social and money management'. Another said: 'I read everything I could get my hands on to do with the business and I did courses, before I got up the confidence to start'. She also felt that women 'set the bar lower' for themselves and err on the side of caution when making business decisions.

According to the director of a new women's business incubator (a suite of offices available for individual lease with add-on services such as a receptionist, fax machines and a photocopier) operated by the Victorian Women's Trust in inner Melbourne, 75 per cent of women-owned small businesses started in 1991 were still operating, compared with 66 per cent of all small businesses.

Incubators are designed to overcome one of the drawbacks of small business, particularly home-based micro-businesses: isolation. But only one woman interviewed mentioned the problem. Retrenched from an office job where her networking, promotional and organisational skills were honed, she turned to helping women get together—and set up a women's network. Her first step had been to survey women living in her area, an affluent Melbourne suburb, about their interest in the concept. Although her survey was not specifically directed at small businesswomen, she found their responses underpinned her belief that isolation was indeed a problem. When she began the network her goal was to attract twenty-five to thirty women on an occasional basis. Barely twelve months later, between three and four times that number meet monthly for a Sunday brunch with a guest speaker. The women are supportive of each other and each other's businesses, with keen interest shown in members' achievements. However, in her extensive dealings with women in small business, the convenor has identified two weaknesses: 'they don't like to push themselves, and they network—but not for good contacts'. She sees one of her tasks as encouraging them to do both.

Women tend to be less assertive about their skills generally. A commonly identified problem with older women returning to the workforce is a lack of confidence in their skill levels. In fact, most women have skills in organisation and management by virtue of the responsibilities they take on both inside the home and out of it. According to a 1991 study by Cox & Leonard, and quoted by Anne Summers (1994: 36):

> . . . women themselves rarely recognise these skills because they are not acquired within the paid workforce. Yet many women develop technical, management, finance, interpersonal and organisational expertise which is transferable into paid work situations.

This is borne out by the views of one respondent to the survey. She had a word of advice for other women contemplating starting up their own business: 'Get a list of your skills, identify them, then put them to work for yourself. Don't be deterred by horror stories'.

Women in their middle years now are certainly more likely to have a long history of employment and a bank of well-developed skills. They are perfectly placed to take advantage of business opportunities. If it is true that women also gain new confidence and strength as they get older, it is no wonder they are succeeding. One woman surveyed talked about a 'burst of creativity' when she had passed through menopause. Another said: 'It's hard (starting a new business) but it's chickenfeed compared to nursing. I'm not making a lot of money but I'm happy doing what I want to do'.

Interestingly, one woman wanted to give the following advice to other women thinking about starting up a small business: 'Tell them not to listen to their families, they'll try to stop you—in a misguided effort to protect you'. And, in fact, a survey on Australian attitudes to small business undertaken for the federal government in the Karpin Report (1995) reported that Australians were less than enthusiastic about the small business sector:

> When asked what they felt it would be like to be in small business, respondents offered overwhelmingly negative opinions. Negative comments made up 84 per cent of responses. The most popular comments were very general in nature, such as 'tough' (41 per cent) or 'tough economic climate' (34 per cent). Interestingly women and older people tended to be more negative. (Survey: 257)

Discussing the positive comments the Report states:

> A theme of independence of some sort pervades the popular positive categories. Interestingly 'being your own boss' and 'control your own time' were most attractive to those in full-time employment, those in the 35–49 age group, those with children and those who left school at 17+. (Survey: 259)

Exactly.

Friends in high places

There are now more than 846,000 new small businesses operating in Australia, with another 40,000 expected to come on stream within the next twelve months, according to Peter Reith, then Minister for Industrial Relations, in a press release of 20 February 1998. The small business sector increasingly attracts the interest of policy makers. Referred to by politicians as the 'engine room of the Australian economy', small business is now recognised as a major job-creating sector. In a speech to parliament in March 1998, Australian Prime Minister John Howard said: 'In the decade to 1994–95, small business accounted for 1.1 million of the 1.2 million net jobs created over that period'.

Both major political parties now seek to woo the small business sector. It appears to be 'flavour of the month' and is regularly touted as the major beneficiary of any, and all, economic reforms. However, there appears to be little understanding of why, or how, women do it. In the federal parliamentary *Hansard* record for the past fifteen years, most mentions of women in small business were in the general context of 'small business men and women of Australia'.

Small business proprietors are depicted as risk-takers and 'macho' in their outlook. The Liberal Member for Cowan, speaking on 6 March 1997 in federal parliament (*Hansard*) on a Bill designed to allow small business greater rights to claim outstanding debt when large companies go into liquidation, extolled the virtues of small business proprietors. He said:

> Risking your money . . . is the ultimate leading edge feeling. The ultimate buzz in anything is risking your own money: putting it all on the line, risking the house, risking the family, risking security, having the will to go through start up, the will to risk it all.

Since all the evidence shows most women err on the side of caution in the management of their businesses and avoid risk at all cost, it's unlikely many women would agree with him. (Hand me a pebble!)

One drawback of the small business sector is its fragmentation. The only thing that most small businesses have in common is their size. But if small business continues to grow, if the trend for women to enter their own businesses continues to rise and their success rate continues, women can expect to make a significant impact in policy terms. There should be scope for women, with their networking skills, to be a force for positive action. Of course, they will need to act as an effective lobby group—not an easy task when most are busy concentrating on their own enterprises.

Older women, with a handful of pebbles at the ready for those who doubt their potential and a warm embrace for women travelling the same road, may yet prove a powerful factor in the growth and prosperity of Australian small business in the future.

Conclusion

So what is the next logical step for older women? Simple: go to work for yourself. Get rid of the boss. Become one yourself and get the best of all possible worlds. Starting up a small business is a challenge but it seems that the odds for success are improved if you are a woman.

Changes in the workforce over the past thirty years have eased the way for women's participation at a higher rate, leading to acquisition of the skills and experiences that can stand them in good stead for the next step: self-employment. It might also be the case that as women grow older their attitudes change—both to themselves and to the outside world.

There is a positive energy about the answers the women gave to the question 'why did you do it?'. More than that, there is an overwhelming feeling of invigoration as a result of the changes brought by increasing years, a feeling of new confidence, new strength of purpose. But even though women talk about a new emphasis on their own needs, they have not forgotten the needs of others: having more time for themselves also means having more time for friends and families.

In short, the women in their forties and fifties embarking on a small business enterprise described here are doing what they have always done, but with one important difference: they are doing it by themselves, for themselves. They are choosing their place on the continuum between Mrs Doasyouwouldbedoneby and Mrs Bedonebyasyoudid according to their own needs—cuddling other people's babies or popping a pebble into the mouths of naughty boys to teach them a lesson—because as older women, they are confident and comfortable in doing whatever seems appropriate.

References

Australian Bureau of Statistics (ABS) 1995 *Characteristics of Small Business* ABS, Canberra, Catalogue No. 8127.0

Cox, Eva & Leonard, Helen 1991 *From Ummm . . . to Aha! Recognising Women's Skills* Women's Research Employment Initiatives Program, Department of Employment, Education and Training, AGPS, Canberra, May

Employment & Skills Formation Council of the National Board of Employment & Training 1994 *Making it Work: Women in Small Business* AGPS, Canberra, December

Greer, Germaine 1992 *The Change: Women, Ageing and the Menopause* Penguin Books, Melbourne.

Jones, Barry 1995 *Sleepers, Wake! Technology and the Future of Work* Oxford University Press, Melbourne

Karpin, David 1995 *Enterprising Nation: Renewing Australia's Managers to Meet the Challenges of the Asia-Pacific Century* Industry Task Force on Leadership and Management Skills (Karpin Report), AGPS, Canberra, April

Kingsley, Charles 1979 *The Water-babies: A Fairytale for a Young Land-Baby* (first pub. 1863) Constable & Company Ltd, London

Mackay, Hugh 1993 *Reinventing Australia: the Mind and Mood of Australia in the 90s* Angus & Robertson, Sydney

Merrit, Chris 1998 'Woman a Part-time Partner' *Australian Financial Review*, 20 February

Robertson, Robin 1995 'Women Opt to Run Their Own Show' *Australian Financial Review*, 25 July

Summers, Anne 1994 *Damned Whores and God's Police* Penguin, Melbourne.

eight

the improvised careers of older women: gendered ageism at work?

ROSSLYN REED

> It is time now to explore the creative potential of interrupted and conflicted lives, where energies are not narrowly focused or permanently pointed toward a single ambition. (Bateson, 1990)

Older women workers are a relatively new social group. Until the early 1990s it was the norm for most women to have left the labour market by the time they were fifty-five years of age. Few remained until the statutory retirement age of sixty years. However, in the 1990s, a growing minority of women is continuing in employment beyond this age to sixty-five, sixty-six and even later.

According to Australian Bureau of Statistics (ABS) figures, in the late 1980s the labour force participation rate for women over fifty-five years of age fluctuated slightly around 15 per cent. In 1990 it jumped to 17 per cent and remained near that level until 1995, when it jumped to 20 per cent (Reed 1996). The rate continued to fluctuate around 20–21 per cent throughout the mid-1990s (ABS 1995, 1996, 1997a, b, c). The trend appears to be established for more women to remain in the labour force beyond the 'conventional' mid-life retirement age, and for a small but stable—and even growing—minority to remain in employment into later life. Why do these women do it? How do they manage it?

Until recently there was little research undertaken on older women as workers. Existing studies from the United States show that older women workers, irrespective of education, qualifications and broken or unbroken careers, have traditionally received lower wages and lower retirement incomes than men (Nuccio 1989; Hollenshead 1982). Given the results of more general research on women and employment, this finding is not surprising. Although researchers are now likely to include older women as well as older men in mainstream research on older workers (Legge *et al.* 1996), we still know very little about the labour-market and on-the-job experiences of the women currently leading the trend to continuing workforce participation.

Since observing the beginning of this trend, I have carried out a study of older women working in Sydney department stores. This study, conducted during 1993–94, is based on ABS statistics and on in-depth interviews with twelve women aged between fifty-five and sixty-six years of age (Reed 1996). Examples and illustrations from this and other research related to older women's employment opportunities (Reed, 1995, 1997) are used to support the claims I am making here in relation to older women's work experiences. I acknowledge that there may be differences in experience both in other industries and for professional women, who might have had more continuity in employment and access to superannuation to support them in retirement. My concern is with those women who are employed in the kinds of jobs that have attracted women returning to employment after child-bearing. Retailing positions are quite typical of these.

Because so many different ages are used to denote 'older workers', it is necessary to define 'older woman worker' as I am using it here. The term 'worker' refers to employment or paid work. The emphasis on paid work in no sense diminishes the value or extent of women's unpaid work. On the contrary, with the life-course approach I am taking, the former cannot be discussed without some attention to the latter. According to Hockey and James (1993: 50–1) the life-course approach moves away from the 'rigidity of the life cycle model' and allows us to see how

> some, but not all, members of certain social categories come to be dependent on or made subordinate to the members of others . . . It allows us to explore how power is continually negotiated . . . as people assert very different social identities during their lives.

Most discussions of older workers take forty-five years of age as the starting point and sixty or sixty-five as the end point. This seems to be related to social security and pension eligibility, and generally ignores the subjects' earlier experiences and aspirations for the future, particularly in relation to paid work. Employers seeking to marginalise segments of the labour force also influence definitions. With the recent trends to earlier retirement, some researchers are pushing the boundary of 'older' back to earlier ages than forty-five. Employers in Britain, for example, are classifying women over thirty years of age as 'older workers' (Bernard *et al.* 1995: 61–4). This shift in classification cannot be ignored by researchers, particularly in relation to questions of power in the employment relationship, but the thirty-year-old group is clearly too young to form the basis of any meaningful discussion of the experience of being an older worker. At the other extreme, there is some interest, particularly in the media, in those exceptional individuals—usually but not always men— who can be found at the shop counter or on the (work)shop floor at seventy or eighty or even ninety-something. Unfortunately, celebration of these extreme or heroic performances obscures rather than illuminates the experiences of most people.

Ultimately, the choice of a starting point for the category 'older' is a matter of somewhat arbitrary judgment depending on the aims of the research. I have chosen fifty-five for two reasons. First, I want to examine the life-course experiences behind the statistical evidence. Second, it makes little sense to define women as older workers at increasingly younger ages, for several reasons. For example, they are remaining in both education and the workforce longer—and, in the latter, on a more continuous basis. Women are also healthier and more active than in the past and enjoy longer life expectancy than men, which makes acceptance of employers' definitions of women as being 'older workers' a decade before men are labelled as such both untenable from a research or policy perspective, and potentially damaging to women's financial security in later life.

I was interested in the obstacles encountered by pioneering older women workers that probably discourage other women. Is it ageism? Or is it sexism—encountered in youth as much as in the present? It seemed to me that the differences between the working life-course of men and women, exemplified in the experience of older women in my study, were best understood as 'gendered ageism'.

The concept of 'gendered ageism' (Ginn & Arber 1995: 7) is much more encompassing of the attitudes to older people than is 'ageism' alone. In the case of paid employment, however, there is a greater need to examine the ways the ageing process influences manifestations of sexism (as well as racism and ethnocentrism; see Bottomley 1994). Women workers face sexism throughout their employment careers. It is present in direct, indirect and systemic discrimination, and it intersects with racism (I have described this in more detail regarding retailing in Reed 1996). This means that some groups of women are excluded from some segments of the labour market at earlier points along the life-course for reasons such as class background or poor English language skills. Young Aboriginal women and recently arrived migrant women, for example, are more likely to be offered process work in factories than sales positions in department stores. Women are channelled into a narrower range of occupations, industries and hierarchical positions on the basis of sex/gender. This experience of sex discrimination and, in some instances, race and sex discrimination, represents another of the uneven accumulations of the life-course alongside family and personal experience. In other words, some groups may not get to experience ageism in paid employment because they have already been excluded on other grounds or marginalised in other ways. We should also remember that age discrimination can be experienced at any time in life (Byetheway 1995: 11). It is not always cumulative. For example, some groups—like young white males working in fast food outlets—may be 'too old' to employ at nineteen years of age without any consequent ongoing detriment to their life chances. Age discrimination, however, appears to be experienced quite differently by women, particularly in terms of interrupted paid employment.

Interrupted careers

As a context for their experience, it is important to note that the cohort in the retailing study entered the workforce in the post-World War II period, and were among the first married women to return to the workforce after child-bearing. They pre-date the 'baby boomers'. Their lives have been framed by the 1930s Depression and World War II; by post-war reconstruction with its emphasis on women as unpaid domestic workers; and by full (male) employment in the 1950s and 1960s, which saw them drawn back to paid work. These women have also benefited to some extent from developments in access to contraception, 'second-chance' education, equal employment opportunity and affirmative action.

In general, a woman's life-course is punctuated by events that disrupt her education and employment opportunities: as a consequence of biological factors such as the birth of children and the death of significant others such as spouses, parents and siblings; and as a result of more gendered social phenomena such as unpaid domestic, caring and nurturing work. Of course, the biological and social are not separate, and disadvantage may accumulate even though some of these events do not occur at all, or occur in a non-disruptive way.

'Broken' or interrupted careers are the major consequence of these life-course events. These apparent employment breaks can actually be periods of diverse work experience. Breaks from conventional employment such as clerical/secretarial work and women's professions like nursing and teaching normally follow the birth of children, but do not always imply a period completely outside the labour force even for women who are now entering later life. Some of the women interviewed in the retail study had long breaks from their career following child-bearing (up to twenty-seven years). On average they were outside the formal labour market for thirteen to fourteen years but not necessarily outside paid work.

Two women had very limited breaks which did not occur immediately after childbirth. One of these women continued to work in a family business following the birth of her first child:

> . . . *my husband . . . was a pharmacist so we built a pharmacy, so I worked there for quite a few years . . . I more or less came home from hospital and went straight to work.*

The other was a recent immigrant who undertook several part-time jobs to fit in with her husband's employment, starting soon after the birth of her first child:

> . . . *I started work on the stock exchange . . . and I was working there for two to two and a half years but it wasn't very practical because I had a little girl. I had no relatives here so I had to do something . . . so instead of being full-time . . . I split it up into two. I had two jobs then. I was working for a shoe importer/exporter . . . Four hours in the morning then I rushed home and picked my little girl up . . . and at*

night I went back to . . . a stock and share broker also for a night's typing.

With the birth of a second child, she 'left the workforce and just did casual work'.

Career breaks are not only related to child care. Care of an elder or a spouse does not preclude all other activity, including paid work, except in extreme circumstances. One of the women who did not leave formal employment after the birth of her first child found it necessary to give up employment during the final stages of her second husband's terminal illness. Most women's caring responsibilities for an elder or a spouse come in later life—although many of the women in the retailing study had been involved in caring for step-children or orphaned children and elders while outside of and marginal to the labour force as a result of normal child-care and domestic responsibilities.

During their break, most women engaged in some form of paid work, including door-to-door sales, running a home-based employment agency, and babysitting, while regarding themselves as being outside conventional paid work. This sort of employment and the experience it provides is not counted as work experience by employers; in fact, employers may see it as detracting from the woman's occupationally based experience gained prior to the 'break'. Women who were previously employed as secretaries or nurses—in the latter case, particularly if they had not completed their training—had to turn to lower status occupations, such as retail sales, when returning to the formal labour force.

A minority of other women in the study used their 'break' to participate in further and tertiary education, one completing the requirements for a second career in secondary school teaching. Opportunities for higher education became more available in the 1970s with the abolition of university fees. This meant some women who did not need to earn additional family income could access higher education in their 'spare time' while rearing children, without drawing on their husband's income to pay fees. This created more equal opportunity with men who, as potential 'breadwinners', were the main beneficiaries of family sacrifices to fund opportunities for further and higher education for this age cohort. Women with tertiary qualifications re-enter the labour force in higher status employment such as secondary school teaching, but this does not mean they benefit equally with men.

The time they are outside employment precludes access to non-salary benefit schemes such as superannuation and means they have lower retirement incomes and are more likely than men of similar occupational status to require government pensions when they leave paid work.

The interviewee who achieved professional status through second-chance education resigned in mid-life to enjoy some time to herself. Some years later she tried unsuccessfully to return to teaching. Seeking an alternative, she applied for management positions and when told she was 'too old' attempted to return to her earlier occupation of secretary. She was unsuccessful on the grounds that she was 'overqualified'. Retail sales provided the opportunity to resume paid work, but it is work with lower status and pay (including non-wage benefits such as superannuation) than either of her previous occupations, despite this woman's promotion to department manager.

Negotiating the workplace

There are many changes occurring in the nature and patterns of paid work in the context of globalisation that shape the conditions of older women's ongoing employment. In retailing this is most obvious in extended trading hours and in enterprise bargaining, which emphasises employer definitions of flexibility as more fragmented part-time and casual employment. Casuals are required to be more or less available across the full seven-day trading period, which is not always possible for younger workers, who are often students. Some experienced full-time employees who resigned to take overseas holidays have been re-employed as casuals who work close to full-time hours. The union has had some success in retaining full-time and part-time work without the requirement to be rostered on Sundays for some existing full-time and permanent part-time employees, but new employees are being recruited to fit the new working patterns, creating uncertainty about the nature of future opportunities for this group. This sort of 'flexibility' as uncertainty is common in other growing service industries, creating employment opportunities for women at the same time as men's workforce careers in manufacturing and similar industries collapse. Some have referred to this as the 'feminisation of employment in later life' (Schuller 1989: 47). This term should not, however, obscure the reality of women's greater willingness to take on lower paid and lower status work at older ages, partly because they have not had the continuing employment that provides for redundancy payments to cushion their departure from the workforce.

Retailing, including employment at the higher status end in department stores, has been a major site of casual, temporary and part-time employment for some time; it has opened up work opportunities for women 'returners'. This does not mean that all employees work under these conditions or that older workers are only employed in these types of jobs. Some older workers seeking part-time work in the past were forced to accept full-time employment, as that was all that was being offered at the time. The paradox whereby older workers are considered less able to learn new technologies and new ways of working, while being perceived by employers as more reliable and stable, operates to limit opportunities for training and promotion for those in full-time or permanent part-time employment.

The variety of education, training, employment and other experience of the older women interviewees working in Sydney department stores did not normally translate into promotion opportunities, beyond the position of department manager, because of the stereotypical views of older women held by employers and managers. Older women were promoted into department management or specialised selling roles only when other younger staff members could not succeed in them. When the older women who achieved success in these positions asked for further training and promotion opportunities, they were denied.

At the same time, other less career-oriented sales assistants—secure and confident in their familiarity with the merchandise in departments where they had worked for a long time—were transferred to unfamiliar departments when they were not seeking a change in status. In their new positions, they were junior and subordinate to less experienced and less qualified sales assistants. Women who were unhappy with their new 'challenges' in unfamiliar departments found they had to work hard to maintain their good relations with other workers ('friends') in their new situation. One woman was able to have her transfer reversed by appealing to higher management.

In these circumstances older women are forced back largely on their own personal resources of determination and grit. Due partly to ideology and household socioeconomic status and partly to shop-floor experience, older women in retailing are unenthusiastic union members—if they are members at all of the largely paternalistic and male-'breadwinner'-oriented union. This is not to say, however, that they are hostile to unions.

Managers have, at best, a 'blind spot' in relation to the potential and aspirations of work-centred older women. At worst, managers are opposed to their employment, preferring to exercise policies of marginalisation and exclusion in the widely held, but generally mistaken, belief that older women's skills are comparable to, or inferior to, those of younger workers. This belief is in turn due to assumptions about ageing as 'decline', even among the 'young old'.

The nature of the hierarchy in retail management—a hierarchy that occurs in other areas of employment—also helps to explain this apparent failure to recognise the career aspirations of some older women while forcing change on others. Retailing has a gendered dual internal labour market. Mature women, including the group I am discussing, and juniors, who are largely still students, are employed in sales. The career ladder here does not extend beyond the position of department manager. Younger people, mainly males, are recruited to management. These younger, less experienced managers can feel threatened by older women's life and work experience even if such experience is not formally recognised; hence the tendencies to deny these women training and promotion opportunities when they seek them.

The distance of union organisation from the shop floor to the State branch (there is no real delegate structure), the long-standing paternalistic practices of retailing management (which are not limited to the industry), together with a trend towards more formalised bureaucratic organisational rules, allow supervisory managers to exercise power over workers. They do so by granting employees 'favours' such as access to their own sick and annual leave to care for ill spouses/partners, and access to business phones to call home during a family member's illness. What are understood as rewards to loyal employees further undermine the potential for collective action, and generate greater loyalty towards and benefits for both the manager and the organisation. To remain in paid work, career-oriented older women are forced to bring all their personal skills and ingenuity to bear to ensure that the sexist and ageist stereotypes of insecure management do not combine to curtail their employment prospects. It's not surprising that few prevail against the tide.

Ambiguous and uneven policies

In recent decades governments have made social security and other benefits available to women as citizens rather than as dependants (Bryson 1994: 192). Citizenship and equality of treatment with men have the potential to benefit older women by extending work and retirement benefits to them in their own right. Unfortunately for older women now in their fifties and sixties, most social and public policies continue to focus on health, housing, caring and tax transfer payments, such as the Mature Age and Partner Allowance. Important as these benefits are to well-being in later life, especially for the 'old old', this emphasis does not facilitate or encourage continued employment for career-oriented older women, particularly those who need and wish to work to make up for the economic disadvantage resulting from career breaks, divorce or widowhood. Some of the women I interviewed had experienced all three events, adding to the accumulation of life-course events such as child-bearing and caring for elders.

In the period of the Howard Liberal–National Party coalition government, so-called family-oriented policies have further undermined women's continued workforce participation. Cuts to child-care funding and the provision for a male 'breadwinner' to make contributions from *his* income to his wife's superannuation fund provide neither income continuity across the life-course nor career development for women in the immediate or longer term. If (nuclear) families from younger cohorts avail themselves of these policies now, older cohorts in the future are unlikely to be much better placed in terms of retirement income than older women are at present. This is partly because divorce or death of a spouse can curtail this route to retirement income, and can compel women to go back into a workforce for which they are unprepared. Women are also likely to be worse off later in life in social terms if age pensions decline in value relative to incomes from superannuation entitlements and more, larger pay-outs resulting from ongoing labour force attachment, especially when combined with some access to age pensions and benefits.

Recognition or otherwise of the value of employment for older workers does not follow party-political lines. The Greiner and Fahey Liberal governments' Mature Workers Program in New South Wales attempted to keep older workers in employment through placement and training programs (Funnell 1994). This program has continued and is to be applauded for including older women as workers. But reference to older women as a 'special needs' group stigmatises them unnecessarily—they have been as, if not more, successful in achieving paid work than men through the scheme. This is not to say that they do not experience considerable labour market discrimination (Encel & Studencki 1997).

Like the Howard coalition government, some trade unions also remain generally locked into a typical (male) lifetime-career breadwinner model when considering policies for older workers. Most union policies I have examined emphasise benefits to be secured on termination of employment whether on retirement or redundancy. Some do include policies on age discrimination, including discrimination in relation to older women. Only where there is significant female representation among union leadership are wider concerns relating to the ageing of the population, the adequacy of current retirement income provisions and the rights to productive work and to contribute to society included in policy formulation. The desire to make unions more attractive to new entrants to the workforce, such as women *and* youth, largely accounts for the generally limited attention given to older women's needs and aspirations. Nevertheless, analysis of policies in terms of union structures indicates that as more women remain in paid work and become more central to union policy making they may succeed in having their demands placed on union agendas.

The complexity of policy concerns in the context of globalisation, and the dominance of masculine interests, have limited both governments' and trade unions' responses to the changes in labour force participation of older women workers. Where they do respond, they continue to assume past patterns of dependence or even to reassert them. While this may change in the future, in the short term older women are forced to negotiate a number of obstacles to benefit from a longer period of paid work.

Avoiding the conflicts

Although they face a number of political obstacles, little formal encouragement and many personal conflicts about priorities, older women are likely to continue to work in the future. To note this is not to diminish or gloss over the potential for conflicts at every level. It is common for managers to try to deflect the vertical conflict inherent in hierarchical organisational relationships towards horizontal conflict in the relationships between workers. In the case of older women retail sales assistants, this means potential conflict with younger workers.

Interestingly, in the retailing study, there was no evidence of lack of solidarity between older and younger sales assistants. This is more remarkable when we consider that, despite the general view that older women's skills and abilities are limited or declining, it is apparent that older sales assistants are expected to provide an informal supervisory and training function in relation to younger workers. In many industries, including manufacturing and retailing, there is a long tradition of the 'sit by Nellie' style of on-the-job training, which involves more experienced workers in training newer recruits. Older sales assistants not only provide tactful assistance in dealing with customers because younger sales assistants ask them to; the evidence is that older women sales assistants enjoy the company of younger staff, and vice versa, and are willing to give assistance and support both in relation to work and personally:

> *Sometimes an older person is more approachable for a younger person. It's like going to see nanna (laughs) . . . Some of our colleagues are younger than we are, younger than my children and . . . some of them don't like calling me Beth. In the workforce you are just 'Beth' or whatever other Christian name you've got. Some of the younger people there are very good, for girls, too. Where I work we're old and young all mixed in. Like a girls' night out . . . There's that sort of relationship with all ages . . . I've got a little girl . . . she's twenty, brilliant . . . at uni . . . I'm her mother sort of, because she can't talk to her mother . . .*

Of course, employers benefit from this support as it minimises the calls on management time to deal with socialising younger workers into desired working norms.

Similarly, employers' assumption that mature women can be called on almost at will because they have fewer demands on their time than younger workers is an almost heroic assumption when the competing time demands of older women's lives as mothers and grandmothers are taken into account. As others have noted, these are the 'elder care years' (Watson & Mears n.d.). Some women are also likely still to have family members living at home. Extended adolescent and young adult economic dependency is a result of higher levels of participation in tertiary education and limited employment opportunities for young people who do not have further and/or higher educational qualifications. High rentals in a city like Sydney are a further obstacle to youth leaving home. Children who have married/partnered may also return home after divorce or separation, sometimes with their own children. All of these situations were evident in the study of older women in retail employment.

To note the constraints and obstacles surrounding older women's workforce participation is not to say that they are not able to manage and organise these competing demands. Most have demonstrated this competency throughout their lives, which flies in the face of managerial devaluation of their knowledge and experience. This is quite different, however, from the notion that their time is their own and that they are 'freer' of time pressures, including at weekends, than are young people.

To retire or not?

Older women have accumulated a large number of experiences and responsibilities by the time they reach sixty years of age. The life-course approach to research alerts us to the differences and discontinuities in women's lives relative to men's experience. These experiences vary also according to the social background of the family of origin, marital status, whether or not children have been reared (and how many), and whether there is a need for elder caring. Experiences of migration and negotiation of ethnocentrism and racism in and beyond the workplace are also determining factors.

Depending on the timing and the rate of accumulation of these fairly general experiences in the lives of older women workers, opportunities for retirement from paid work may be enthusiastically or unenthusiastically pursued. A major factor appears to be the woman's relations with a spouse or partner. Separation and/or divorce may be a factor pushing older women back into paid work, even after a long absence necessitated by child-rearing, caring, domestic and other activities. This was true for two of the women interviewed in the retailing study, who had taken twenty-four- and twenty-seven-year breaks from paid work respectively:

> *After my husband retired from work we went to live on the Gold Coast and we lived there for two years . . . I thought oh, I couldn't stand it any longer and thought no, I'm going*

> back to work . . . He's not living here. He's gone back to Queensland . . . I don't want to live there. (61 years of age)
>
> When we separated I'd always said I felt treated like the sixth child . . . So we had to shut the doors (of my shop) and have a massive sale . . . David lost lots of money on it, but he was very nice about that . . . so that's when I thought I have to work because by this time I was divorced. (58 years of age)

On the other hand, widowhood, or the imminent disablement or death of a long-time partner through a chronic illness or disease, might precipitate a decision either to retire fully or, more likely, to pull back from full-time to part-time or casual employment:

> My husband will be the next thing; he's got emphysema . . . I was really thinking of complete retirement and then when we found out James wasn't as well as he was expected to be and then saying to me they wanted me (to do something special) . . . I looked at the way James is, I decided I'd be stupid to cut my nose off . . . I'm not going to do the full week like I'd been doing. (62 years of age)

Other women with different life-course experiences are less willing to relinquish or limit their involvement in the labour force. Some have continued to work despite spousal retirement. Where women have had a more manageable or controlled experience of balancing paid and unpaid work they are more likely to be seeking ongoing employment, including full-time work:

> I feel I'm moving into a new phase. I enjoy my job, I love my job but I do need a challenge . . . so I've put the word out that I'm looking for management jobs . . . (62 years of age)

Women over sixty years of age who accessed second-chance education in the 1970s, which opened up new areas of interest for them, and who also took strategic breaks from paid work to ensure they did not feel tired and overburdened, might not be interested in retirement. They might even be seeking new opportunities and challenges. Like men in higher status employment, such as management and the professions, they want to continue to enjoy the satisfactions of paid employment.

The retailing study showed that the choice of a preferred retirement age had little to do with pension and superannuation eligibility. Women with lowest entitlements (Superannuation

Guarantee Charge (SGC)/Award Superannuation) but with the highest accumulation of life-course events—such as migration, widowhood, divorce, family caring, and overall low income across an employment career—are most likely to be interested in 'early' retirement at around sixty years of age. Those who have had most opportunity via personal or employer (occupational) superannuation—for example as in an earlier career in teaching—are least likely to be seeking retirement.

Women from lower income households who accumulate a large number of debilitating life-course events feel more 'tired' or 'worn out' at about age fifty-eight to sixty. Policy makers urging greater self-provision for retirement income need to listen to low-income workers who have major family-related demands on their often negligible discretionary income.

Conclusion

Women who now remain in employment beyond fifty-five years of age are 'survivors' or even 'victors' over cumulative life-course events that both propel them into and repel them from the workforce. They have been relatively privileged through gaining access to paid work but, once there, they have had to negotiate ongoing structural constraints, and unsympathetic policies and personal treatment. Men with similar or lesser skills and knowledge are unwilling to allow themselves to be treated in this way.

To some extent the results of my study of the experiences of older women workers may reflect a cohort effect of a period in Australian industrial and social history that privileged the male breadwinner and saw women as secondary wage earners, if they were employed beyond marriage or even employed at all. If we accept this, however, we also accept the validity of claims of 'pipeline effects and other excuses' (Castleman & Allen 1998), which are used by managers and others to obscure the lack of appropriate attention given both to award changes following equal pay decisions in the Arbitration Commission, and to race, sex and age discrimination. Affirmative Action/Equal Employment Opportunity legislation has rarely taken account at the organisational level of the employment potential of women with interrupted careers and conflicted lives.

Current interest in 'family friendly' and 'work and life' policies in organisations should also take account of a wider range of factors than just the needs of parents to combine work with child-rearing; as well, some attention needs to be paid to elder care given the ageing of the population. The principal effect of the latter is a shortage of new entrants to the workplace, and attention to the needs of experienced and knowledgable older workers may therefore be an act of enlightened self-interest by employers. The research evidence is, however, that older workers are not necessarily the solution to possible labour shortages.

The labour market and workplace experiences of older women and the related strategies and accommodation into which these women are forced are best explained as primarily processes of accumulated sexism, sometimes interestected with racism. They result in lower wages, benefits and other rewards than those received by men of similar status and ability. Over time, that is, during the life-course, 'age effects' or discrimination based on age in its direct, indirect and systemic forms also informs the judgments and decisions made by more powerful others, such as managers and policy makers.

Ageism becomes a more salient form of discrimination in later life, but cannot be understood simply as a response to older people due to their age. Gendered ageism takes account of the differential treatment of men and women, but it underplays the effects of other dimensions of social inequality and division. Social class in terms of family of origin and household status is a major determinant of life chances for older women. The intersections of the forms of inequality and discrimination that are experienced by women throughout the life-course, and the nature of those experiences for different groups, also need careful analysis. At the same time, gendered ageism is a useful starting point and is a major advance on the view that discrimination in employment in middle and later life is based solely on ageing.

References

Australian Bureau of Statistics 1995 *The Labour Force Australia, October 1995* Catalogue No. 6203.0
—— 1996 *The Labour Force Australia, October 1996* Catalogue No. 6203.0
—— 1997a *The Labour Force Australia, January 1997* Catalogue No. 6203.0
—— 1997b *The Labour Force Australia, June 1997* Catalogue No. 6203.0
—— 1997c *The Labour Force Australia, October 1997* Catalogue No. 6203.0
Bateson, M. C. 1990 *Composing a Life* Plume (Penguin), New York
Bernard, M., Itzin, C., Phillipson, C. & Skucha, J. 1995 'Gendered Work, Gendered Retirement' in *Connecting Gender and Ageing* eds S. Arber & J. Ginn, Open University Press, Buckingham

Bottomley, G. 1994 'Living across Difference: Connecting gender, ethnicity, class and ageing in Australia' in *Australian Women: Contemporary Feminist Thought* eds N. Grieve & A. Burns, Oxford University Press, Melbourne

Bryson, L. 1994 'Women, paid work and social policy' in *Australian Women: Contemporary Feminist Thought* eds N. Grieve & A. Burns, Allen & Unwin, Sydney

Byetheway, B. 1995 *Ageism* Open University Press, Buckingham

Castleman, T. & Allen, M. 1998 'The "Pipeline Fallacy" and Gender Inequality in Higher Education Employment' *Policy, Organisation and Society* (Issue 15, Summer & nhsp, pp. 23–44

Encel, S. & Studencki, H. 1997 *Gendered Ageism: Job Search Experiences of Older Women* Department for Women/NSW Committee on Ageing, Sydney

Funnell, S. 1994 *'Somebody listened, Somebody cared, and Somebody did something about it' or What makes the Mature Workers Program Successful: An Evaluation of the Mature Workers Program* Department of Industrial Relations, Employment, Training & Further Education/NSW Office on Ageing, Social Policy Directorate, Sydney

Ginn, J. & Arber, S. 1995 '"Only Connect": Gender Relations and Ageing' in *Connecting Gender and Ageing: A Sociological Approach* eds S. Arber & J. Ginn, Open University Press, Buckingham

Hockey, J. & James, A. 1993 *Growing Up and Growing Old: Ageing and Dependency in the Life Course* Sage, London

Hollenshead, C. 1982 'Older women at work', *Educational Horizons* vol. 60(4), pp. 137–46, 195–6

Legge, V., Cant, R., O'Loughlin, K. & Waite, H. 1996 *Issues of Absenteeism and Occupational Health and Safety: A Research Report Focussing on Older Male, Female, and Non-English Speaking Background Workers* NSW Consultative Committee on Ageing, Sydney

Nuccio, K. 1989 'The Double Standard of Aging and Older Women's Employment', *Journal of Women and Aging* no. 1, pp. 1–3, 317–38

Reed, R. 1995 'Social Policy for Older Women is Not Working' *Social Policy and the Challenges of Social Change: Proceedings of the National Social Policy Conference, Sydney, 5–7 July 1995, vol. 2* eds P. Saunders & S. Shaver, Social Policy Research Centre, Sydney, pp. 167–81

——1996 *The Invisibility of Older Women Workers: Women Aged 55 and over in Retailing* WEETAG Monograph, AGPS, Canberra

——1997 'Older Women Workers: A challenge to unions' *Proceedings of the 5th Women and Labour Conference* eds M. Oppenheimer & M. Murray, 29 September – 1 October 1995, Macquarie University, Sydney

Schuller, T. 1989 'Work-ending: Employment and ambiguity in later life' in *Becoming and Being Old: Sociological Approaches to Later Life* eds B. Byetheway, T. Keil, P. Allatt & A. Bryman, Sage, London, pp. 41–54

Watson, E. & Mears, J. (n.d.) *Women in the Middle: Care Givers with a Double Burden of Care* University of Western Sydney, Macarthur, NSW

nine

social capital, volunteerism and older women

CONCETTA BENN, THERESE MCCARTHY
& WENDY WEEKS

The extent of social contribution made by older Australian women to the delivery of human services within the community is inestimable. Women of all ages give voluntary and unpaid time to community health centres and rural women's organisations, to the home-based economies of child care and to the care of elderly people or those with disabilities. It is increasingly clear that women's unpaid voluntary work makes a major contribution to the economy, and that conservative governments are capitalising on this as they decrease government funding and support for services designed to maintain communities and promote the rights and well-being of citizens.

This chapter will attempt to develop a critical discussion of the tensions and contradictions regarding the social and economic value of older women's volunteering. Within a discussion of the contemporary social and political context, we will discuss a small empirical study of women volunteers that illustrates the particular significance of older women's volunteering activity and contribution to the community. We will also explore the alternative discourses that seek to understand and explain 'volunteer work'. The case example presented is a Victorian service called Victorian Court Information and Welfare Network (Court Network), which is dominated by the contribution of older women. The volunteer activities within this organisation focus on the provision of information and support to people across all court jurisdictions. The Court Network survey was undertaken in 1995 as part of

social capital, volunteerism and older women / 135

an organisational development process. At the time of the survey, 77 per cent of the volunteers were more than fifty years of age and 46 per cent were over sixty. The volunteers were predominantly women. In working with the organisation, and in writing about the women's voluntary contribution, we found ourselves debating questions such as 'why do women volunteer?', 'who benefits?' and 'what is the cost—and to whom?'. What does the phenomenon of volunteering tell us about women and gender relations, age, social class and ethnicity?

There are many organisations or associations through which older women contribute volunteer time—to lobby government, represent women's interests or in other ways actively contribute to the community. Aboriginal women's organisations and councils, the Older Women's Action Network, the Women's Electoral Lobby, Women with Disabilities Australia, and the National Council of Women are examples of groups of women who work voluntarily within long-standing organisations to influence public policy. In the human services there are volunteer organisations such as Australian Red Cross or Lifeline, which operate relatively cheap human services with a great number of volunteers. The particular interest of the case example we are using here is that it is a volunteer organisation of mainly women volunteers, who work to fill a serious gap in the provision of information and support for people attending courts. The justice system is an extremely expensive and well-resourced system where (mainly male) judges and lawyers are highly paid, in stark contrast to the unpaid volunteers. Cuts to Legal Aid have made it even more likely that people attending courts will be stressed and distressed, and more likely to be in need of accurate information, interpreters, support and referral to associated community or human services.

Women's volunteering is full of contradictions. We have been aware as we worked together that we span three generations of professionally qualified women who work in human services; we, too, have often been caught up in the contradictions of 'volunteerism'. We have all worked in both paid and unpaid capacities with a wide range of government, government-funded and community organisations. Sometimes we have encouraged citizen service-users to become more actively involved in running their services, thereby expanding citizen participation or active citizenship. When we noticed that voluntary participation cost money—as well as time, effort and care, especially if the volunteers were living on pensions or social assistance benefits—we found ourselves trying to obtain funds so that their participation would attract an economic benefit, a supplementary or living wage. We wrote grants to expand professional programs, education and training for volunteers, not only because they said they wanted skills and knowledge, but because we valued standards of professional practice, accountability and quality services. Yet we ourselves have spent hours of our personal or family time in the evenings and over weekends contributing unpaid or voluntary work to our communities, hoping to make a contribution to a more socially just Australia.

Volunteering in the contemporary context

Conservative governments in Australia in the 1990s, both State and federal, have explicitly championed the use of volunteers, the value of family and a caring community. Buzz words such as 'partnerships' between government, business and 'the community', are associated with the political drive towards smaller government, fewer publicly funded services and constructed customer choice. The underpinning economic liberalism or public choice theory assumes, in apparent contrast to the rhetoric of 'care', that society is composed of self-interested individuals on a level playing field, and that competition will increase service effectiveness and economic efficiency. Governments in the wealthier Western countries are in agreement that the publicly funded welfare state has become too costly. In Australia, industrial relations deregulation, introduced in the 1990s, has been associated with lower trade union membership, with enterprise bargaining, and with increasing contract, casual or what has been called precarious employment (see, for example, Campbell 1997). Older workers are particularly affected by the changes to the labour market and employment policies, although women of all ages have always been overrepresented in casual and part-time work, and in unpaid or underpaid community and family care work (see, for example, Romeyn 1992).

Human service organisation managers within the state are now increasingly required to demonstrate the extent to which volunteers will be used to fulfil the goals of government-funded programs. 'Work for the Dole' was introduced by the federal government in 1997 to encourage unemployed people to join volunteer programs in exchange for subsistence-level benefit payments. Educational programs in human services seek 'volunteer' experience which bring merit points and a better chance of access. In this context, competition across the community for the opportunity to volunteer in human services is becoming tougher. It is not a citizen's automatic right to volunteer, or to participate in human service decision making. Volunteering in human service organisations is becoming more professionalised, though informal care, neighbourhood work and home-based community care proliferate, and draw heavily on women's time and labour. Healy (1997: 94) notes that

> Volunteerism is contentious since professional staff oppose amateurs intruding upon their domain, and paid staff see volunteers as a threat to their jobs. Volunteers offer several advantages: they do some things better than professionals, undertake complementary tasks, do routine tasks cheaper than paid staff, and provide services that are otherwise not offered.

However, the dismantling of community infrastructure and state deregulation have led to some activist volunteering becoming more politicised—in citizens' associations and movements, civil and human rights campaigns, and public demonstrations and rallies.

The past three decades of attention to women's unpaid work in families and communities have made women's voluntary social and economic activity more visible. In the 1970s the emphasis was on 'wages for housework'. In the 1980s the value of women's contribution and its official exclusion from national accounts were popularised by Marilyn Waring's *Counting for Nothing* (1988) and by international time-use studies. 'Satellite accounts', to use Waring's terminology, are now kept of women's household, volunteer and community work following the 1993 new United Nations System of National Accounts. Australian data indicate $227.8 billion of unpaid work, with 92 per cent undertaken in the household and 8 per cent in the community. Women are estimated to contribute two-thirds of the household work and 51 per cent of the voluntary and community work (Australian Bureau of Statistics (ABS) & Office of the Status of Women (OSW) 1997: 105). The Industry Commission (1995: 121) reported the estimated extent and cost of volunteers to be more than 1.3 million people contributing 95 million volunteer hours. Women's work is therefore more visible, if still unpaid!

Who are 'volunteers'?

The concept of 'volunteer' arises from a history of welfare liberalism that values philanthropy and giving from the 'haves' to the 'have nots'. Within liberal welfare states there is no clear consensus about what should be done as an act of friendship or neighbourliness, and what citizens might expect the state to provide: for example, a community service like child care or attendant care for disabled people. In social democratic states, such as the Scandinavian countries, the goals of full employment and equality are pursued by a developed public sector and public services covering a wide range of work-related policies and human services for women and men. Such policies and programs provide much greater social protection for women at all stages of their lives and, as a result, older women's circumstances are better resourced.

In Australia, the Victorian Community Services and Health Industry Training Board (1996: 3) defined a volunteer as 'a person who performs a service, task or work for the community other than their family; out of their own free will; and without monetary reward'.

The Australian Council of Social Services (ACOSS) (1996: 5) uses a similar definition, but excludes out-of-pocket expenses from the 'no monetary reward' criterion.

The first ABS national survey of voluntary work, completed in 1995, defined a volunteer as 'someone aged 15 years and over who willingly gave unpaid help, in the form of time, service or skills, through an organisation or group'. As a sign of its contemporary significance, the *Australian Women's Year Book 1997* devotes a new section to voluntary work. In giving this form of work prominence, the authors also identify the contradiction between voluntary work supposedly being 'by definition, a discretionary allocation of time' (ABS & OSW 1997: 105), yet widely discussed internationally as 'unpaid work'. We would argue that in the context of explicit government policies, such as 'Work for the Dole', some volunteer work is, in fact, no longer voluntary!

It is, by now, well substantiated that the social organisation of paid and unpaid work, care and community services is highly gendered; that is, it operates very differently for women and men (see, for example, Sassoon 1987; Sainsbury 1994; Pascall 1997). There is a sexual division of volunteering, with women volunteer workers tending to predominate in the areas of health and welfare, typically areas of 'women's work' and women's caring labour (Baines *et al.* 1991; Vellekoop Baldock 1995). Men tend to be located in the voluntary industries of sport and recreation, for example in football coaching and Scouting, or in positions of authority and community decision making, such as in municipal councils. When men's volunteer labour falls outside these areas, it is often described in terms such as a *pro bono* contribution to the community—as, for example, when men work as volunteer treasurers or legal advisers to service organisations. As one volunteer in our study commented:

> *It is often claimed that only men do* 'pro bono' *work to promote their careers but so do professional women. Perhaps the motivation is slightly different—men because it looks good on their curriculum vitae and women to feed back new knowledge into their jobs.*

It appears that the social capital accrued by such contribution is also linked to the financial capital of career reward, a less likely prospect for the vast majority of women volunteers in community services.

Older Australian women are still likely to be overrepresented in poverty or low income categories, having been predominantly responsible for child and other family care and subject to lower wages and overall earnings in the paid labour force throughout their lives. They are overrepresented in part-time and casual work and in discontinuous labour force participation. Until the 1980s women were predominantly excluded from superannuation schemes (ABS & OSW 1997). It is, in fact, difficult to calculate women's economic circumstances as individuals because family income will vary for women as wives, partners or daughters. Independent or single women, widows, single parents and Aboriginal women will be likely to have lower incomes and access to less money. There are some outstanding exceptions of wealthy Australian independent women who have used their family inheritance for the common good, but statistically these are rare exceptions in Australia.

Court Networkers—an example

Court Network is a state-wide service providing support to people going to court. The organisation is mainly staffed by volunteers, but also had some paid staff at the time of this research. Having operated for sixteen years by 1995, the organisation's structure, recruitment processes and elements of operations required review. A survey was conducted to elicit the volunteers' views about the organisation and we took the opportunity to examine the volunteer make-up of the organisation at the same time.

A survey of 111 court volunteers was undertaken as part of an organisational process that included individual interviews and group discussions. The mail return question sheet was designed to give volunteers an opportunity to express their views and speak of their experience. For comparative purposes we used questions from Vellekoop Baldock's West Australian study, which at the time was one of the largest studies of Australian volunteering in community services.

RURAL/METROPOLITAN LOCATION

The sample comprised eighty-five (76.6 per cent) metropolitan volunteers, twenty-five (22.5 per cent) rural, and one whose location was unspecified. It was clear that the volunteers in rural Victoria were confronted by specific issues in their work, related to the size of their communities and to the difficulties of providing confidential services to people they might also know socially. With a high unemployment rate in rural Victoria, there was also more consciousness of the opportunities involved in volunteering as a route to paid work. A number of rural volunteers spoke of difficulties associated with training 'younger' people who then left the organisation to pursue paid employment. This was viewed negatively as a drain on the organisational resources allocated to recruitment and training. Because of the small size of the rural sample we were unable to pursue a full comparison between rural and metropolitan volunteers.

GENDER

The sample reflected the gender composition of the organisation; that is, mainly women (105 women, or 95 per cent) and only six male volunteers (5 per cent), all of whom replied to the mail survey.

The data for Court Network reflect other studies, which show that women predominate as volunteers in direct care and service contributions. The first ever ABS study of volunteering conducted in November 1982 (and published in 1983) used Victorian data and suggested that women's and men's rates of volunteer community work were very similar. On a closer look, however, men were coaching the sports teams, fundraising through service clubs, and sitting on community decision-making committees and councils. Women were involved in direct care work—helping in schools, hospitals, nursing homes and community services. Vellekoop Baldock's study of volunteers in welfare organisations in Western Australia showed that women comprised 80 per cent of the 392 volunteers in the study (Vellekoop Baldock 1990: 29). The Victorian study of the non-government community organisations, *Welfare as an Industry,* reported 85,000 volunteers (Community Services, Victoria 1992) but did not collect data by gender. The ABS (1996) study of voluntary work in Australia showed women and men to have similar rates of volunteering, but with the sexual division of volunteering discussed earlier.

AGE

Nearly half of the volunteers in our Court Network study were sixty years and over (fifty-one volunteers, or 45.9 per cent). In 1995, there were no volunteers under twenty; one between twenty and twenty-nine years; none between thirty and thirty-nine years; twenty-five, or 22.5 per cent, between forty and forty-nine years; and thirty-four, or 30.6 per cent, between fifty and fifty-nine years. The 76 per cent of volunteers over fifty indicates the service as a site for older women's voluntary participation and activity, in contrast to other larger studies. For example, in Vellekoop Baldock's Western Australia study, only 30 per cent of women and 36 per cent of men were past paid-work retirement age (Vellekoop Baldock 1990: 31). The national ABS study found the peak age for volunteering to be between thirty-five and forty-four years (ABS & OSW 1997: 107). From an organisational perspective, the age spread means that policies need to respond to people at different life stages. The older volunteer age group, in contrast to the numbers of younger people in court, raised questions for recruitment policy. For our purposes in this chapter, the study provides a window into the experience of older women volunteers. Most of these volunteers were not seeking paid work.

RACE AND ETHNICITY

The volunteers in our study were predominantly English-speaking people, although a small number were multi-lingual. Sixteen per cent of them spoke one or more languages in addition to English, but these were generally other European languages—French, Dutch, Italian, German, Greek, Spanish and Yiddish—or Hebrew. This finding is also consistent with Vellekoop Baldock's study, and with the ABS national study, which found that a predominance of volunteers were born in Australia or in a mainly English-speaking country. Only 10 per cent of female volunteers and 8 per cent of male volunteers were from non-English-speaking backgrounds (ABS & OSW 1997: 107). The Court Network organisation, therefore, had a shortage of languages that reflect the newer immigrant populations in Victoria, and a complete absence of members from Asia or Aboriginal Australia. This finding suggested that use of interpreters might be significant in training. Our survey alerted us to the racial and ethnic divisions in volunteering within the mainstream court or justice system. However, it was also apparent to us that the legal system itself was highly classed and gendered. As the Australian Law Reform Commission so aptly put it:

> The operation of the law by courts, police, lawyers and judges is largely the product of men's ideas and actions and largely remains in the control of men. The needs of women, where they differ from men's are still not being fully met by the system. (1994: 7)

Our experience with other volunteers suggests that immigrant groups are fully occupied with providing welfare programs within their own immigrant communities, such as the Chinese Welfare Organisation or the Turkish Women's Association.

Given the composition of the legal system itself, and the relatively contemporary challenges to the ethnic and gender mix of the judiciary, it is clear that organisations like Court Network, because of their location within this highly classed and gendered context, may be more reluctant to recruit from those who would be less educated, spoke less English or were overall more discriminated against within such a system.

In summary, it is clear that the type of service being provided—its purpose and its locality—has great bearing upon *who* does volunteer work for the service.

Socioeconomic and occupational background

In an attempt to obtain information on the socioeconomic and occupational background of volunteers, some questions on 'last paid employment' and 'partner's last paid employment' were drawn from Vellekoop Baldock's study. The author makes a lengthy apology to women for including partner's job as relevant, but explains that women's social background is hard to measure given the cultural dominance of paid work. Nevertheless, in order to identify gaps for recruitment, and given the number of poor people in the courts, we decided to include this question.

Sixty-nine (or 62.2 per cent) of the Court Network volunteers surveyed reported having had a paid job. This is higher than the 52 per cent (3,823,000) of all Australian women over fifteen years of age who were in the Australian paid labour force at the time of the survey (Department of Labour and Industrial Relations, Women's Bureau 1996: 6). The comparable percentage of Australian men at the time was 74.1 per cent. So the volunteers in our sample were more likely to have worked in paid employment than Australian women in general, although less likely to have done so than Australian men. Given there were only six male volunteers in this organisation, the figures are most interesting in relation to women. Using a combination of Vellekoop Baldock's categories and the Federal Women's Bureau figures we compared our sample with all Australian women in 1996, and with the Western Australian figures for women and men. The outstanding finding was that the Court Network volunteers were twice as likely as Australian women in general to have held professional or managerial positions (twenty-eight, or 40.6 per cent compared with 20.5 per cent), and four times as likely to have held a para-professional job (eighteen, or 26 per cent compared with 6.6 per cent). Our volunteers were less likely to have been clerical workers than the average Australian woman (only fifteen, or 21.7 per cent compared with 29.4 per cent), and less likely to have been in sales and personal service (eight, or 11.6 per cent compared with 25.3 per cent of Australian women). There were no women volunteers at Court Network who had been employed in working-class jobs in trades or labouring positions, though 18.2 per cent of Australian women's occupations are in this category.

The Western Australian study showed only 10 per cent of the women volunteers to have had their 'last paid job' in upper professional and managerial occupations, so Court Network volunteers were four times as likely to have been professionals when last in paid employment. They were less likely than the Western Australian volunteers to have been in any other occupational category. The Court Network volunteers who had been in the paid labour force were senior professional women, although there was some occupational range. The job titles reported included the following: shop manageress, editor of historical records, Commonwealth public servant, nurse, theatre nursing sister, director of a human service organisation, manager of a government-funded telephone advice service, university librarian, retired school principal, and high school teacher.

The volunteers' own paid work experience suggests that they are predominantly middle class. However, given the age and gender profile, the 'partner's job' is likely to give more of a clue to actual socioeconomic position, as women's lifestyle and social class are frequently related to partner's income and occupation, as mentioned above.

Only forty-seven (42.3 per cent) answered the question about partner's occupation. Several responded that it was 'irrelevant'. We did not ask for marital status, on equal opportunity grounds that it was irrelevant to 'doing volunteering'. The low response rate means, however, that the respondents who remained silent might be widows, divorced or single—or just consider it irrelevant to their volunteering. Although the number is small, thirty-eight (81 per cent) of the forty-seven who spoke about the occupation of their partner reported professional and managerial occupations—doctors, surgeons, lawyers—in other words, a strong upper-middle-class presence. The other nine partners were spread across the occupational categories, including two trades and labouring people. This contrasts with the Western Australia study where 58 per cent of the volunteer partners were professional and managerial, 26 per cent from trades and labouring jobs, and 16 per cent in clerical or sales.

Overwhelmingly, then, the Court Network volunteers were more likely to have held professional occupations than all Australian women, and more likely to be partnered by upper professional people, if they have partners.

REASONS FOR VOLUNTEERING

Survey respondents typically reported more than one reason for volunteering. The percentage of respondents (111) who gave each reason is reported below. Categories used were drawn from Vellekoop Baldock's study for purposes of comparison, although the steering committee refused to use 'altruism', substituting,

social capital, volunteerism and older women / 145

instead, the wording below: 'desire to help people/make a social contribution'. The following lists in descending order the reasons given.

Desire to help people/make a social contribution	104 (93.7 per cent)
Personal growth	74 (66.7 per cent)
Skill development	54 (48.6 per cent)
Social interaction	51 (45.9 per cent)
Other	11 (10 per cent)
Developing skills for paid work	10 (9 per cent)
Total number of reasons given	*304 (100 per cent)*

Some examples of 'other' reasons given were:

I believe there is great need for those ever familiar words 'May I help you?' and someone to show that there are people who care—beside the Court staff who are very good, but very busy.

I have skills and I want to use them.

Awareness of need to make the court more user-friendly.

Alternative activity after retirement.

To remain a useful member of society.

The major theme of 'desire to help people/make a social contribution' warrants our emphasis on older women's social contribution. It is, however, likely to have been partly generated by the steering committee's choice of words, which captured the organisational ideology about their purpose. This response was much higher than in the national survey, which reported 41.8 per cent of women volunteering to 'help others/community' (ABS & OSW 1997: 111). The Western Australian study found 85.6 per cent reported 'altruism' as their main motivation. Social interaction was the second reason, being reported by 40.1 per cent. The Industry Commission (1995: 124) reported on a study completed by the Australian Volunteer Centre of retired and senior volunteers whose main reasons for volunteering were 'to stay mentally alert and to feel useful'.

Our sample were skilled and experienced women strongly motivated to continue to use their talents to contribute to the community in their later years. They were not seeking paid work, and nor were they likely to get it if they were, given the current labour market. Court Network showed up in our study as a place where people could contribute, and perhaps enhance the community 'social capital'.

'Personal growth' was also much more frequently reported in our sample than in the national study. Sixty-six per cent of our sample gave 'personal growth' as a reason for volunteering. This contrasts with 35.3 per cent of women and 31.2 per cent of men volunteering for 'personal/family involvement', or 26.7 per cent of women and 26.5 per cent of men volunteering for 'personal satisfaction' in the ABS 1995 study (ABS & OSW 1997: 111). 'Personal growth' was a reason for 35 per cent of the Western Australian sample, and 'developing skills for paid work' applied to 10.5 per cent—a similar percentage to the Court Network volunteers.

TIME SPENT VOLUNTEERING

The ABS (1995) national study of volunteers found that women over fifty-five years and men over sixty-five years were likely to volunteer for 150 hours or more, or a minimum of three hours a week (ABS & OSW 1997: 109). Volunteers in the Court Network contributed long hours. Two spoke of their time commitment as follows:

Volunteering takes up most of my week.

I am the only person in my street who does voluntary work, and I do it 3 days per week. I like to learn new things, belong to an organisation, and to be able to talk with all sorts of different people.

Fifteen per cent gave between eleven and twenty hours a week; 10 per cent contributed five hours or less; and the great majority, seventy-eight volunteers, or 74 per cent, volunteered between six and ten hours weekly. This suggests an intensive, regular volunteer commitment, similar to a part-time job in human services. In terms of 'in-kind' donations this is a major contribution to the community, without economic remuneration for the volunteers, which saves the human service system thousands of dollars.

We now turn to explore the discourses that seek to understand the phenomenon of volunteering.

Volunteering as social capital?

The economic and social restructuring of the Australian welfare state, supported by both Liberal and Labor governments, has been associated with a revived interest in civil society. One stream of research and discussion concerned with civil society explores 'social capital'. A large international study of 'social capital' originated from Robert Putnam's work at Harvard University and compares social capital in Sweden, the United States, the United Kingdom, France, Germany, Spain, Japan and Australia. Putnam's study of regional Italy argues that 'the existence of community networks outside of government is a key feature in making governments effective' (Robinson 1997: 2). According to Eva Cox

> We will be looking for measures which can demonstrate comparatively the levels of trust in the community. The social capital thesis is that social and economic disintegration occur when the levels of trust drop. Business operates effectively on high levels of trust, even though competition is often over-emphasised. The social and political spheres cannot operate with low levels of trust. (1996: 2)

In analysing the pathways to a civil society, Cox argues that such voluntary contributions, most particularly by women, are critical to the establishment of a civil society, one that values social capital alongside the economic. A common theme in our study at Court Network was that women who had completed their unpaid child-bearing and child-rearing saw volunteering as a way of contributing something to the community. This was also true for those professional women volunteering after they had retired from the paid labour force.

Volunteering as unpaid labour?

The close connection between volunteer work and other unwaged labours has been researched extensively in the past two decades of research and literature on women's paid and unpaid work. Cora Vellekoop Baldock (1995: 15) argues that women are available for volunteer work in those contexts in which they are structurally and ideologically marginalised from waged work—in other words, when their primary role is seen to be that of (house)wife and mother, and when they are not seen as having the right to paid work.

As mentioned earlier, older women who are able to enter

or re-enter the labour market often do so in casual or part-time positions, and are frequently seen as taking jobs from young employed people. In this context, volunteering provides a particularly legitimate form of work, which is highly functional in economic terms, and relieves the economic burden of government. In providing meaningful 'caring' roles for thousands of women—who are physically fit and reliable managers with a lifetime of skills developed in the family, household and community—volunteering offers a social alternative to these competent women re-competing in the labour market. It does so with low economic cost to the human services, and with no wages paid to the women volunteer workers.

Volunteer work as 'women's work' and caring?

Much of the research and discussion of women's unpaid labour has been cast in terms of 'women's caring' or gender relations and care work within welfare states (see, for example, *Social Politics* 1997). The concept of women's caring has been useful in describing women's overrepresentation in the 'caring professions' of health and welfare, in particular the predominance of women in nursing, social work, primary school teaching, and volunteering in direct care services (see Baines *et al.* 1991). Caring behaviour has been linked to women's traditional familial roles as daughters, wives and mothers. 'Caring for', an activity that women do, has been differentiated from 'caring about', which is more likely to be how men care. More men have the financial means to ensure paid care for those they 'care' about. The concept of 'caring' is useful in understanding older Australian women, though less useful in understanding younger women's lives and work patterns.

The concept is sometimes used ahistorically and essentially to imply that women do and can care more than men. This is not helpful for social change in family or community gender relations, nor does it help explain the younger fathers and husbands who are trying to learn to share the caring responsibilities. A number of writers have broadened the debate on gender and caring to pursue a 'social model of caring' for community care generally, and particularly for funded human services for elder care, care for persons with disabilities, child care, and family-related workplace policies and programs. This makes the debate central to human service provision and raises issues about community support services for carers, carer abuse, the costs of caring work, and implications for housing and employment policies and programs (see, for example, Dalley 1988; Baines *et al.* 1991).

Hilary Graham's (1993) classic work on the 'social divisions in caring' critiques the feminist caring debate as being too preoccupied with the similarities of gendered caring within families. She points out that poor and working-class women undertake 'care' work for others, often for low wages, and then go home to assume their own family care responsibilities. This throws light on the economic and social divisions among women. One volunteer referred to the class composition of volunteers when she said:

> *Volunteers should be different sorts of people, not only ladies from Toorak [an affluent Melbourne suburb], particularly when you are helping people who are in trouble.*

In understanding older women's experience as volunteers these traditions of research, analysis and debate raise questions about the extent to which volunteering further marginalises women, making them less powerful and influential. Or is it another way by which women express their social citizenship, access their social, political and community decision making, and facilitate their social contribution?

Conclusion

> *The type of people who volunteer have changed over the years. Once it used to include young women after their children had gone to school—now they go to work instead of volunteering. The other type were grandmothers whose family commitments had diminished—now they babysit their grandchildren whilst their daughters work.* (Personal interview)

As can be seen, the nature of volunteering—as unpaid labour or citizen participation—changes according to government social and labour market policies, and the associated patterns of work and everyday life. Economic policies and constraints drive the extent to which volunteers are used in the human services, even though volunteering is presented to citizens in the high moral terms of 'care' and 'giving to the community'. As services have been cut and the community restructured according to business principles to become a quasi-market, there has also been a lot of interest in reviving social capital, and building trust and community towards the creation of a more civil society.

Our small sample of older women presents one snapshot, at one point in time, of a particular volunteer organisation within the justice system. The volunteers could be seen as upper-class and upper-middle-class stereotypical 'charity ladies' or hand-maidens to the court. Their contribution has to be appreciated within the white, male, ruling class system in which they volunteer. They could be described as cheap and uncosted labour within the human services. Yet we know them to be dignified, intelligent, well-educated, talented, hard-working women, many of whom have retired from senior professional positions in paid employment, who give generously of their time, skills and knowledge through this volunteer service network.

The strong theme reported in the 'reasons for volunteering' was the wish to make a social contribution, without economic reward. This is the stuff of women's social citizenship: an example of women who silently, often invisibly, contribute to building 'social capital' or trust and goodwill. Women are, by law, political and social citizens, yet they are markedly under-represented in positions of political and other public decision making and influence. They must, therefore, express their social citizenship, their right to participate and make a contribution, in other ways. In the court system the volunteers are filling the gaps in services, responding to needs, and keeping the justice system running smoothly.

Our exploration of older Australian volunteers calls for a costing, accounting and valuing of all Australian women's social contribution. We suggest there is also a need to maintain space for older women within the voluntary sector, despite the competition that is growing within the community for unpaid work, particularly with schemes like 'Work for the Dole'. We argue for the maintenance of this space because older women's contribution is particular and valuable—they have a lifetime of skills to contribute. The valuing of this contribution is necessary as a major step towards socially just human services, and towards an Australian constitution for the next century that counts women 'in' and gives them their fair share of resources and recognition.

References

Australian Bureau of Statistics (ABS) 1983 *Provision of Welfare Services by Volunteers, Victoria, November 1982* ABS, Melbourne, Catalogue No. 4401.2
—— 1996 *Voluntary Work, Australia* AGPS, Canberra, Catalogue No. 4441.0
Australian Bureau of Statistics & Office of the Status of Women 1997 *Australian Women's Year Book 1997* AGPS, Canberra, Catalogue No. 4124.0
Australian Council of Social Services 1996 *Volunteering in Australia* ACOSS paper no. 74, ACOSS, Sydney
Australian Law Reform Commission (ALRC) 1994 *Equality before the Law: Justice for women* report no. 69, part 1, ALRC, Melbourne
Baines, Carol 1991 'The Professions and an Ethic of Care' in *Women's Caring: Feminist Perspective on Social Welfare* eds Carol Baines, Pat Evans & Sheila Neysmith, McClelland & Stewart, Toronto
Baines, Carol, Evans, Pat & Neysmith, Sheila (eds) 1991 *Women's Caring: Feminist Perspective on Social Welfare* McClelland & Stewart, Toronto
Baldock, Cora Vellekoop 1990 *Volunteers in Welfare* Allen & Unwin, Sydney
—— 1995 Victorian Court Network 1996 The New Year Plan, unpub. report, Court Network, Melbourne
Campbell, Iain 1997 'Beyond Unemployment: The challenge of increased precarious employment' *Just Policy* no. 11, December, pp. 4–20
Community Services, Victoria 1992 *Welfare as an Industry* Community Services, Victoria, Melbourne
Cox, Eva 1996 'Social Capital: Australia joins international study' *ANZTSR (Australian & New Zealand Third Sector Research) Newsletter 1996* no. 2, pp. 1–2
Dalley, Gillian 1988 *Ideologies of Caring: Rethinking Community and Collectivism* Macmillan, London
Department of Labour and Industrial Relations, Women's Bureau (1996) *Women and Work Newsletter* DLIR, Canberra
Graham, Hilary 1993 'Social Divisions in Caring' *Women's Studies International Forum* vol. 16(5), pp. 461–70
Healy, Judith 1997 *Welfare Options: Delivering Social Services* Allen & Unwin, Sydney
Industry Commission 1995 *Charitable Organisations in Australia Report No. 45, 16th June 1995* AGPS, Melbourne
Odendahl, Teresa & O'Neill, Michael 1994 *Women and Power in the Non-profit Sector* Jossey-Bass Publishers, San Francisco
Pascall, Gillian 1997 *Social Policy: A Feminist Analysis* Routledge, London & New York
Robinson, David 1997 'Social Capital and Policy Development' *ANZTSR Newsletter 1997* no. 3, pp. 2–5
Romeyn, Jane 1992 *Flexible Working Time: Part-time and Casual Employment* Industrial Relations Research Monograph no. 1, June, Department of Industrial Relations, Canberra

Sainsbury, Diane 1994 *Gendering Welfare States* Sage, London
Sassoon, Anne Showstack (ed.) 1987 *Women and the State* Hutchinson, London
Social Politics: Special issue on gender and care work in welfare states vol. 4(3), Fall 1997
Vellekoop Baldock, *see* Baldock
Victorian Community Services & Health Industry Training Board 1996 *Volunteer Policy Paper* CS & H Training Board, Melbourne
Victorian Court Network 1996 'Who are the Networkers: A profile of networkers at Victorian Court Network, from the 1995 survey' *VCN Newsletter*, Melbourne
Waring, Marilyn 1988 *Counting for Nothing* Allen & Unwin, Sydney

part three

relating

ten

making the most of my life: a conversation with Dot Peters

MARILYN POOLE & SUSAN FELDMAN

Throughout this book, the contributors have looked at issues that support a number of the principles as stated by the United Nations in the International Year for Older Persons 1999: older people should be integrated into society, have the opportunity to share their knowledge and skills with other generations and continue to be of service to their communities.

All the chapters in this book, with the exception of this one, report on research studies undertaken with older women. This chapter, a conversation with Dot Peters, is somewhat different. While one woman does not represent the geographic, cultural and spiritual diversity of the Indigenous people of Australia, her narrative contains many of the themes and issues explored and analysed in other chapters.

Indigenous and non-Indigenous populations in Australia have very different age structures. Aboriginal people do not have the same demographic profile of ageing as the rest of Australia, living on average 15–20 years less than non-Indigenous Australians. This means that there are fewer opportunities for Aboriginal communities to engage in active interactions with their older people.

We approached Dot Peters to contribute to this book because she is an older Indigenous woman who remains intimately involved with and committed to her community. She is an activist, educator and spokesperson who lives in a semi-rural location near metropolitan Melbourne. Her observations alert us to the importance of older people in transmitting the history and culture of their people to future generations. Her narrative provides us with a snapshot of issues which are central to her own life as she grows older and which are reflected in other chapters in this book.

The following is an edited conversation between Dot Peters, Susan Feldman and Marilyn Poole.

TELL ME ABOUT YOUR EARLIER LIFE

Well, I was born in Healesville in 1930. My grandparents were Yarra Yarra people and they lived on the Aboriginal reserve at Healesville. My mother was born there at Coranderrk, which means Christmas Bush because it used to grow a lot around that area. My dad was born at [Cummergunga Reserve] and later came to Healesville. We were reared as children in Healesville, and I've lived here most of my life except for when I moved away for a couple of years or so I went to school in Healesville, first off at the Badger Creek School. It's a tiny little old building near the Sanctuary up there, and that used to be the whole school where everybody went. After a year I went to Healesville Primary, and then on to Lilydale High for two years, which was quite good for me in those days.

I left school at thirteen or fourteen. That's about the age everybody left school in those days not like these days. Fourteen seemed to be the age to go to work in those days, unless you were going to be academic, and there weren't very many women around like that. Anyway, I worked as a telephonist most of my life, starting off at the Healesville Telephone Exchange in 1946. I actually finished up there again just before it closed in 1970.

As a family we grew up happily in Healesville. Brothers played football, girls played tennis and we all loved the weekly dances. I played competitive tennis in Healesville. I loved my tennis and put my back into it. I was honoured as a life member of the tennis club, which was great. I don't play tennis now; I think I'd fall apart if I tried playing!

I've gone through the good and bad things with family, just the things that families go through with the grief and that sort of thing, you know. A brother was killed when he was sixteen in an accident and another brother at twenty and a couple of years ago, my other older brother was killed in a car accident.

Anyway, my girlfriend worked on the *Fairstar*, she was the head stewardess there, and she said, 'Come on, work as a stewardess'. So I went on the *Fairstar* for a few trips to the islands. It was lovely, yes. And they put me in the cocktail bar where all the really nice moneyed people came and had their drinks. And we went to Tahiti and the islands, and that was really lovely, yes.

My son was born in 1969. I was in Sydney and it was hard. I was working on the Ansett switchboard, and getting him [Andrew] minded. Also my mum had died in the February before my baby was born in the March. She didn't even know I was having him. My family didn't know either. And with mum going, I thought, 'Well, God meant me to keep Andrew, so I'm going to'. But it was just too hard trying to work, and I thought, 'I don't want him to grow up in a city like this'. And I remembered Healesville and what it was like growing up there myself, and I took him back there. It was the best thing I ever did. My son is now twenty-nine and he's back at college studying marketing and managing. He's in his last year and doing very well at it, so I'm quite proud of that. Now, whether anybody thought ill of me or anything like that, I don't know, because I never ever heard anything. It's the same with being Aboriginal and growing up in Healesville. We never experienced any racism or anything like that. I had a wonderful time in Healesville growing up. I grew up in that town knowing and loving Aboriginal and white people. I never even thought about being Aboriginal. It didn't dawn on me; never thought about it. I'd always got friends, I played tennis, I loved dancing, I loved singing. Sometimes when we had a local band in, I'd get up and sing 'Goodnight Sweetheart'. And whenever the football was on in those days, they'd always have a party on the Saturday nights, and there was always a sing-song, you know. My mum played piano, she only learnt to play it by ear. Of course, there was always a gathering around the piano on the Saturday night, and a sing-along. And I think that's what brought people together.

TELL US ABOUT YOUR LIFE NOW AS AN OLDER WOMAN

I've become more involved in the Aboriginal community. I don't know whether you realise it wasn't until 1967 that Aboriginal people got the vote and were recognised as Australian citizens. After this Aboriginal education started to move forward, so, at

Healesville Primary School, they advertised for what they called an Aboriginal teacher aide at the school. So I applied for it and I got the job, at fifty years of age. And then I realised that I didn't know a thing about Aboriginal history. We were never taught it at school. I never listened to gran or mum talking, you know, you don't listen to old people! It's a terrible thing to say, but it's the truth. So like a lot of Aboriginal people I had to start reading up about my history. And then it dawned on me just what my grandparents and my mum and dad must have gone through in their lives. And I thought, 'Well, this is what God meant me to do'. So I got involved and worked at the primary school for ten years. I retired at sixty-one from paid work because it was just getting too much to work there every day, come home and clean up house and look after a son who leaves things all over the place. And then I got involved with the Healesville RSL, and I was actually president of the ladies' auxiliary there for a couple of years. I didn't find that terribly satisfactory. I don't know why, but I guess because what I'm doing now, working with Aboriginal people, is more rewarding. I joined some consultative Aboriginal groups, and went around Victoria talking to and listening to Aboriginal communities, about what they needed and what they wanted. I go out quite often to Ballina, which is an Aboriginal cultural centre at Healesville. They have school groups in there, and they ask me to go and talk to the kids. I also demonstrate the baskets, and try and show them how to make them. Other kids come out there, too, and I've actually had people that have been there once request that I go and talk to them again. I talk about my experiences at Healesville, and what it was like. I'm also working on a number of committees to work towards Reconciliation in the local area. I tend to get involved with the younger people more, though some of the older ones, too, because they need the help. And every now and then I think, 'Oh, I'm sick of this, I'm just going to go and do my own thing. I'm going to sit and make my baskets, and just sit quietly and watch television'. But someone rings up, or something happens, and then you get involved again. I help whenever I can.

AS AN OLDER WOMAN DO YOU WORK WITH YOUNG PEOPLE?

Yes, definitely, but not just within Aboriginal culture. I don't even like to use the terms Aboriginal and white as I think that's divisive. Our children don't know about their Dreamtime, they don't know about where they actually came from, and they've lost identity. And that not only applies to Aboriginal children today, I think that applies to a lot of children. Now, I was lucky enough to have gran on the Coranderrk Reserve, and we used to go out there as young people. She actually taught me basket coiling when I was about seven, and we were also taught respect. We were taught to respect our elders, to respect the water, the trees, the animals, everything around us, but mainly to respect each other. Now, my sisters and my brothers, we've all grown up, and we've never had an argument. It wasn't that we couldn't, but we remembered what gran would say: 'You say something in anger, and you can never take that back, you should walk away from it, and if you still want to say it, well say it quietly'. Respect to me is understanding what another person is all about, I guess. They might have different ideas to you, they might not agree with what you say, but you should at least believe that they have the right to say and feel the way they do. Respect to me is caring for the other person and their feelings. I think that's why there is a lot of drinking with the younger ones today, because they've lost that respect for themselves, actually. They're in a twilight zone, they're in limbo. And I always say that what people don't understand they don't like, and a lot of them don't understand themselves. They don't understand where they are going because of this lack of identity and, therefore, are caught in between two worlds. There's the Aboriginal culture, but they've now all got houses and televisions and phones and cars and things. They still expect to have that Aboriginality coming forth, or using that, I guess, as something they can do in their lives, but they haven't really got that feeling in their heart, and that's where it comes from. I was lucky enough to be brought up when respect and discipline were very much a part of our lives, and I think that was right. I know, yes. I guess we need to turn it around and call it respect and not discipline now.

DOES THE LACK OF RESPECT AND DISCIPLINE IMPACT ON YOUR LIFE?

Well, it doesn't on mine, but I can imagine it does with some grannies who just give in to their grandkids ordering them around. My sister turned seventy this year, and we were talking the other day about how we're glad our lives are nearly over, because I don't know what it's going to be like in fifty years or a hundred years time. She said she worries about her grandchildren because we've seen such changes, you know? When we were growing up in Healesville, it was still the horse and cart days and only about a dozen people could afford a car. You walked everywhere, and everybody knew everybody. And you could not be sick in your house on your own and definitely not be lying dead there for days, because somebody would be calling in. You could go out and leave your door open for months, six months even, and you'd come back and it would still be the same. Young people today have not seen the changes we older people have experienced, so they will cope perhaps!

I think there are changes in attitudes today, you know. I don't like bad manners, I don't like swearing, and I think that sort of attitude impacts on me more than anything. I mean everybody can do something wrong once or twice, but if they keep doing it, then it's a problem. But even they can turn around, I guess. I don't like to see drunks, even though I love a drink myself. In fact, I think a couple of times the ground has moved when I've had a couple of drinks!

DO YOU THINK IT'S DIFFERENT NOW FOR A YOUNG ABORIGINAL PERSON GROWING UP IN HEALESVILLE?

Well, because of the structure of Aboriginal life, a lot of them didn't have the chance for an education. Marilyn and Susan, like you would have been born in a house where your mum and dad would have had plans for your future. With Aboriginal children, some of them would still have been born in huts, and even today it's nothing for ten or fourteen people to be living in one house because of the family structure. They take in other people and their relations' children, and they don't think that education is that important. Now, I guess I do, because that's the way I was brought up. My mum said to us from the word go, 'Be educated, be nice, and always wear clean underwear in case you have an accident'. Mum would say things like, 'Wash your clothes and always look tidy. Just because you are poor, there's no need to look poor'. And when I look back now, I think she was teaching us to be proud of what we were in ourselves.

TELL US ABOUT YOUR INVOLVEMENT IN YOUR COMMUNITY

Well, it's not really a big town, and because I was involved in tennis, and worked at the primary school, and my son played football, your name gets around and you hear all these things. And, of course, when something is happening, somebody either rings me up to say, 'Will you get involved?', or you hear it on the grapevine. I get very involved if I think something is unfair. Then I will go for it, but I go quietly. I don't rant and rave and swear and carry on. Normally, I can help get things straightened out in a quiet way. I get a few telephone calls now and again from the different Aboriginal groups that need a bit of help, and I guess they know that I'll help them. We've got organisations up there that are supposed to help, but some of them are too busy looking after themselves I'm afraid. I've been up at Glenrowan over the weekend to see the Aboriginal Cultural Officer there who wanted me to go up and do the basket coiling at the festival. A fortnight before, the young man from the Museum of Victoria asked me to attend a meeting at Toolangi in regard to the new museum that is going to be built saying they were doing this new section called 'Four Seasons' and they needed an Aboriginal input. Apparently I was involved in a workshop there three or four years ago, but I'd forgotten about it. What I'm getting at here is that if I do something, I sort of tend to forget about it, but then somebody remembers me and says, 'Oh, we'll get aunty Dot'. They know they can ask me to do something, and rely on me to help if I can.

DO YOU SEE YOURSELF AS POWERFUL?

I've never thought of myself as being powerful. I don't like the word power. It sounds like you fight over it, you know I have a friend and he calls me influential. I guess I'm more involved in Aboriginal things now, and they sort of look upon me in that light, too. My family was respected in the Healesville community.

ARE OTHER OLDER ABORIGINAL PEOPLE ALSO RESPECTED?

Oh, yes, very much so. But a lot of the older ones now have become senile, you know. I think I'm getting that way myself, actually. But it comes down to the respect of the community for their elders. It wouldn't matter where I went in Australia, when I was introduced anyone younger than me would all call me aunty Dot or if the same age, sister. No one would ever call me Dot on the first day. I don't like the word elder. I believe that it belongs in the past, you know. I like to be referred to as an older woman of the community, and that includes me in the wider community as well. And I don't like it when I see some of our younger people being cheeky to the wider community. There's a young lass that works in the bank, and one day two young Aboriginal kids aged about fourteen approached her. One of them wanted to know the time, and the other one said, 'Don't ask that white bitch'. And I said to her, 'Who were they?', because I would have torn strips off them. To me, at my age, it's a responsibility to be a role model for younger ones. And I mean that in every respect. I remember one young mum swearing madly at the kids all the time, but when one of the kids swore at her, she threatened to wipe his mouth out with soap. And I said, 'You can't do that, you were swearing in front of him'. 'It doesn't matter aunty, he's not allowed to swear.' And I said, 'Well, you've got to not swear, too'. That's the sort of double standard that I'm trying to fight. I've got to the stage where if anyone swears in front of me, they apologise. And I also say to them, 'Don't do it in the first place'.

I think that older people with their experience have got a lot to offer young people these days. It's crazy for them to sit back and not offer. I mean you don't go barging in telling people what they should be thinking and what they should be feeling, but you should try to get the message across to us. I believe this needs to come along with our young ones, too. And I think the young ones need it today. We have street kids, and everyone says, 'Oh, they're sorry for the street kids'. But I don't feel sorry for street kids, except for the ones who have probably suffered abuse at home. I would say six out of ten of them have left home because they don't like mum and dad telling them what to do. They forget that parents have got rights, too. Just because you're older doesn't mean you haven't got any rights, no.

IS BEING RESPONSIBLE A BURDEN?

I don't find it as such. I think to myself sometimes, 'Oh, I'm never going to get anywhere with this'. Because even a little thing like using a knife and fork, a lot of Aboriginal children don't know how to do it. They don't know how to even sit at a table and have a meal. I guess there are a lot of kids like that these days. And that astounds me, because with Andrew we always sat at the table.

I'm at the stage now, that instead of being free to do what I want to do, I'm more involved with the community. I can't really sit down and do what I want to do personally. I don't know how many times I've said, 'I'm not going to get involved with this Aboriginal community any more', but there I am involved again, as a teacher, and I get paid for it.

WHAT ISSUES CONCERN YOU MOST NOW?

I think I would like to see the caring come back into life at all levels. I get very concerned when we have governments that put a machine in, which puts six or seven people out of work. I think of the families that are struggling, and I can understand how people can get desperate. I'm on an age pension, I haven't got any money in the bank, and about two or three days before pay day, you're always wondering if you've got enough for a meal. It's just Andrew and me, so usually there is a tin of spaghetti or an egg or something like that, but I can appreciate what a young family must go through when they've got kids. So I would like to see really honest politicians who care for the people, and for everybody in those positions to get back to caring for people. But when you see them spend all this money sending things up in space—and they're going to cover that up before long—when kids are starving. All that people need is love, all they need is someone to say, 'I love you', every day. And I don't think that costs money, does it? I can honestly say I don't sort of think about what I want for myself, you know. I've never sat down and thought about what I want from life. I'm happy with what I've got, I guess, in my life—a beaut family and good friends . . .

HOW DO YOU SEE YOUR LIFE IN THE FUTURE?

I have thought of that. I guess, eventually, I'm going to be sitting in a chair and not being able to move around, or go and play a poker machine if I want to, or make the baskets, or go to my bingo once a fortnight and I love that. I'll probably get to the stage where I won't be able to hop in the little car that my son gave me and go for a cup of coffee. I never get lonely, but I can feel alone sometimes. And when that happens to me, I just hop in the car and go and have a cup of coffee and a talk with somebody. But I've never been one to be lonely, and I don't think I've ever been one to just sit around lots of the time. I've got the gift of the gab, and I'll always love to sit and talk about things. So when it comes to something personal for myself, and where I'm heading, I guess, eventually it will be up there, to Heaven, I hope, but I don't sort of think about that very much. I'll just continue with what I'm doing, hopefully to help someone in need.

eleven

'no more dinners only lunches': older widowed women relating to the world

Susan Feldman

> 'Widow' is a harsh and hurtful word. It comes from the Sanskrit and it means 'empty'. I have been empty too long, I do not want to be pigeonholed as a widow. I am a woman whose husband has died, yes. But not a second-class citizen, not a lonely goose. I am a mother and a working woman and a friend and a sexual woman and a laughing woman and a concerned woman and a vital woman. I am a person. I resent what the word widow has come to mean. I am alive. I am part of the world. (Caine 1974: 221)

Why widows?

While the ageing of the world's population is a key global issue, it is less well recognised as primarily a female concern. Australian women, on average, are living beyond eighty years and have exceeded the average male life expectancy by approximately seven years (Clare & Tulpule 1994). This trend is expected to extend well into the next century, resulting in a significant population of older women for whom widowhood will mark a 'normal' transitional phase in the life-cycle.

The experience of the death of a spouse is understood to be one of the most stressful and disruptive events within the human life-cycle (Murrell *et al.* 1988; Prigerson *et al.* 1995). For older women, coming to terms with such an event entails confrontation with a complex array of issues within the dynamics of daily life. It can also have a negative impact on their health and well-being (Barrett & Schweis 1981; Wenz 1977; Mendes de Leon *et al.* 1994; Guohua 1995; Lund 1989; Prigerson *et al.* 1995), even leading to profound bereavement and serious mental health problems. Because of this, Gee and Kimball (1987) have expressed concern that widowed women have been stereotyped as little more than women who have lost their spouses, and that widowhood has been constructed within the context of crisis and personal affliction. Similarly, Friedan (1993) has argued that in the past researchers into widowhood have focused on deterioration, loss and decline, refusing to confront the possibility of any potential for further growth in old age. She insists that this trend must be overcome before it is possible to envisage new possibilities for ourselves or our society.

However, more recent research indicates that, in the longer term, the majority of older women find that widowhood is accompanied by a positive shift into a new life phase (Byles *et al.* 1998; Feldman *et al.* 1998; Lopata 1987; Martin-Mathews 1987; McCallum 1986). Many widows discover that the transition from 'wife' to 'single person' provides them with opportunities for development and re-establishment within their particular communities (Lieberman 1997; Walker-Birckhead 1985). Several important studies have focused on the challenges that confront older women after the death of a long-term marital partner, and have explored the changes that accompany the experience of widowhood beyond those of the initial bereavement (Lopata 1987; Patterson & Carpenter 1994; Silverman 1986; Walker-Birckhead 1997; Wenz 1977). As women age, informal social support becomes especially important because it creates continuity and stability through group membership. The death of a partner might easily diminish social support, especially if a spouse was 'a central part of the woman's support network' (Murdock *et al.* 1998: 6). As McCallum (1986) argues, widowhood is a central event of ageing, which is the process of moving through life transitions that have been socially constructed. Like others, Harrison (1983) has identified the potential for social stigmatisation that is often associated with widowhood and which can impact directly on the quality of health and well-being of these women. There is a perception that widows are older women who are unproductive, isolated and without meaningful roles or relationships in society beyond those linked to the family.

Although the shift from the status of married to widowed is often accompanied by a freedom from the responsibilities of caring for an infirm spouse or the restrictive conventions of marriage (George 1980; Lopata 1987), the challenges faced by older women after the death of a husband may 'comprise a new and uncharted journey' (Lieberman 1997: 3). Murdock *et al.* (1998: 17) emphasise that we can gain a greater understanding about the stress associated with the loss of a spouse by exploring how older widowed women negotiate the daily, small life events, such as '. . . making minor repairs to household appliances . . .'. Reinharz quotes from Lopata's exemplary work on widowhood written in 1973, in which she describes herself as being 'so infuriated at the lack of preparation women have for living lives without their husbands . . .', because to her 'the helplessness of (some) widows revealed the effect of their socialization as women' (as quoted by Reinharz in Pearsall 1997: 74). However, Walker-Birckhead's studies (1985, 1997) of Australian rural women have provided a positive view of widowhood as a time that has been anticipated as empowering and liberating, while Alston (1995: 60) describes the period of widowhood as '. . . the most powerful time in a farm woman's life, because it may be the only time she achieves autonomy in her productive life'. The perspective offered by these studies is of widowhood as a process of change; but importantly they introduce a level of theoretical analysis to a body of work that has in the past been largely policy driven, descriptive and atheoretical (Arber & Ginn 1995; Gee & Kimball 1987; Martin-Mathews 1991).

This chapter details a research project in which a group of older women were given the opportunity to share their experiences of how the death of their spouse impacted on their lives.[1] Many of them agreed that in the short term there were negative consequences associated with the death of their husband and the 'crisis' of bereavement, but overall they viewed their life as one of positive negotiation, transition and change. The women who participated in the study confirmed that the social consequences of the death of a spouse were considerable. For them the most dramatic change was the acquisition of a new social status as one shifted from being identified as married to being a 'widow'. They also spoke of how they faced the challenge of overcoming the stereotype of widowhood as a prolonged period of bereavement, depression or social isolation. As Freda, a 75-year-old woman widowed for less than twelve months, exclaimed, 'You must learn to be alone'.

Although these women spoke of family life as integral to their sense of well-being and security, they were quick to make the point that relationships and interaction with their peers was of equal importance—life must go on! Their comments confirmed that few women grow old or experience widowhood in total isolation; however, they may be forced unwillingly to confront the reality of living alone, often for the first time in many decades. Like other older women, those in the study had outlived a spouse and perhaps siblings, or seen their children move away. The women described the day-to-day obstacles they faced as single older women, particularly regarding their desire to continue membership in their established social networks. But as Mary, aged sixty-five, saw it they were now 'the odd woman out in the world of couples'.

In this chapter I refer to the women for their perspective on life after the death of a spouse, paying particular attention to any comments concerning the physical and emotional relationships between themselves and their family, friends and community. I subject the observations from this group of women to a thematic analysis, because it is a 'subjective and interpretative process' (Kellehear 1993: 39) about 'the speaker's experience of the past, present, and anticipated future set within an extended dialogue with its own history . . .' (Luborsky 1993: 207). Such an analysis is also conducive to the coding and systematic comparison (Luborsky 1993) of comments from these older women, for it is in their comments that we gain a more detailed picture of 'the extraordinary variability that characterises the experience of widowhood' (Martin-Mathews 1991). Here I recognised the importance of integrating the experience of the women themselves for an account of their lives (Daly 1997: 1), and turned to them for an 'insider's view' (Luborsky 1993) of widowhood. Echoing an idea that reverberates in other studies (Feldman *et al.* 1998; Byles *et al.* 1998), these women presented widowhood as a process of change, and '. . . one cannot interpret the nature of those experiences by mechanically assigning subjects to groups such as . . . male or female, young or old, married or widowed' (Gubrium & Sankar 1994: viii). It is the women in this project who provide us with extensive accounts of 'the multifaceted and complex nature of human experience' (Gubrium & Sankar 1994: ix) from their own perspective.

Who are these women?

Fifty-six women, including twenty-four from rural Victoria, responded to advertisements in local and State-wide publications inviting women aged sixty years and over to participate in small discussion groups about their experiences of widowhood. The project was widely advertised through community organisations which included the Older Women's Network (Vic.), The Older Person's Action Group, and Chesed (Jewish widow/ers' support group), and in the *Rural Women's Network Newsletter*, the publication *50+ News* and the *Health Care Australia Journal*. The women who joined the project ranged in age from sixty to ninety years. On average they had been married for thirty-eight years and widowed for fourteen years, although a few women had experienced the death of their spouse less than two years previously. The majority were of Western European origin, owned their own homes and relied on a pension of one kind or another.

During day-long meetings, the women were split up into one rural and three urban groups, with up to sixteen participants in each. They were then asked to discuss how their lives had been altered by the death of their spouse and to identify the significant factors in their lives now. There was much discussion in the groups about larger structural issues—such as health, financial, housing and transport concerns—but without exception these women emphasised that continuing relationships with family, neighbours and wider social groups were especially important to them. As a group these women talked about the small life events, about the daily hassles, that went hand-in-hand with their experiences of becoming widowed.

During the course of our days together the women were encouraged to reflect on how their personal commentaries might add to the limited body of knowledge about the emotional, psychological and social impact of widowhood. The groups from Melbourne included a substantial number of women from multi-cultural backgrounds, who stressed that language and cultural barriers also impact enormously on their experiences of widowhood. To date very little work has been undertaken with this specific group of ageing women, and we know almost nothing of their particular circumstances, needs or concerns.

Approximately one-third of the women in this project currently lived with a son or daughter, while the rest lived alone. All of them participated in social activities of one type or another ranging from church and formal club membership to interactions with friends and family. Many of them contributed to a wide range of organisations through their voluntary efforts, while others were active and ongoing members of groups like the University of the Third Age or Legacy. Some of these women continued to be members of sporting or fitness clubs, both as active or social participants.

Initially I faced difficulties in recruiting women into the groups. Some women were reluctant to participate in 'widows' research', commenting that they found the term 'widow' demeaning and defining. As Elizabeth, aged eighty years and widowed for the past seven years, declared, 'I am more than a dead man's wife'.

Other women worried about whether I might find what they had to say useful or valid. The following comment from Iris, a highly articulate woman in her late seventies, reflected the initial concerns of some of the women in the group: 'I can't see how my ordinary life can help you with your research'. I explained to the women that only by working together with them, by taking seriously their life experiences and opinions, could I locate my analysis of widowhood within a life-cycle framework, and possibly avoid developing only a negative perspective of what is a normal life experience for most women. In her extensive work on older, widowed women Martin-Mathews (1991: 113) argues that a woman's past life greatly influences her attitude to and experience of widowhood: 'no single stage of a person's life can be understood or viewed apart from its antecedents and consequences'. Markson (c. 1983) and Daly (1997) argue that for women, the later years represent a life stage often dominated by social and cultural expectations of appropriate behaviour that does not reflect the realities of their lives. Markson (1983) also observes that the lives of many older women, particularly after the death of a spouse, might no longer fit a predictable pattern or an expected norm.

The shift to singleness

What stood out in the women's comments was their attitude to life, their courage, strength and stoicism. These women were survivors, with their collective experiences including those of war, depression, migration, of outliving family and friends. They all described the period immediately after the death of their husband as a time of shock and bewilderment, and told of how it took time for them, as older women, to re-establish their life. The women emphasised that in time, they believed, 'things will be better'. They did not place time limits on the process of learning to live alone, to manage existing relationships or to develop new ones. As Joan, aged seventy-nine and widowed for less than one year, put it:

> *I have needed to have time to mourn and adjust to my new single life without pressure and this includes time to be alone . . . but with help and encouragement from family and friends I will build a new life . . . as a single older woman.*

Joan's comment was echoed by others in the group, revealing that the women know it is the passage of time that allows for healing and for other things in life to fill the space left by the death of a spouse. However, the women were adamant that while the pain of their loss diminished with the passing years, the death of their husband never lost its saliency. Even women whose husbands had died up to thirty years earlier still wanted to talk about the experience of becoming widowed and the impact that it had had on their lives. Jane, now aged seventy-eight and a widow for more than twenty years, says:

> *I was very independent. I was independent since I was a young child because I was the only child. The thing was that I was the queen of my home, my husband was the king of the household. The house was my castle. My kids were the princes and princesses and all the things outside in the world didn't matter. My education began, ladies, when I became a widow, and believe me it was not an education I advise you to undertake . . . It was almost a change of identity.*

But while all the women, regardless of their age, agreed that the death of a long-term partner is accompanied by difficulties, sadness and loneliness, many of them also spoke of the following years as being a time of new-found independence, often accompanied by positive life changes. For these women, such as Alice who is well over seventy years of age, it was the small, seemingly unimportant experiences of daily life that provided them with a positive outlook and a sense of future:

> *I do small things like eat peanuts in bed, read for a long time, cook when I like. I've become an independent woman.*

Change and restriction

As for other women, life for these older women is dependent upon a series of complex interactions, an intricate web of past and present circumstances, experiences and expectations built up over a lifetime, with each element affecting the other. Here I refer not to the grand events, but rather to the everyday experiences, the mundane, the obvious or the taken-for-granted minutiae of daily life that these women must grapple with. For example, Voula, a Greek woman of sixty-eight widowed for only six months, found that relationships with family, and her routine activities, changed after the death of her husband:

> *My importance has gone since I lost my husband . . . I lost myself too. I don't feel alive. I've lost everything, the house, because before my husband died everything I need I have . . . lucky I have good sons who look after me . . . I don't have any friends now, no more cooking dinners because the Greek tradition, as soon as you lost your husband you're not allowed dinner parties, you no go out . . . so it's all the time not just for a year. No make-up, you no go to the different places, you no go to the party, you no invite people except your brothers, your sons, no actual dinner parties any more.*

Another woman asked Voula: 'Why don't you kick the tradition?'. 'Impossible', was Voula's reply.

A child all over again

Like Voula, other women recounted experiences that conveyed a sense of a new life evolving, of change in their position within the family, and an understanding that the balance of these past relationships may have been tipped. In her study about the social world of older women Matthews (1979: 123) notes that, in general, as widowed women age their relationship to family becomes even more central.

> For the older widow, rewards may be available from other sources, but circumstances change, usually in the direction of limiting the number of relationships available. Offspring may be the only source of acceptance, approval, and instrumental services.

Nowhere is this change illustrated more vividly than in the descriptions from the women themselves about their relationships with sons and daughters. All the women agreed, to a greater or lesser degree, that while their families generally provided them with moral, physical and financial support that may not be available from other sources, new tensions between them sometimes surfaced, particularly regarding expectations about the future roles and responsibilities for both themselves and their families. The source of these tensions could also be described as:

> a direct result of the recent loss and role transitions for these recent widows, their children and other family members as they adjust to their husband's, father's or family member's death. (Murdock *et al.* 1998: 17)

A degree of family tension is reflected in the comments of Ann, one of the more recently widowed women in the group. Aged sixty-eight, she has been widowed for eighteen months. In the following observation she contemplates her future:

> *My children see me differently to my friends—they don't want to hear what I am doing outside the family. They think others drain me, they are protective of me, they don't like to think that I can and will continue to make adult choices about my life. They think I am being manipulated because I want to make a new life for myself as a single older woman.*

And Janet, aged seventy-three and widowed for five years, adds:

> *Because of my age, they (my grown up children) think they know better than I do. They forget that experience counts and that I am not a child . . . I can make my own decisions about the rest of my life.*

The matter of friendships

The women in this project emerged as articulate and assertive, and unwilling to accept a passive, declining role in society even after the death of their lifelong partner. They talked about the challenges of maintaining and developing their relationships to the world around them, particularly in the early days of being on their own. Jenny, widowed for less than twelve months, takes a pragmatic view of her future, declaring that even at seventy-five years of age, 'you have to find your own personhood'.

For Ellen, aged eighty-three and widowed for nine years, it was the loss of the social activities she had shared with her husband, especially their shared love of dancing, that caused her the most grief. 'The hardest thing for me I think was that I lost a dancing partner.' And it was with an air of resignation, of sadness, that others described how after the death of a spouse some old friendships and relationships were closed to them. As Hilary explained: 'I used to be included in dinner parties with my partner; now I am left out'. Other women agreed and her comments sparked off an animated discussion between three other women.

> *Funny, a widow often gets invited for lunch but not so often dinners. Do you think so?*
>
> *That's right.*
>
> *So the lunches go up and the dinners go down.*
>
> *I think it's safer with lunches anyway.*
>
> *I think they're [lunches] much safer too.*
>
> *Oh yes, I mean I notice that you don't get as many invitations for dinner with women and their husbands, but rather lunches with the girls.*

There was much speculation between women as to why they were no longer included in outings and activities that they once shared with their husband and their married friends. There was agreement between them that as single women they might be a threat to their married women friends, a point explained by Pam, seventy-nine years old and widowed for four years.

> *And I think that they (my friends) are frightened that you are going to make eyes at their husbands or something. But it's very disappointing when you have old friends who have always included you and your husband and then you find out that you've been left out.*

The matter of sex

And quite unexpectedly the discussion about friendship turned to their relationship with men and the pressure of unwanted sexual advances. Some of the women were saddened by the fact that not only had they experienced the death of a husband, but that they also had to cope with the diminishing opportunities to mix with men, including those who might have been friends of long standing. Or as Mina, aged seventy-four, said:

> *I wish that I could have some relationships with men without being misunderstood. It all has changed now. I want friendly, fun relationships . . . No, I just had to realise that they [men] misunderstood . . . it all happened after he died . . . it all changed.*

Other women agreed with her and confirmed that they, too, had become wary about maintaining some of their male friendships, because of the pressure they felt from men. Ruth was quite blunt in the way she described the difference in how one married man, who had been 'their' friend, now approached her.

> *Oh, yes, we taught him golf. I am sorry that I did because he loves his golf now and he loves coming up to the hills to play, but I put a stop to that in the last six weeks because he comes up and I would be home and he . . . I have to say to him that friendship is more important to me than sex.*

Other women also recounted experiences with married male friends who pressured them for sex, saying that they often restricted their social activities because they were seen as 'moving targets' or as 'hussies'. Some said that they have come to prefer the world of women, rather than be subjected to unwelcome attention from men they feel can no longer be trusted. Mina put it this way:

> *You need to belong to a mixed group of people who accept you as you are and not someone to hop into the cot with. Wherever you go that's what men have in mind. I discovered that after my husband died . . . We need friends that we can trust.*

But although only some of the women spoke about this distressing aspect of their life, as a group they were adamant that older women have few opportunities to talk 'frankly and freely with their peers about their own sexual feelings, attitudes and behaviour' (Anike 1995: 19). Bernice, a seventy-year-old woman who had been widowed for just over two years, pointed out to the group that 'nobody here has raised the word intimacy . . . or said that as women they have still got sexual needs'. In response to Bernice other women opened up. Their talk was tinged with sadness about how the death of their husband had deprived them not only of the loss of a sexual partner, but of someone to touch them, to provide intimacy and physical closeness. Some said that now the only people who gave them the comfort of physical touch might be their doctor, or a grandchild, or perhaps even a stranger who shakes their hand. In her timely piece on older women and sexuality, Anike (1995: 21) notes that: 'This body hunger has a great deal of sadness in it as touch is one of our human needs'. Or as Joan, aged seventy-one, put it so poignantly, 'my body is just needing a hug, to be touched'. But other women, living alone after the death of a lifelong partner, confessed to a sense of relief now that the pressures they had felt during their marriage had ceased. The pressure that they talked of was related to the physical sexual activities that had never been a pleasure to them anyway.

I want to get out and about again

All of these women said that they wanted to continue relating to, and engaging with, the world around them despite their limited financial resources. Most of the group relied on a pension or benefit of some kind, but still wanted to take holidays, eat out in restaurants, and meet socially with friends and family. At the age of eighty, Beryl takes trips away with her church social group but is aware that:

> *If you want to share a room when you travel, are old and single, it's impossible because it is only geared for couples. I can't afford to pay for a double room alone and I don't want to share with a stranger . . . why should I?*

Dulcie said going out and about on her own often caused her aggravation because:

> *You can't get a table in a restaurant if you're on your own particularly in the tourist area, because they don't want a table being taken up by one woman so either you get refused or you get put near the kitchen door.*

But throughout our days together the women were clear about the importance of maintaining a positive attitude to life. A strong theme throughout our discussions was humour and how they used it as a coping mechanism. This is illustrated nicely by Gwen, one of the older members of her group, who at eighty-two years of age thumbed her nose at the stereotypes about older widowed women and declared that 'their opinion of me is no concern of mine'. Taking up the challenge thrown down by Gwen, 78-year-old Alice made it clear that despite the grief associated with the death of her husband five years previously, life right now presented her with new opportunities for 'adventure'.

> *I look at us all, older women as almost like loose cannons. No one's telling you when to come home. You can do whatever you like. You can stay in bed until lunchtime as I found out, you're single . . . you could turn this town on its head if you wanted to.*

And in the end

We know that the death of a loved one is a stressful event regardless of age and personal resources. In this chapter I have raised some of the primary concerns of this group of older widows and the daily challenges that they face. Through their voices we have heard about their desire to continue to live fully engaged lives through relationships with family and community. These women have told of how the death of their spouse did bring about dramatic lifestyle changes, particularly their shift to singleness, and the subsequent effect on their continuing relationships with children and friends. But they have also described how they have been forced to 'cope' with the change, and how this has made some of them 'stronger'.

The older women in this project have generously provided us with wide-ranging insights into daily life after the death of their spouses. Daly, in discussing experiences of menopause, argues that 'it is important to note that women cannot be located within one or other of these experiences in any static way since their experiences can change radically over a relatively short period of time' (1997: 164). Similarly, Martin-Mathews (1991) advocates that widowhood be viewed as a process of transition. The comments from this group of women have certainly strengthened my understanding about the process of transition associated with the changes of widowhood. Their comments have provided a window into their lives by pinpointing factors that promote or inhibit positive outcomes for them after the death of their spouse. The stories from these women have challenged the dominant underlying assumptions about the impact of widowhood on an older woman's life.

The richness of the qualitative data has revealed the ability and desire of this group of older women to contribute to our understanding about their life experiences, particularly their expectations about the future and what it might hold for them as they grow older. Through their accounts these women have provided a retrospective view of life after the death of a husband, their comments reminding us of the complex and integral relationship between many factors in their lives including the physical, emotional and social circumstances. While most of the women looked towards a positive future, their stories also tell of the ongoing struggles of daily life. Here I would suggest that to adopt a negative/positive split in relation to their observations is simplistic and does not take account of the fact that, as with other experiences of life, widowhood is positioned somewhere on a continuum, with 'some good days and some bad days'.

And finally, we have seen resilience emerge in a group of older women, all of whom have experienced the death of a husband, and we recognise their determination to continue to engage with the world around them regardless of their age or particular circumstance. As 84-year-old Rose reflected, they have no choice but to continue to meet life's challenges: '. . . but I think it's about being single again, and it's as a single older woman this time round that I face the world'.

References

Alston, M. 1995 *Women on the Land* UNSW Press, Sydney

Anike, L. 1995 'Older Women, Relationships and Sexuality' in *Age Cannot Wither Her: Older Women's Sexuality* ed. R. Sorger, Healthsharing Women's Health Resource Service, Melbourne

Arber, S. & Ginn, J. (eds) 1995 *Connecting Gender and Ageing: A Sociological Approach* Open University Press, Buckingham

Australian Bureau of Statistics 1998 *Australian Social Trends* Catalogue no. 4102.0, AGPS, Canberra

Barrett, C. & Schweis, K. M. 1981 'An Empirical Search for Stages of Widowhood' *Omega—International Journal on Aging and Human Development* vol. 12, pp. 97–104

Bernard, M. & Meade, K. (eds) 1993 *Women Come of Age: Perspectives on the Lives of Older Women* Edward Arnold, London

Byles, J., Feldman, S. & Mishra, G. 1998 'For Richer, for Poorer, in Sickness and in Health: Older widowed women's health, relationships and financial security' (accepted for publication in *Women and Health* journal)

Caine, L. 1974 *Widow* William Morrow & Co. Inc., New York

Clare, R. & Tulpule, A. 1994 *Australia's Ageing Society* Background Paper no. 37, Office of EPAC, AGPS, Canberra

Cole, T. R., Achenbaum, W. A., Jakobi, P. L. & Kastenbaum, R. 1993 *Voices and Visions of Aging: Towards a Critical Gerontology* Springer, New York

Daly, J. 1997 'Facing Change: Women speaking about midlife' in *Reinterpreting Menopause: Cultural and Philosophical Issues* eds P. Komesaroff, P. Rothfield & J. Daly, Routledge, New York

Erikson, E., Erikson, J. & Kivnick, H. 1986 *Vital Involvement in Old Age—The Experience of Old Age in Our Time* Norton, New York

Fahey, C. J. & Holstein, M. 1993 'Toward a Philosophy of the Third Age' in *Voices and Visions of Aging: Toward a Critical Gerontology* eds T. R. Cole, W. A. Achenbaum, P. L. Jakobi & R. Kastenbaum, Springer, New York

Feldman, S., Byles, J. & Beaumont, R. 1998 '"Is Anybody Listening": The experience of widowhood for older Australian women' (accepted for publication in *Research on Aging* journal)

Finch, J. 1989 *Family Obligations and Social Change* Polity Press, Cambridge, UK

Friedan, B. 1993 *The Fountain of Age* Random House, London

Gee, E. & Kimball, M. 1987 *Women and Aging* Butterworths, Toronto

George, L. 1980 *Role Transition in Later Life* Cole Books, Monterey, CA

Gilligan, C. 1982 *In a Different Voice* Harvard University Press, Boston

Gubrium, J. R. & Sankar, A. 1994 *Qualitative Methods of Aging Research* Sage, Thousand Oaks, CA

Guohua, L. 1995 'The Interaction Effect of Bereavement and Sex on the Rise of Suicide in the Elderly: An historical cohort study' *Social Science and Medicine* vol. 40(6), pp. 825–8

Gutmann, D. 1987 *Reclaimed Powers. Towards a New Psychology of Men and Women in Later Life* Basic Books, New York

Harrison, J. 1983 'Women and Aging: Experience and implications' *Ageing and Society* vol. 1(2), pp. 209–35

Heaven, P. 1992 *Life Span Development* Harcourt Brace Jovanovich, Sydney

Jones Porter, E. 1995 'The Life-World of Older Widows: The context of lived experience' *Journal of Women and Aging* vol. 74, pp. 31–46

Kellehear, A. 1993 *The Unobtrusive Researcher: A Guide to Methods* Allen & Unwin, Sydney

Lieberman, M. 1997 *Doors Close, Doors Open: Widows Grieving and Growing* Putnam, New York

Lopata, H. 1987 *Widows, Volume II North America* Duke University Press, Durham

Luborsky, M. R. 1993 'The Romance with Personal Meaning in Gerontology: Cultural aspects of life themes' *The Gerontologist* vol. 33, pp. 445–52

Lund, D. A. (ed.) 1989 *Older Bereaved Spouses: Research with Practical Applications* Hemisphere, New York

McCallum, J. 1986 'Retirement and Widowhood Transitions' in *Ageing and Families: A Support Network Perspective* ed. H. Kendig, Allen & Unwin, Sydney, pp. 129–48

Markson, E. W. c. 1983 *Older Women: Issues and Prospects* Lexington Books, Lexington, Massachusetts

Martin-Mathews, A. 1987 'Widowhood as an Expectable Life Event' in *Aging in Canada: Social Perspectives* ed. V. Marshall, Fitzhenry & Whiteside, Ontario

Matthews, S. H. 1979 'The Social World of Old Women' *Management of Self Identity* Sage, Thousand Oaks, CA

—— 1991 *Widowhood in Later Life* Butterworths, Toronto

Mendes de Leon, C. F., Kasl, S. V. & Jacobs, S. 1994 'A Prospective Study of Widowhood and Changes in Symptoms of Depression in a Community Sample of the Elderly' *Psychological Medicine* vol. 24, pp. 613–24

Murdock, M. E., Guarnaccia, A., Hayslip, B. & McKibbin, C. L. 1998 'The Contribution of Small Life Events to the Psychological Distress of Married and Widowed Older Women' *Journal of Women and Aging* vol. 10(2), pp. 3–22

Murrell, S. A., Norris, F. H. & Grote, C. 1988 'Life Events in Older Adults' in *Life Events and Psychological Functioning: Theoretical and Methodological Issues* ed. L. H. Cohen, Sage, London

Patterson, I. & Carpenter, G. 1994 'Participation in Leisure Activities after the Death of a Spouse' *Leisure Science* vol. 16, pp. 105–17

Pearsall, M. (ed.) 1997 *The Other Within Us: Feminist Explorations of Women and Aging* Westview Press, Boulder, CO

Prigerson, H. G., Frank, E. & Kasl, S. V. 1995 'Complicated Grief and Bereavement-Related Depression as Distinct Disorders: Preliminary empirical validation in elderly bereaved spouses' *American Journal of Psychiatry* vol. 152, pp. 22–30

Reinharz, S. 1997 'Friends or Foes? Gerontological and feminist theory' in *The Other Within Us: Feminist Explorations of Women and Aging* ed. M. Pearsall, Westview Press, Colorado

Reinharz, S. & Rowles, G. D. 1988 *Qualitative Gerontology* Springer, New York

Silverman, P. R. (ed.) 1986 *Widow to Widow* Springer, New York

Wainrib, B. 1992 *Gender Issues across the Life Cycle* Springer, New York

Walker-Birckhead, W. 1985 'The Best Scones in Town: Old women in an Australian country town' in *Australian Ways* ed. L. Manderson, Allen & Unwin, Sydney

—— 1997 ' "You Just Go on Day to Day": Understanding health and independence in old age' *Aging Beyond 2000: One World One Future, Book of Abstracts* 16th Congress of International Association of Gerontology, Adelaide, pp. 76, 77, 456

Wenz, F. V. 1977 'Marital Status, Anomie, and Forms of Social Isolation: A case of high suicide rate among the widowed in an urban sub-area' *Diseases of the Nervous System* vol. 38(11), pp. 891–5

---

1   An outcome of this project has been the development of a larger sub-study on Australian widows in the Longitudinal Study on Women's Health, Women's Health Australia, University of Newcastle. The aims of the larger study are to examine the short- and

older widowed women relating to the world / 181

long-term effects of widowhood on the health and well-being of older women, and to explore the process of change that they experience after the death of a spouse. The names of the women quoted in this chapter are pseudonyms.

twelve

the ache of frequent farewells

CORA VELLEKOOP BALDOCK

This account has been inspired by my personal experiences. It began for me without theory, without the kind of systematic reading and preparation on which research is meant to be based. It came from an urge to document my own feelings and to talk with others to find out whether they had resolved issues that I have faced over the last few years.

I left my home country, the Netherlands, at the age of twenty-eight to take up an academic job in New Zealand. When I departed, my parents were in the 'prime of life', looking forward to retirement among friends and relatives. My only sister was a busy professional in a full-time career. I returned home to visit regularly over the years, but I never returned to live there; instead I moved on to the United States, and eventually settled in Australia. My father died in 1990, and after this my mother's physical and mental health deteriorated quite rapidly. My sister—now retired—who lived close to her, became the primary caregiver. However, for a period of seven years, until my mother's death in 1997, I also became increasingly involved in the caregiving, both from a distance and during frequent visits back home.

I realised that I had never read any descriptions of such experiences, even though I knew many other 'new Australians' who like me travelled regularly to their country of birth to visit ageing parents. I decided to document my experiences and talk to others about theirs. This chapter, then, is an autobiographical account by an ageing migrant, who cared from a distance for an ageing mother back home, and also cared about an ageing primary caregiver (my sister) in the home country. In it I talk about the practices and emotions of *caring* (as in caring about)— exemplified in frequency of contact, the sense of loss when apart, the importance of visits—but also about the practices and emotions of *caregiving* (as in caring for), through participation in decision making about issues of health and well-being, and actual 'hands-on' caregiving during my return visits back home. I speak also about questions of identity—my sense of Australianness, and the notion of 'home' as tied to family connections—and the likelihood that I would never return to my country of birth to care or to be cared for. I follow this with the results of a pilot study based on interviews with a small number of women who had similar experiences in caring from a distance.

Caring from a distance: an autobiography

I departed from my country of birth nearly thirty-five years ago, leaving my parents, my sister, aunts, uncles and many friends behind, all healthy, active people busy with their own affairs. I did not see myself as a migrant and claimed I would stay away for at most three years. There was some sadness at my departure, one elderly aunt among the many who farewelled me at the airport crying that she would never see me again—in fact she lived to the age of ninety-five and saw me off many more times. But generally people went on with their own lives, and although later my mother often said she had not believed I would ever return, no one expressed the feeling that I should not go.

Leaving home and staying in touch

Having settled in my new environment I soon established patterns of staying in touch with my distant family. When I moved to New Zealand in the 1960s, the common mode of contact was by mail. Telephones were used sparingly in those days: connections were not always good, and it was the convention to reserve the phone for Christmas, New Year or birthdays, and of course for emergencies. Every letter I wrote was immediately responded to by my mother, which meant we each received mail once a fortnight. The telephone gradually came to be used more, and by the 1990s we had established a pattern of letter writing combined with phone calls. Staying in touch was especially important on birthdays and at Christmas time, and involved letters also to other relatives.

The other major pattern of staying in touch involved visits by my parents (and other relatives or friends) and return visits back home by me. I had two visits from my parents, one after the birth of my first child when I lived in New York, the other to Australia when they came to meet their second grandchild. My sister also visited in New York and Australia. The return trip home, however, was a much more frequent occurrence, initially undertaken—three years after I had left—on my own, later also with husband and children, and in recent years usually on my own again. The long Christmas break in the southern hemisphere allowed return visits at that time, as did sabbaticals, conference and research travel, and long service leave.

The chance I had for study leave and conference travel provided an opportunity not only to combine visits to my parents with paid work, but also to defray some of the costs, as the university usually granted the money to travel. The fact that there was free accommodation at the other end helped: initially, when I travelled on my own, I would stay with my parents; later it became a matter of course that my sister would provide accommodation. Notwithstanding the benefits of university subsidy and free accommodation, the trips were costly and I used up a great deal of time and money on these return visits.

Caregiving from a distance

Realisation of the fragility of life and the probability that parents will age and need caregiving did not come to me until my father died. I had been aware of my parents' health problems for some years prior to my father's death. My mother had written about any personal health issues and deaths in the family in her regular letters, and my sister kept me informed of our parents' illnesses and hospitalisations. In fact, the timing of my very first return trip in the late 1960s had been motivated by my mother becoming seriously ill and having to undergo surgery. During a visit in 1987 (combined with outside studies leave) I helped my sister in attempts to persuade our parents that they should move to a hostel. These were clearly instances of involvement in caregiving. I was, however, not consciously aware of this and had no sense of a major responsibility. There was also a certain element of protectiveness towards the absent family member. Unexpected telephone calls were introduced with the words 'Nothing serious . . .'. When there was a death in the family or some other crisis I was not always told immediately; usually my mother would use her fortnightly letters for a carefully worded account of such events. It was my sister who provided support and assistance when my mother had a hip operation and my father was hospitalised with pneumonia; she also eventually helped my parents move to a hostel close to her own residence.

My father's death brought a drastic change more than twenty-five years after I had left home. He died suddenly, but I was able to attend the funeral, help comfort my mother and assist my sister with some of the financial and other arrangements. This close contact and involvement with the family continued after my return to Australia. I started a pattern of weekly phone calls with my mother, and my sister began to provide me with detailed information about my mother's well-being, financial matters and any other issues requiring action. In this she sought my advice, and it appeared that she appreciated my involvement. Return visits also began to accelerate, sometimes combined with conferences and research travel but also specially arranged for family occasions. For example, I had not attended my parents' fortieth and fiftieth wedding anniversaries, but now I made a special effort to attend my mother's ninetieth birthday.

As my mother's health deteriorated, my emotions and experiences of caring for and caring about my ageing mother became a source of anguish. As I travelled back home more frequently, each farewell became more painful. The decision of how often and when to visit was a particularly difficult one. Should I visit each year, or wait until an emergency? What if I travelled, and she died soon after my return to Australia? Contact with my sister had become more intense, regular letters back and forth replacing the correspondence my mother was now no longer able to engage in. From my sister's letters it became quite apparent that for her, as the only close relative, caregiving was becoming increasingly stressful. Travel back home, then, also became an effort to relieve the caregiver, to provide support to my sister and not just to my mother. Together we visited nursing homes, sorted my mother's belongings, and created a 'living memory' photo album in anticipation of our mother's move from hostel to nursing home. Again, the final visit to attend my mother's funeral was an occasion to deal with practical matters as well as mutual support. When my father died, my sister spoke at the funeral on behalf of the family; at my mother's death she specifically asked me to share that responsibility.

Notwithstanding my close involvement in the caregiving process, my role as a caregiver was at all times only partial. I did not have to deal with the day-to-day issues my sister was concerned with. Even when we visited mother together, my ability and my willingness to provide assistance with personal hygiene were very limited, and I often left it to my sister to help mother to the toilet. In any case, mother—not feeling confident with my attempts at such caregiving—would not ask or accept much help from me. Where I participated it was primarily in comforting her when we visited, and in decision making related to accommodation needs and some purchases. My participation may have been of some comfort to my sister, but it seemed to me that she also involved me in a deliberate effort to ensure I would not feel left out; major decisions had sometimes already been made, and my advice was sought for confirmation only. Was this because I lived so far away, or because I remained the younger sister?

My preoccupation with the caregiving of my mother developed a special intensity during the seven years following my father's death. This was possibly due to the immediacy of the situation; my mother required a great deal of care, and my sister and I were in frequent contact to talk about mother's well-being. The intensity of my response, however, indicated that there was more at play. Most important here was my newly gained consciousness that it saddens parents when their children live so far away. I had never felt this, but I now began to be aware of it because my *own* children travelled abroad, and my daughter had decided to settle in the Netherlands. My sadness about my daughter's absence gave a special edge to my relationship with my mother. She would often comment on this: 'you moved away', she would say, 'and now your own daughter has moved away to come and live here'. Notwithstanding such comments, she really never complained that I lived so far away. Only once—in her final year, when she was often severely depressed and confused—did she say with great clarity: 'Ik wou dat je hier kon blijven wonen' (I wish you could stay and live here).

Identity and distant care

Having lived in many countries I had always defined myself as a 'citizen of the world' with limited allegiance to one nation. I had to give up my Dutch nationality when I married and later became an Australian. I found, however, that when I reaffirmed my connection with my mother and sister after the death of my father I also rediscovered my home country. I took increased pleasure in 'going home' and experienced, as I wrote once in my diary, 'a sense of well-being, of being in the right place'. In fact, I seriously began to consider the possibility of spending more time there, maybe even living there. This culminated in a genuine crisis about my sense of identity at the time of my sixtieth birthday, which I tried to resolve through a month of long-service leave back home, a visit that coincided with the arrival of my daughter to settle in the Netherlands.

Nonetheless, during this visit I wrote in my diary 'the more I am here, the more Australian I feel', and on my return to Australia I felt a greater sense of belonging than I had for some time. I wrote this chapter while again in the Netherlands on a three-month sabbatical, which I combined with a visit to my sister and daughter. Again, I experienced a sense of ambiguity. For example, I speak better Dutch than my daughter, and could 'pass' for Dutch while she can't. But in Australia people recognise my accent, and I will never be able to 'pass' for Australian in the way my daughter can. I recognise the voices of uncertainty expressed by Modjeska (1990: 261) in *Poppy* when she said: 'I still don't understand what it means to consider myself Australian when I know I am not'. I would add that I also don't know what it means to consider myself Dutch when I know I am not.

The question as to whether I would ever return to the Netherlands to live has resolved itself for the time being; my sense of Australianness has prevailed. But my caregiving work for my ageing mother back home—and now the ongoing close contact with my sister and daughter there—has made me realise that I remain bound to that other place for the remainder of my life. I do not have to be present to be an active participant. Although a migrant and absent from my home community in a physical sense, I am an integral part of that community.

Studying the accounts of others: the anguish of distant care

I began this project from a need to document my own experiences of caregiving from a great distance. I followed this with a small number of interviews with university colleagues who had faced the same concerns of distant care. Among these were five women who, like me, had departed from their home country as single women (four of them marrying afterwards in Australia), and had cared for ageing parents from a distance. Two of them migrated to Australia from the United States, one came from Great Britain, one from the Netherlands, and one other had a mother living in Canada. They were all in their mid-twenties to early thirties when they left their home country and at the time of interview they had lived in Australia between fifteen and twenty-five years. One had lost both parents since her move to Australia, three had only one parent (their mother) and only one still had both parents. There were many similarities in their experiences, but also some differences.

Like me, these women had not been consciously aware at their time of departure that their parents one day might require caregiving or might die. One said: 'you don't think when you are thirty, that your parents are going to [die] . . . you just don't think about it'. But they had stayed in close touch with their parents by mail and phone, and had travelled back home frequently to visit. As their parents aged, and they aged themselves, caregiving issues began to emerge for them as they had for me. While at a distance, they took a close interest in health-related matters, making certain they were kept informed by relatives or neighbours back home about any problems. During visits, they checked up on the support systems available to their parents, and took them on outings and holidays. One told me she had 'played detective' by phoning relatives about the side effects of some medication her father had been taking; during a subsequent visit she accompanied him to his doctor and ensured this medication was discontinued. Another woman who had increased her visits to her elderly mother from once every three years to yearly visits and had spent every holiday over the last four years back home, said she would hire a car and take her mother on holidays or visits to friends and relatives. Yet another said that when her father became terminally ill 'she put everything on hold and went back to be with him for the year of his illness . . . it was part of my responsibility to go back'.

What stood out in the accounts these women gave me was a sense of anguish and guilt, anguish about their parents' well-being and quality of life and their own uncertainty about the question of how often they should travel back home, guilt about not doing enough. For example, one woman who visited her mother nearly every year, said: 'it takes quite a bit of my income, but it is something we'll have to try and build in our budget because otherwise I know I will be feeling ever so guilty'. Another commented: 'It's like a guilt thing, that if you don't go, you'll be regretting it the next year'. A third, whose parents were no longer alive, regretted strongly not having been able to attend her mother's funeral, saying: 'I was feeling guilty I guess that my sisters were having to do this all the time . . . that they had to take care of all the decisions of cleaning up, even clothes and all these sort of things'.

Several of my interviewees had experienced some ambiguity about their national identity. For two women, this ambiguity was resolved through the death of a parent, rather than aggravated, as in my case; they said they began to feel *more* Australian after the death of their parents. Both women had received a great deal of resistance from their parents when they first decided to move away from their home country. As one said: 'they did not really want me to go. I think every time that I went back they always asked, "Well, when are you coming back?"'. In her case, 'my mother's dying was probably one thing that made a difference . . . somebody who's all the time telling you [you] have to come back home is no longer doing that'. The other woman told me that after her father's death her mother put less pressure on her to return home, and this also consolidated her own sense of Australianness. One other, whose parents were still alive, had retained a sense of ambiguity similar to what I had experienced myself. As she commented: 'You don't really belong there, you don't really belong here. Or you belong in both. On your good days, you think you belong in both. But I certainly sometimes think that I won't grow old here'.

Interestingly, all *five* women had considered the possibility that they would permanently return to their home country. It appeared to me that this was associated with their awareness that they might end up alone in later life. Four of them had seen a parent die, and the surviving parent (usually the mother) live alone; they knew this could happen to them. They made comments such as: 'if my children migrate there, and there is no one else here, then I'll probably end up going there myself'; and 'if my sister and I would end up being alone, we might live in the same community'. It was clear that where their children, other close relatives and friends lived as they grew older was an important consideration given the possibility that their partners might die before they did.

Discussion and conclusion

In recent years many studies have been conducted on the needs of the aged and the quality of care given by their adult children (Remnet 1987; Bengtson & Harootyan 1994). It is recognised in this literature that people who are caregivers for elderly parents within their own residence or in the close vicinity face extreme burdens on a day-to-day basis (Ungerson 1990). Their caring responsibility may even affect their ability to remain in paid work.

I have in this chapter tried to narrate my caring and caregiving emotions and experiences as an adult child who for many years lived at great distance from my parents. I have suggested that I have been involved in their caregiving. Interviews with women who like me moved away from their home country suggest the same for them; a close and ongoing involvement in caring for and about their ageing parents back home. Our caregiving differs from that of adult children who live in close proximity to their ageing parents. While we care from afar, in letters and telephone calls, our stress and anguish remain invisible. At a practical level it is not likely to affect our paid work. On the other hand, as distant carers we use all our long service and annual leave, not to relax and restore our energies, but to 'go home' and become caregivers for our elderly parents. Other people might see these return visits as holidays, and the fact that the travel is actually an instance of compassionate leave is not acknowledged. Our contribution to caregiving is, then, usually intermittent and only partial; but—as I found in my own experience, and that of others—it is nonetheless of great significance.

My findings, although based on the accounts of only a few people, have, in my opinion, broader significance. Studies of caregiving (Aldous & Klein 1991; Lin & Rogerson 1995) have generally assumed a close connection between caregiving and geographic proximity, arguing that only adult children who live close to their ageing parents will provide care. However, my findings suggest that older people are not necessarily bereft of the support of children who live at great distance. Transnational migrants do not lose their sense of moral obligation towards their parents even after many years of residence in a very distant location. Further, my findings reinforce theoretical insights developed by researchers such as Baldassar (1997) that the migration experience does not stop at settlement, but involves an ongoing dialogue and interaction with the 'homeland', which might even result in the contemplation of re-migration back home after many years. I believe that the particularly important finding here is that such re-migration may be considered in the context of, and as a consequence of, family obligations and the perceived needs for caregiving of family members in the home country.

In fact, my observations provide direction for further research of extended family relations and obligations across countries. Such research would add to the spate of recent family studies (Gubrium 1990; McDonald 1995; Blieszner & Bedford 1995) that attempt to break away from conventional, narrow-based concepts of 'The Family'. Blieszner and Bedford have drawn attention to the need for a more inclusive concept of the family through greater emphasis on family relations *in later life*. I suggest that to focus on family relations in later life implies the study not only of connections and obligations between family members who live in close proximity, but also of family interaction and caregiving that occurs across vast geographical distances.

My interviews were exploratory, and many questions remain to be formulated and answered. My decision to interview only female 'migrants' like myself working within the context of a university is a limited approach to the issue of distant care. What anguish and guilt are experienced by older women who do not have the financial means to make frequent visits to their home country? And what are the processes of negotiation between siblings as to who plays the central role in caring for parents if one of the siblings lives at great distance? I was particularly fortunate in having a sister who, as primary caregiver, encouraged my involvement in caring for my mother. Several of the women I interviewed had no sisters to connect with; did this bring an extra burden of responsibility? And what if primary caregivers resent the efforts of the distant caregiver to be involved?

Finally, there is the issue of gender. Literature on carers (Ungerson 1983, 1990) tends to see caring as a gender-specific issue. I did interview some male colleagues, but the numbers were too small to draw any meaningful conclusions at this point. The few men I interviewed also retained close communication and support networks with their parents; sons as well as daughters made the frequent trips home to care for and comfort these parents. What I did observe, however, was that the women expressed a sense of guilt at not doing more, and a sense of obligation to caregiving not expressed nearly as strongly by male interviewees.

Whatever the focus of further research on distant care, I believe one of its main objectives must be to render visible what has until now remained invisible and unacknowledged: namely, that caregiving of ageing parents is not limited to adult children who live in close proximity; that it may occur across national boundaries, at great distance over long periods of time; and that those who participate in such caregiving do so at considerable emotional cost. Indeed, I suggest that there are many older women in Australia who experience the 'ache of frequent farewells', travelling back and forth to their country of birth to provide care to their parents as they age.

References

Aldous, J. & Klein, D. M. 1991 'Sentiments and Services: Models of intergenerational relationships in mid-life' *Journal of Marriage and the Family* vol. 53, pp. 595–608

Baldassar, L. 1997 'Home and Away: Migration, the return visit and "transnational identity"' in *Home, Displacement, Belonging* eds I. Ang & M. Symonds, RCIS, Sydney

Bengtson, V. L. & Harootyan, R. A. 1994 *Intergenerational Linkages* Springer Publishing Company & AARP, New York

Blieszner, R. & Bedford, V. H. (eds) 1995 *Handbook of Aging and the Family* Greenwood Press, Westport, CT

Gubrium, J. F. 1990 *What is Family?* Mayfield Publishing, Mountain View, CA

Lin, G. & Rogerson, P. A. 1995 'Elderly Parents and the Geographic Availability of their Adult Children' *Research on Aging* vol. 17, pp. 303–31

McDonald, P. 1995 *Families in Australia. A Socio-Demographic Perspective* Australian Institute of Family Studies, Melbourne

Modjeska, D. 1990 *Poppy* Penguin, Melbourne.

Remnet, V. L. 1987 'How Adult Children Respond to Role Transitions in the Lives of their Aging Parents' *Educational Gerontologist* vol. 13, pp. 341–55

Ungerson, C. 1983 'Women and Caring: Skills, tasks and taboos' in *The Public and the Private* eds E. Garmarnikov, D. Morgan, J. Purvis & D. Taylorsson, Heinemann, London

——1990 *Gender and Caring* Harvester Wheatsheaf, Hemel Hempstead, UK

thirteen

the expectation of love in older age: towards a sociology of intimacy

ANNE RIGGS & BRYAN S. TURNER

> *I find now not sexual intimacy but intimacy with friends . . . is getting better as I get older, or I'm working at it, or I'm appreciating it more or something—but just with women friends. I mean I have got some wonderful women friends now and I think they feel the same, but I don't think men understand . . . what a good friendship women can have and how intimate a friendship without sex or anything . . . I've got a few friends, we can talk very intimately about certain things you know and I find that is very good.* (Age 67)

This woman clearly explains the many meanings that the term intimacy has for the individual. Ageing as a process does not necessarily bring about a decline of sexual desire, interest or capacity, and there are many other ways of being intimate with a partner. Our research project was primarily concerned to understand the impact of loss of traumatic illness or partners, and the problems these situations posed for sustaining intimacy, identity and health. This chapter presents the results from interviews with thirty-seven older women, and explores the many and varied ways in which intimate relationships are sustained in older age. In recent years, much has been written about the considerable changes in the expectations of both men and women in intimate relationships, changes that are reflected in altered attitudes towards marriage, adultery and divorce. Despite these considerable social changes, trust and reciprocity continue to be important in the maintenance of satisfactory emotional or intimate relationships.

The study

For the study we interviewed thirty-seven women between fifty-five and eighty-nine years of age.[1] Of the women, thirteen were currently married or in a de facto relationship and twenty-four were single because of widowhood, divorce or never having been married. The majority were Australian born; six were born in the United Kingdom, two women were from the Netherlands, one came from Germany and one from Greece. The participants were recruited from a variety of community organisations within the Geelong region of Victoria—including University of the Third Age (U3A), exercise/activity groups, church groups, and sporting clubs—and from Health and Community Care (HACC) recipients and people living in a retirement village and an aged-care hostel, also in the Geelong region. Some of these women had lived all their lives in the Geelong area while others had lived there for part of their lives; the remainder had retired to the Geelong region from rural and metropolitan areas. Many designated their main occupation as housewife, but a significant number had continued working outside the home after marriage and the birth of their children—some from necessity when left alone through widowhood or divorce, others because 'they wanted to'. Their occupations were in the traditional female areas of teaching, nursing, secretarial work, sales and factory work.

We talked to these women about their lives and how they understood their sense of self-identity. This question about selfhood was difficult for them to articulate, because they were from a generation not given to self-reflexivity; rather, they were concerned with the practical issues of getting on with life. Personal relationships were most important in giving these women a sense of who they were as individuals—their self-identity. Intimacy with a spouse, children, sisters and friends was for most the way in which they defined themselves. When, as for some, these relationships broke down or were disrupted—through death, divorce or from a physical trauma—the women were thrown back on their own resources and were more inclined to be aware of themselves as individuals, that is, to be self-reflexive. This study, then, presents the story of how these women described intimate relationships and how they talked about the place these relationships had in their lives.

Intimacy

Sexuality is no longer regarded as a natural or inevitable condition or activity that an individual accepts as a preordained state of affairs. Sexual relationships have become increasingly problematic, and in successful relationships have to be discussed and negotiated. In contemporary society, the complementarity of gender roles in what might be called a traditional marriage has been transformed into a 'pure relationship' in which individuals are forced to negotiate rights and responsibilities (Giddens 1992). Whereas the traditional marriage was an economic relationship, which excluded romance and intimacy, the pure relationship is not based primarily on economic exchanges. It involves mutual assumptions about sharing emotional supports. Of course, romantic dating involves implicit negotiations of an economic character, but there is an underlying emphasis on mutual affection and emotional support (Illouz 1997). These assumptions are supported by patterns of sexuality that have been freed from the needs of reproduction, facilitated by the introduction of modern contraception. Within a modern relationship, the principal basis for continuing personal domestic social relations is the satisfaction of desire and intimacy. The companionate marriage, which emphasised companionship rather than reproduction as the basis of a successful marriage, has, of course, been a topic of discussion since the 1930s (Nimkoff 1934). In contemporary debate, however, emotional and sexual intimacy have become the foundations of marriage.

This emphasis on intimacy places new expectations and tensions on marriage, as one respondent put it when speaking of her first marriage:

> We were talking about divorce changing your life. Well, the thing was I was an adulteress while still married to my other husband, the marriage was nothing . . . I never had any intention of spending the rest of my life with him. We didn't have any sex by this time, I mean I thought there was something wrong with me but he didn't seem to care much either. So I thought, 'Oh well, perhaps it is a whole lot of nothing just to sell things you know?'. Anyway I was

approached by G., who I had known some years before, and he started saying all sorts of lovely things to me, which I had never heard before or not for a long time, and I was ripe for picking. He swept me completely off my feet.

This woman's disillusionment with her marriage clearly illustrates this notion of sexuality mediating body, self and social norms. Trust must somehow be incorporated into a relationship in which each partner seeks to change and grow as an individual, while at the same time remaining committed to a relationship. As this woman found, it does take two to make a relationship work:

. . . I think what happened in the marriage [was that] I very quickly realised I'd made a mistake, and he was not a very responsible man even after the children came . . . And I thought, 'Well, I'm married now I've got two children I'll just try and make the marriage work'. But, you know, one person cannot make a relationship work. So I was just hoping soon that he might go away.

The fact that relationships can be volatile and unpredictable was evident in the number of participants in this study who had had multiple sexual relationships. Trust, or the lack of it, was an important element in the breakdown of these relationships. This woman's sense of betrayal is palpable, when she says:

One big self-reflection I had . . . when I was forty-six or forty-seven and trapped in this marriage, was what an absolute worm I am to put up with it because he was seeing other women . . . I didn't necessarily know about all of them but all the neighbours knew . . . When it got so bad I thought I'm an absolute worm to put up with this but what can I do? . . . [T]he choice was not a lot because I had no money at all. I'd never had control of any money from the time I'd left work in 1951, but I eventually took the big step and initiated the divorce, which restored my self-respect to some extent.

Recent research on adultery also raises questions about the importance of trust in modern marriages. In her book *Adultery: An Analysis of Love and Betrayal*, Annette Lawson (1988: 62) explores the meanings of adultery in modern relationships and concludes that 'marriage remains built on sexual exclusivity that is interpreted in modern times as part of the very structure of love'. Marriages are not so much measured as happy or miserable, but are assessed on the basis of how they share or fail to share a story. In law, adultery was for centuries defined exclusively as the act of a married woman, because first she was the property of her husband, and second she might bear another man's child whom she would 'pass off' as legitimate (Lawson 1988: 40). Contemporary definitions of adultery continue to follow this theme. Because it is the possibility that a child might be born that suggests adultery, the woman over fifty, being unlikely to conceive, will not 'count' as an adulterous partner. She is defined from the man's point of view as non-sexual, that is, as not really a woman (Lawson 1988: 41). In conclusion, Lawson (1988: 301) suggests that while the nature of adultery has changed its 'shape' still remains unchanged:

> It has changed because women's roles, both as wives and in the world of paid work, have changed; because beliefs and attitudes about what marriage is or should be, about sexual freedom and restraint have all altered. In this sense, it is appropriate that we rarely now speak of 'adultery', for adultery is a feminist issue where the affair, sometimes is not. Yet the shape of adultery does not change, and it is this that gives it its permanence and a certain fascination.

Forty years ago the only grounds upon which the women in this study were able to obtain a divorce quickly was by proving adultery:

> *There was no way of divorce unless you were prepared to wait three years and get it on the grounds of separation. You could get it on adultery, which I did and I had to go to tremendous lengths to get the adultery. I got it within six months but before that I had no money to move out and take the children. So I thought, 'Well, it must stay as it is until it can be different'.*

Despite the violence within her marriage, this woman was unable to divorce until adultery was proven:

> *It was no good at all. Before I was married my husband promised to take me to England and once we were married he decided that he would go out while I looked after the children, it was quite a different thing all together. Then at one stage he really raped me. He finished up living with someone else and I was able to divorce him.*

The success of modern marriages depends wholly upon the emotional satisfaction felt by each partner within the relationship. In this case, such a relationship can be terminated if either one or both partners are dissatisfied with the marriage relationship, whereas in the traditional form of marriage the contractual arrangement is likely to be stronger and more obligatory. In a more traditional context, economic ties, legal relations and religious assumptions worked to make marriage a binding agreement. Modern marriage relations are hence more volatile, uncertain and unpredictable. When the marriage did not work, as for these women, the legal difficulties and social stigma were greater than they are perceived to be today:

> *1965, yeah, I was thirty-five then . . . [I]f you got a divorce then, oh it still wasn't a nice thing to happen, it doesn't happen in good families. Now it happens in all families, but it was something that, you know . . . wasn't the proper thing to do.*

Many of the women found that once they became single women again, through divorce or widowhood, they were abandoned by some of their married friends. The social stigma associated with divorce also produced social isolation:

> *That's true too. I felt that people, I wouldn't say looked down on me, but if they knew you were divorced I think it did make [a difference]. And another thing I did find [was that] I lost a lot of friends because I was a threat.*

Ann Ferguson (in O'Connor 1995) recognises that, for the majority of women, particularly in the early child-rearing stage, Giddens's concept of a 'pure relationship' is not a particularly helpful perspective: '[t]heir sexual as well as their procreative lives are firmly located within a network of domestic and family responsibilities'. Furthermore, 'to prioritise sexual pleasure over such demands, is socially, culturally and psychologically difficult' (O'Connor 1995: 344). This woman clearly explains the difficulties that arise in forming new relationships when children are involved:

> *If you mean between two partners, married partners, let's say while I searched for Mr Right, hoping to have a companion in my old age, when I did marry it was, sadly, a disappointment in many respects. Partly because of that and partly*

because the children were difficult enough to rear without added complications, I felt that I couldn't impose anything or anybody else upon them. So I didn't seek a replacement after the marriage broke down. I needed it, I'm not saying I didn't, but I didn't seek it and I didn't look for it or whatever.

It is not only in forming new relationships that difficulties occur when children are involved: after a divorce, the need to support a family emotionally and economically also increases the complications. For this woman, the negative emotional consequences of her divorce were paramount:

About feelings and moods I found it difficult to bring the children up by myself and working besides, (a) I felt so guilty about the divorce, (b) I felt more guilty than ever because I've been teaching child care to other people. I couldn't cope with my own but of course they had all this backwash from the divorce, their own confusion and pain, while I tried to keep them and myself on the straight and narrow. The children often suffered, consequently, so that was a very difficult time and often I was near enough to a breakdown.

For this woman, economic considerations and the necessity of supporting her children were the most difficult consequences:

I had to work hard. I had three children by this stage and there was no supporting mothers' pension or anything like that. That's when I went to work on the trams. I had two boys at . . . College; my little daughter was three. I had someone to look after her.

Not only are there gender differences in expectations of satisfying love relationships, but there are also generational differences. This woman explains her perception of the difference between intimate relationships when she was young and those of the present generation:

[An intimate relationship means] having jokes with, you know, laughing and talking. Sex has its place but I'm not sure that the young don't put too much stress on it, it's important in a way. In my day, of course, he had to have his licence first, not that it always happened. But now I think the young ones are freer, they live together for a while, in our day that wouldn't be heard of. Sex [was] more of a mystery at the beginning, it was not for everybody, of course, everyone's

different. I think with everybody, there's that closeness really. Yes, I think it's important.

One of the main features of the new era is a collision of interests between love, family and personal freedom (Beck & Gernsheim-Beck 1995). The autonomy of the nuclear family is being undermined by the intrusion of public issues, such as emancipation and equal rights, into our private lives. The result will be a different family system incorporating 'new arrangements after divorce, remarriage, divorce again, new assortments from your, my, our children, our past and present families' (Beck & Gernsheim-Beck 1995: 2). 'Good communication and trust between the marital pair . . . make for the security and integrity of a marriage' (Lawson 1988: 229). Equality is also demanded, because marriage is now supposed to be a relationship between equal partners. However, the notion that communication, trust and equality are important between married partners is not a new assumption as this woman illustrates:

> *No, it was a big nothing; it was a big nothing. He didn't want to know about things like that. I wanted to talk to him if I had a worry or I wanted to talk about just anything, [but] he didn't really want to talk much. He would just go out to his shed or look at the television. I wanted a soul mate, I felt that I had no one . . . [and] a mother shouldn't be looking at a daughter for a soul mate. I knew that wasn't it and the silly part was when I finally left him, his remark said it all. He said, 'Well I was happy, I thought you were'. I thought that's just it, you didn't want to know whether I was happy or whether I wasn't happy. I was completely unhappy for 10 years at least . . .*

This woman also regrets the lack of communication in her current marriage:

> *. . . but he's not one to discuss that's another thing. [W]e're not compatible, put it that way, very secretive. He never discussed that he was having troubles in the business. He's still secretive, very, and I talk too much, well I don't go telling people all the private business.*
>
> *Well that's what it should be, communication, but there isn't any. But we struggle through, [and] if you asked him he would say he had a good marriage. [H]e said, 'Well we've had a good marriage', and I said, 'Do you think so?'. Oh, yes, he thought so, but he'd never talk to me.*

the expectation of love in older age / 201

Beck (1992) believes that high divorce rates, multiple employment careers and changing household forms are consequences of advanced modernisation. He describes this form of modernity in terms of a 'risk society', which requires greater reflexivity about our lifestyles. 'Risk society' requires a new relationship between the individual and society in which personal biographies are less dependent on external social control and traditional moral laws. Interpersonal relationships are more open, transparent and individually negotiable. Stability in personal relationships cannot be taken for granted; interpersonal communication requires reflexivity (Beck & Gernsheim-Beck 1995: 5). More and more, the individual is required to take the initiative and make choices about shaping their own biography.

The notions of risk society, reflexivity and individual decision making suggest that there are enhanced opportunities for self-development, but these possibilities are set within broad functional changes in social arrangements. These tensions are reflected in the contradictory nature of love: 'love is pleasure, trust, affection, and equally boredom, anger, habit, treason, loneliness, intimidation, despair and laughter' (Beck & Gernsheim-Beck 1995: 12). Love is the essential element in modern intimate relationships (Hunt 1994). It is in the expectation of love that individuals continue to seek out partners and re-partner despite the disappointments and failures of previous relationships. As one woman said, 'then I was silly enough to marry again', and as this woman found:

> ... [D]uring the war ... I met my first husband ... We were married in 1942, we never lived together. He was in the army and then he was killed in 1944 and I had one son who was four months old.
>
> I was working in the office ... and a certain young man came circling around. [H]e was interested and I was at the point of my life where I'd been a widow for six years and I could see my young life slipping away. I never went out much but something pushed me. The first date we went on he said, 'What about getting engaged?'. I said, 'You're crazy'. Anyway he kept on and on pushing this marriage business, and in the end I thought why not and I married him within six months. Complete disaster, shouldn't have done it.

These new codes of behaviour have their own strict norms. While rejecting marriage and the family as a model for their own lives, the majority of young people seek a stable partnership and 'faithfulness often seems to be taken for granted, without the official pressure of law and religious beliefs' (Beck & Gernsheim-Beck 1995: 16). Lawson also suggests that 'two people in a committed and loving relationship may take for granted that they will be faithful; for the majority this belief provides the basis for the "trust" they place in their relationship' (1988: 40). In living together, a man and a woman create a cosmos of 'shared attitudes, opinions and expectations' which develop in 'a continuous interplay between one's other half and oneself' (Beck & Gernsheim-Beck 1995: 50).

Intimacy, sexuality and ageing

Ageing as a process does not necessarily bring about a decline of sexual desire or capacity. Emotional changes between couples express a fundamental change in the level of interpersonal expectations, which in turn is an outcome of a radical transformation of marriage. These interpersonal transitions reflect larger structural changes in marriage and divorce. In Australia, both divorce and remarriage rates remain high. The quest for the 'pure relationship' based upon intimacy and emotion has produced highly unstable marriage relationships, with women demanding more satisfactory marital relations based upon intimacy and trust. These changes in expectations about intimacy, friendship and love have had an important impact on the way in which we approach the issue of intimacy and ageing. From the 1950s to the 1990s, a number of major social surveys concluded that men and women remain sexually active into old age. Continuing sexual activity often contributed to better health and sustained marital satisfaction in the later years (Kinsey *et al.* 1948; Kinsey *et al.* 1953; Palmore 1981; Masters & Johnson 1966; Starr & Weiner 1981). This woman would agree:

> We could be very intimate in lots of other ways. I mean G. doesn't talk about some things that I would like to, but at least he talks. We still have very good sex, which I think is great at sixty-seven.

Despite research that asserts that older people can be sexually active and attractive, ageism and ageist attitudes continue to be prevalent in relation to older people and their sexuality and sexual behaviour; the general public perceive sexual behaviour in old age as being 'perverse'. The importance of sexual satisfaction in old age has been celebrated in a number of classics such as *The Fountain of Age* (Friedan 1993). As Rhonda Nay says:

> Despite all evidence that sexuality in all its forms is essential to health and identity, society continues to make aged sexuality invisible: aged people continue to suffer guilt for having sexual feelings or acting sexually and many aged people internalise the misconception that they are asexual. (1991: 92)

There are, however, two problems with ageing. Ageing is a funnel, which constrains the choice of partners. More often, women give up sexual activity, not through the lack of sexual desire, but through the absence of an appropriate partner (Harris 1990). This woman describes how she felt after her husband died:

> *Well they [sexual feelings] were [important] when my husband was alive but the source has gone. The first six months was hard. I thought I was crawling up the wall, but I got used to that, you just have to. The initiation isn't there any more so it's hard. It is that long ago it doesn't matter any more . . . I bought myself a vibrator, well you have to or you would go crazy, I mean you've still got your feelings. I'm nearly sixty, . . . yeah, denial is only being stupid isn't it . . . I'm very broad minded because I was brought up that way. I wouldn't tell anybody this but you have to. You've still got feelings and you've got to have a release for them and that's all there is to it, otherwise you go up the wall.*

The second problem with ageing is the increasing incidence of both acute and chronic illness, which increases the experiential gap or tension between the objective or physical body and the lived experience of the subjective body. There is an important difference between my chronological age and how I feel about myself. Thus, with ageing there are growing tensions between chronological age, how I feel (subjective age) and how I look (body image). As a consequence of her husband's illness, this woman's sexual life came to an end:

> *. . . [S]exually it wasn't very good before anyway so that just fizzled out . . . I used to cry a bit and say my prayers a bit, but I got through it, didn't worry me eventually. I mean I was lucky, you see, I had the two children so they compensated for that. If I hadn't had any children, well that might have been a*

lot harder to cope with. [B]ut, no, as that fizzled out, well I
don't worry about that.

Intimate sexuality is usually understood to mean having
sexual relations or being active sexually in a physical sense. 'In
our society, romantic love is equated to intense physical desire
whose only appropriate sexual expression is characterised by
passionate lovemaking and the achievement of sexual union
through simultaneous orgasm' (Rice 1989: 252). Most people,
whether old or young, are unable to live up to these expectations, at least on a permanent basis. Older women especially
feel they cannot compete and are reluctant to be sexually active
at all, because it is a constant reminder of their real or perceived
inadequacy. 'Cessation of sexual fantasy or of interest does not
necessarily follow illness or ageing or both' (Renshaw 1985: 636).

Intimacy, sexuality and change

A sexual relationship is important in sustaining satisfactory marriage or marriage-like relationships. Marriage is also the traditional
social arrangement in which sexual activity is normatively sanctioned. Consistent with this expectation, older married people
are far more likely than singles of the same age to report
engaging in sexual intercourse (Levy 1994: 294). For obvious
reasons, the availability of a partner is crucial for the continuation
of sexual activity in old age. Gender differences in the conception
of intimacy affect the marital relationship, despite significant
changes in sexual norms and attitudes. Husbands and wives often
have different conceptions of intimacy. Husbands are more likely
to view sex as a separate component of their relationships. For
men, sexual activity is equated with sexual intercourse and
penetration. It thus appears to be a separate and distinct activity.
Women more closely associate sexual fulfilment with marital
intimacy and, hence, with the quality of their marriages (Edwards
& Booth 1994: 242).

These women describe their marriage relationships in various
ways. As friendship:

> . . . *my husband was my best friend as well as being my
> husband and a fantastic person. I had a very, very good
> marriage and relationship. Probably that's why I'm not inter-
> ested in any men that ring me up now.*

The conventional marriage:

> We were the normal nuclear family. The mother and the father and the four children. My husband was a teacher and he felt that he needed to be the breadwinner. He was older than me and very conventional and I was happy to go along with that and be the good housewife, particularly while my children were young and growing up.

And the power relationship:

> A husband who was away from home, that didn't bother me at all, I could like the quiet. [B]ut when he came home it was different, the atmosphere changed. I was the one who was on the bottom and he was the one with the power and quite dominant, not nasty or anything but quite dominant.

Despite the advantages and normative expectations that surround it, marriage does not guarantee a partner for life. Health problems that develop over the course of a marriage can interfere with the ability of one or both partners to engage in sexual intercourse. The death of a spouse also ends marital opportunities for sexual partnership. Because men tend to have more serious health problems in old age and women tend to marry older men, women are more likely than men to be widowed or paired with a sexually incapacitated spouse. This woman gives an especially poignant account of her perception of intimacy in a relationship:

> I think a loss of a friend [was the hardest thing when husband died], because we hadn't had any intimate relationship since he'd had his stroke because he sort of lost interest in that . . .
> [That] didn't worry me, no. I don't know why but it didn't really; we still shared the same bed but it didn't really worry me . . . [We] had such a good relationship, you know, just even as friends, very good friends, and I suppose I missed his companionship . . . I think it was more companionship.
> You see lots of people they get divorces and that when there is a trauma, but . . . if you're really good friends and really love a person then you will accept that person. [I]t is the same person that you got married to, and just because there is no sex, well, it doesn't matter you are still good friends . . . somebody who you could talk to and who looked after you and you looked after them.

With the death of a partner or divorce, older persons may find themselves back on the dating market. The person who is fifty or older typically experienced courtship and marriage prior to birth control pills and the sexual revolution. They now face the dilemma of how to be sexually active outside of marriage in a dating market that has changed considerably since their youth. Opportunities for partnering are also governed by the cultural assumption that equates sexual desirability with such youthful features as slim bodies, flawless complexions, firm muscles and smooth skin. By these standards, older people with their sagging bodies, white hair and facial wrinkles are no longer considered attractive or desirable (Levy 1994: 295). They have lost what we might call their 'sexual capital'. Neither of these women felt ashamed of their old and wrinkled bodies—in fact both were positive about the changes, as they said:

> *Oh, the wrinkles, yes, the wrinkles and I think, 'Oh, I wished I'd have used more cream' . . . Only just occasionally I think, 'Oh gosh, I should've used more cream that would've stopped the wrinkles', but that's about all. It hasn't stopped me physically . . .*
>
> *For the first time in my life I love my body, I really love it. And I've put on weight and my breasts are sort of sagging and all the rest of it, but I really enjoy my body. I'm comfortable with it. I think the only thing I've thought about is, well I have to wear glasses but that's OK. I can see all this but that's OK. I see the grey hairs and I think, 'Oh, I might put a colour through it', then I think, 'I couldn't be bothered wasting my time on that'.*

The ageing body does not fit into the romantic ideology of youthful love or equate with the standards of a sexually attractive body. Looking good and feeling good in our society mean looking and feeling sexually attractive. In contemporary society with its emphasis on appearance, the self is a representational self, whose value and meaning are ascribed to the individual by the shape and image of their external body, or more precisely through their body image (Turner 1996: 23). Body image is a social construct, which is incorporated into the individual's self-identity and sense of self-worth.

Conclusion

Many of the women in the sample had experienced various relationships including marriage, widowhood, divorce and de facto relations. For them, there was more to a satisfactory relationship than compatibility in desire and sexuality. Trust, commitment and shared biographies were as important or more important, as illustrated by their responses to the loss of health and subsequent sexual desire of their husband or partner.

Giddens maintains that trust is more important than ever in a couple relationship when the emphasis is on the individual and self-discovery. Sacrifice or selflessness do not sit well with the notion of the 'pure relationship', depending as it does on the acceptance of rights and responsibilities, and the importance of developing an individual self-identity. Individual choice and individual responsibility are important values in contemporary societies. These values underpin the importance of self-reflexivity of the individual within intimate relationships. Risk society is seen as open, flexible and challenging, because it places an emphasis on responsibility for our own destiny. However, within our sample, self-reflexivity in any depth had not been a significant feature—except in the case of emotional disruption when the individual was forced to reassess her sense of self, or in the event of physical trauma where the body's ability had been limited and it was necessary to overcome or accept these limitations. In the everyday world, disruptions through accident or illness tend to compel individuals into self-reflection.

The need for love and intimacy does not decline with age, but the imbalance in the male/female ratio in an ageing cohort and the likelihood of increasing frailty nevertheless make this search more difficult. Good health (but not necessarily perfect health), financial security and an available partner contribute to the ability to maintain intimate relationships. Intimacy and sexuality are dependent upon this unstable and unpredictable combination of social, personal and economic circumstances. Sociologically speaking, it is not true that all you need is love. One needs a set of conditions (including health, some degree of physical mobility, financial independence and, above all, partners) to make love a possibility.

References

Beck, U. 1992 *Risk Society: Towards a New Modernity* Sage, London
Beck, U. & Gernsheim-Beck, E. 1995 *The Normal Chaos of Love* Polity Press, Cambridge, UK

Becker, G. 1997 *Disrupted Lives. How People Create Meaning in a Chaotic World* University of California Press, Berkeley, CA
Edwards, J. E. & Booth, A. 1994 'Sexuality, Marriage and Well-Being: The middle years' in *Sexuality Across the Life Course* ed. A. S. Rossi, University of Chicago Press, Chicago, pp. 233–59
Friedan, B. 1993 *The Fountain of Age* Simon & Schuster, New York
Giddens, A. 1992 *The Transformation of Intimacy: Sexuality, Love and Eroticism in Modern Societies* Polity Press, Cambridge, UK
Harris, D. K. 1990 *Sociology of Aging* Harper & Row, New York
Hunt, M. 1994 *The Natural History of Love* Doubleday Anchor Books, New York
Illouz, E. 1997 *Consuming the Romantic Utopia: Love and the Cultural Contradictions of Capitalism* University of California Press, Berkeley, CA
Kinsey, A. C., Pomeroy, W. B. & Martin, C. E. 1948 *Sexual Behaviour in the Human Male* Saunders, Philadelphia
Kinsey, A. C., Pomeroy, W. B., Martin, C. E. & Gebhard, P. H. 1953 *Sexual Behaviour in the Human Female* Saunders, Philadelphia
Lawson, A. 1988 *Adultery: An Analysis of Love and Betrayal* Basil Blackwell, Oxford
Levy, J. A. 1994 'Sex and Sexuality in Later Life Stages' in *Sexuality Across the Life Course* ed. A. S. Rossi, University of Chicago Press, Chicago, pp. 287–30
Masters, W. H. & Johnson V. E. 1966 *Human Sexual Response* Little, Brown, Boston
Nay, R. 1991 'Asexual, Depersonalised and Worthless: The lived experience of old women?' in *Women's Health in Australia* ed. A. Smith, University of New England, Armidale, NSW
Nimkoff, M. F. 1934 *The Family* Houghton Mifflin, Boston
O'Connor, P. 1995 'Understanding Variation in Marital Sexual Pleasure: An impossible task?' *The Sociological Review* vol. 43(2), pp. 342–62
Palmore, E. B. 1981 *Social Pattern in Normal Ageing: Findings From the Duke Longitudinal Study* Duke University Press, Durham
Renshaw, D. C. 1985 'Sex, Age, and Values' *Journal of the American Geriatrics Society* vol. 33(9), pp. 635–43
Rice, S. 1989 'Sexuality and Intimacy for Aging Women: A changing perspective' *Women as They Age: Challenge, Opportunity, and Triumph* eds J. D. Garner & S. O. Mercer, The Haworth Press, New York, pp. 245–64
Starr, B. D. & Weiner, M. B. 1981 *The Starr/Weiner Report on Sex and Sexuality in the Mature Years* McGraw Hill, New York
Turner, B. S. 1996 *The Body and Society: Explorations in Social Theory* 2nd edn, Sage, London

---

[1] We thank those who took part in this study for their time and for sharing their lives with us.

index

absence, focus on, 81, 83
adultery, attitudes towards, 193, 196–97
affirmative action, 131
age
  chronological, 5
  cohorts, 5
ageing
  and loss, 75
  and status, 11
  continuum of, 79
  global, 5
  healthy, 88, 89
  negative aspects of, 6
  physical manifestations of, 4, 9–10
  population, 5–7
  public debate on, 6
  representations of, 77
  role models for, 102
ageing process, 3
  tolerance of, 4
ageism, 20, 22, 132
  education and, 74
  gendered, 119–20, 132
  sexuality and, 202
  work and, 117–33
anti-ageing remedies, 105

at-risk women, 8
Australian Red Cross, 135
autonomy
  ageing and, 11
  home and, 41
  see also independence, in daily living

baby boomers, 102, 120
balancing home and work, 106
beauty
  dominant norms of, 91
  exercise and, 90–91
  youth and, 91
body image, 91–92, 99, 203
  as social construct, 206
  see also beauty

carers, 105–6
  abuse of, 149
  community support services for, 149
  see also child care; elder care
change, ageing and, 102, 104, 105–6
child bearing, impact on work, 126

child care
  impact on women, 3, 107, 122
  women's contribution to, 134, 148
class struggle, ageing as, 11
communication, in marriage, 200
communications technology, 21–22
  as form of surveillance, 32
  globalisation and, 33
  society and, 32–33
community care, 8
consumerism, 24–27
  consumer goods as artefacts, 32
  older women as consumers, 23–24
contraception, 121
Council of Adult Education, 74
Court Network project, 134, 139–46, 147
  age of volunteers, 141
  gender composition, 140–41
  occupation of volunteers, 142–44
  race and ethnicity of volunteers, 141–42
  reasons for volunteering, 144–46
  socioeconomic background of volunteers, 142–44
  time spent on, 146
cultural expectations of older people, 10
culture
  issues of, 20
  warp, 20

daily living
  assistance with, 44
  independence in, 9, 10, 36, 41–43, 51, 52
definitions, of older people, 4–5
demographic changes
  implications for social planning, 6
  relating to age, 6, 7
dependency, 6, 23
disability, age-related, 36

divorce
  attitudes towards, 193, 197, 198
  children and, 198–99
  rates of, 202
  social stigma of, 198
domestic labour
  division of, 49
  women and, 38–39

economic
  insecurity, 20
  spectrum of older women, 19
education
  older people and, 73–86
  second-chance, 121, 130
  women and, 122–23
elder care, 122, 126, 128, 148
  from a distance, 182–92
  women's contribution to, 134
  work and, 132
employment patterns, changing, 27
entrepreneurs, older women as, 101–16
equal opportunity legislation, 131
equal pay, 3
exercise
  beauty ideal and, 90–91
  benefits of, 90, 93
  feminist view of, 95
  reasons for, 89–90, 91–92, 93
  social aspects of, 96–98
  well-being and, 96, 99
  see also health
experience of ageing, 9–10

family, changes to, 200
feminism
  ageing and, 3
  impact on older women, 104–5
fertility rates, decline in world's, 6
frail aged, 8
friendship, widowhood and, 173–74

gender, ageing and, 7–9
gerontology, 6
  biomedicalisation of, 8

glass ceiling, 3, 108
global ageing, 5
  see also population ageing
globalisation, communications technology and, 33
Greer, Germaine, 64

health, 9–10, 20, 94–96
  fitness and, 91–94
  fitness instructors study, 88–99
  fitness programs, 87–100
  physical, 9–10
  self-confidence and, 94, 99
  standards of health care, 20
  see also exercise
healthy ageing, 88, 99
home
  as domain of older women, 36, 50, 52
  as place, 40, 49, 52
  as private sphere, 36, 37
  as space, 40, 49, 52
  attachment to, 46, 48–49
  building and renovation of, 46–47
  commitment to, 42
  family life and, 46
  gender and, 39, 44–45
  identity and, 41, 44
  lived experience of, 41
  making of, 45
  meanings of, 40–41, 51
  men and, 37, 52–53
  practical use of, 37
  psychosocial significance, 39
  satisfaction with, 38
  significance of, 19, 36–55
  site of exploitative social relations, 38
  subjective dimension of, 36
  symbolic significance of, 40
hormone replacement therapy (HRT), 56, 57–58, 60, 68
housebound older people, 43
household economy, as economic contradiction, 26–27
  see also women's knowledge
housing, public issues of, 37

Howard, John, family policies, 126

identity of women, 7
incomes
  fixed, 20
  significance of personal income, 10–11
  women's, 118
independence, in daily living, 9, 36, 41, 43
  home and, 41–43, 51, 52
  personal income and, 10
Indigenous older women, 155–64
Indigenous women's organisations, 135
inequalities
  gender, 8
  systemic, 8
  see also sexism
International Year for Older Persons, 155
intimacy, 193, 195–204
  changes in, 204–6
  changing expectations of, 202
  gender and, 204
  impact of health problems, 206
  trust and, 207
  see also friendship; love; sex
invisibility of older women, 4, 18, 27, 29

knowledge
  conceptual, 28–30
  devaluing of, 20
  women's, 25–27, 30
  working, 29–30

learning
  critical/collaborative, 75–77
  lifelong, 73–86
Legal Aid, 135
life choices, 104
life-course development, 9, 10, 118
life expectancy, 6
Lifeline, 135
loss, ageing and, 75
love, older people and, 193–208

mammography, 57
marginalisation of older
  women, 29, 34
  through educational practices,
    73
  see also invisibility of older
    women
marital status, income security
  and, 10
marriage, 19
  as economic relationship, 195
  attitudes towards, 193
  communication in, 200
  companionate, 195
  decision-making in, 49
  power relations and, 39, 52,
    205
  remarriage, 202
  success of, 198
  see also intimacy; sex
Mature Workers Program, 126–27
media
  as communicators of
    knowledge, 28–29
  focus on youth, 20–21
  images of ageing in, 17–35
  influence on public policy,
    17–35
  marginalisation by, 18
  representations of older
    women, 17, 22–24
  role in creating stereotypes,
    12
  role in silencing women, 18
memory work, 76
menopause, 4, 56–69, 109
  as biological marker, 4
  as catharsis, 65
  as end of reproduction, 61, 63
  as hormone deficiency, 56, 58
  as life transition, 58–61, 68
  as lived experience, 61–62
  as loss and grief, 62–66
  clinics, 57, 58, 68
  colours of, 66
  depressive signs of, 62–63
  medicalisation of, 57, 58,
    68
  negative associations of, 64
  privacy and, 63, 64

  problems of, 61–62
  spectrum of, 57
  symptoms, 57
  visual representations of,
    56–69

National Council of Women, 135

old-old aged, 6, 126
Older Persons Action Group,
  169
Older Women's Network, 24,
  135

pedagogy of relocation, 75, 76
pensioners, 20
pensions, 119
  potential decline of, 126
Peters, Dot, 155–64
  community involvement, 161
  early life, 156–57
  life as older woman, 157–58
  power, 151
  respect, 159–60, 161–62
  responsibility, 162–63
  work with young people,
    158–59
photographs, role of, 87
policy
  agenda setting in
    policy-making, 20–21, 22
  as inclusive process, 33
  culture of, 23
  development on ageing, 6,
    21–22
  gender and, 7
  mass media and, 22
political culture of older
  women, 29–34
  artefacts of, 32
  rituals of, 30–31
  see also women's
    knowledge
population predictions, 6
positive images of elderly, 12
power
  ageing and, 11
  relations in society, 23, 33, 77
privatisation, impact on older
  people, 8

public housing, 42
public life, structural exclusion of women from, 23
public sphere, older women and, 23

quality of life, 11

racism, work and, 132
relationships, older people and, 194–95
retirement, 10
 decisions about, 129–31
 incomes, 123
 of spouse, 130
 villages, 47
retrenchment, 108
risk society, 201
roles
 for aged, 10
 of women, 7

self-confidence, fitness and, 94
self-funded retirees, 20
self-identity, 194
services for aged, 11
sex
 changes to, 204–6
 older people and, 193, 195–204
 patterns of sexuality, 195
 sexual capital, 206
 widowhood and, 174–76
sexism, 20, 22
 work and, 119, 132
 see also ageism, gendered
small business
 attrition rate, 111
 definitions of, 110–11
 fragmentation of sector, 115
 government attitudes to, 114–15
 growth of, 110–14
 older women in, 101–16
social capital of women, 27–28, 134–51
social expectations of older people, 10
social knowledge, 21–22
 false, 22

social planning, 6
social security, 119, 126
social systems, 22
socioeconomic factors, impact of, 10–11
spheres of authority, 21
spouse care, 122
stereotypes, 102–5
 challenging, 13–14
 negative, 4, 9, 12–13, 22–23, 24, 88
Stories of Ageing project, 73–85
superannuation, women and, 118, 123, 130–31
support services, 6

trade union membership, 124–25, 127
transport, 20

University of the Third Age, 73, 74, 194
unpaid work, 11
 see also volunteer work

value systems, divergence of, 25–27
voluntary work, 11, 19, 121, 134–51
 as caring, 148–49
 as citizen participation, 149
 as social capital, 27–28, 134, 135, 147, 150
 as unpaid labour, 147–48, 149
 as women's work, 148–49
 beneficiaries of, 135
 class composition of volunteers, 149
 contribution of older women, 28
 cost of, 135, 137, 150
 discourses of, 134
 dismantling of community infrastructure and, 137
 economic value of, 134
 formal, 27–28
 funding for voluntary sector, 27–28
 government advocacy of, 135

in contemporary context, 136–37
increasing visibility of, 137
industrial relations deregulation and, 136
informal, 27
inherent contradictions of, 135
organisations, 135
participants, 138–39, 150
politicisation of, 137
professionalisation of, 137
reasons for, 135, 150
recognition for, 28
sexual division of labour, 138
social value of, 134, 150

well-being, 9–10
widowhood, 7–8, 39, 97, 130, 165–81, 198
as new social status, 167
challenges of, 166
dealing with death of spouse, 165–66
families and, 168, 172–73
friendship and, 173–74
independence and, 171
negative aspects of, 167
positive aspects of, 166, 167, 177
restrictions of, 172
sex and, 174–76
single status and, 170–71
social stigmatisation and, 166
social support and, 166
stereotyping of, 166, 167, 176
Women With Disabilities Australia, 135
Women's Electoral Lobby, 135
women's knowledge, 25–27
artefacts of, 26, 30
women's movement, impact on older women, 104–5, 106, 107
work, 19, 106–8
casual, 123, 139
changing patterns of, 123
child-rearing and, 131–32
constraints on, 128–29
employment revolution, 106, 115
enterprise bargaining, 123
female participation rate, 117
feminisation of, 123
flexibility in, 123
globalisation and, 123
interrupted careers, 120–23, 139
job satisfaction, 107
older women and, 108–9, 117–33
paid employment, 106
part-time, 106–7, 121, 123, 124, 139
policies on, 126–27
retailing as site of, 124
traditional female patterns of, 10
workplace negotiation, 123
see also voluntary work
Work for the Dole, 136, 150
writing
as critique, 80–83
as political project, 77–79
as representation, 79–80

young-old aged, 6